Cecile J. Picou was born in San Diego, California, and worked in the banking industry for over thirty-some years. She worked in a local newspaper as a journalist at the *San Diego Voice* and *Viewpoint Newspaper* for two years. She placed as a 2nd rounder for the *Austin Film Festival* on September 2022, and won as a quarterfinalist for a screenplay entitled *The Jazz Age*, in 2016.

With the 8th Annual Story Pro's screenplay contest, she won an award for *Apex Blues*. At the *Colorado Film Awards*, she won for a screenplay entitled *The Otherworld of Fionn Mac Comhaill*, and received honorable mention for a screenplay entitled *Apex Blues*, in 2013. At the *Austin Film Festival*, a screenplay entitled, *American's Famous Slave-Frederick Douglass*, in September 2022.

Dedicated to the late Jimmy Noone, Jr., who without his knowledge of his father's work, I would not have been able to write this biography.

To the New Orleans Jazz and Heritage Organization, who gave me the knowledge and assistance to further write this book.

To my three children, who encourage me to continue with this book: Andre J. Walker, Leslie Walker, and Chris Walker. Thanks for your encouragement.

To every jazz musician that struggles daily to make a living and keep jazz alive.

Cecile J. Picou

APEX BLUES

A Biography of Jimmie Noone
Sr. and His Son, Jimmy Noone Jr.

AUSTIN MACAULEY PUBLISHERS™

LONDON * CAMBRIDGE * NEW YORK * SHARJAH

Ordering Information
Quantity sales: Special discounts are available on quantity purchases by corporations, associations, and others. For details, contact the publisher at the address below.

Publisher's Cataloging-in-Publication data
Picou, Cecile J.
Apex Blues

ISBN 9798891552524 (Paperback)
ISBN 9798891552531 (ePub e-book)

Library of Congress Control Number: 2023922244

www.austinmacauley.com/us

First Published 2024
Austin Macauley Publishers LLC
40 Wall Street, 33rd Floor, Suite 3302
New York, NY 10005
USA

mail-usa@austinmacauley.com
+1 (646) 5125767

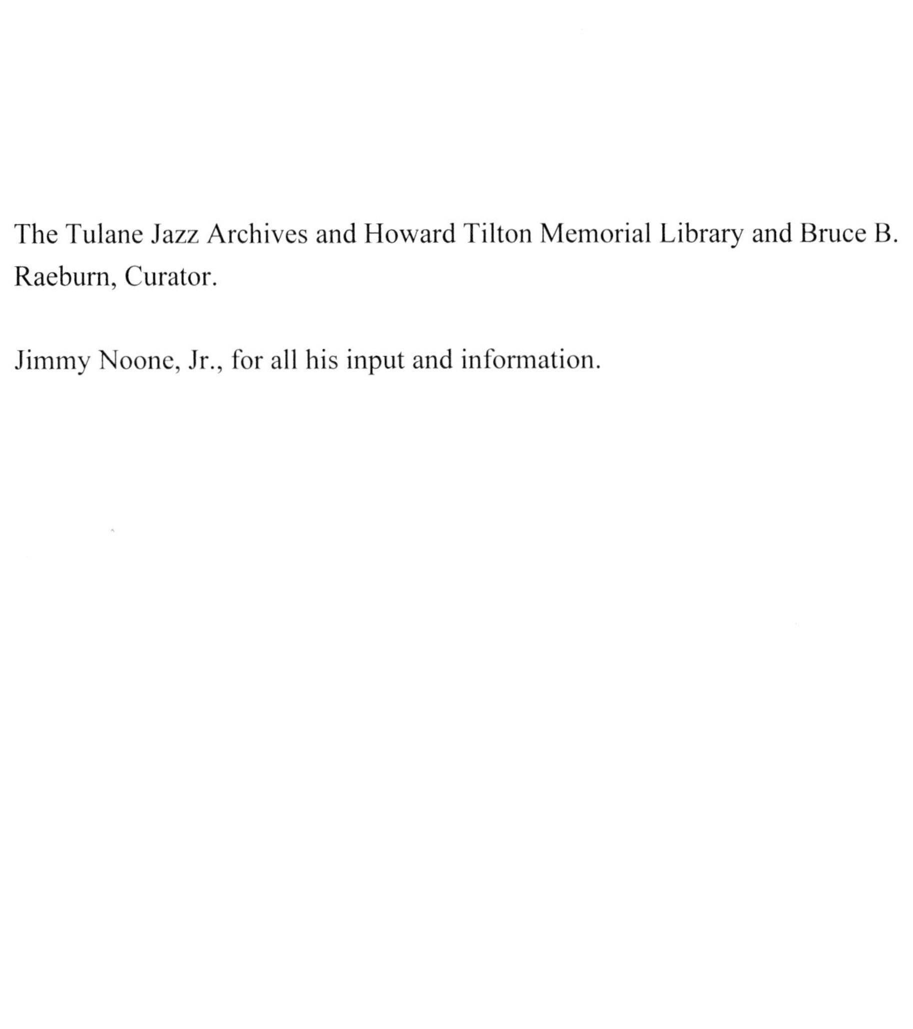

The Tulane Jazz Archives and Howard Tilton Memorial Library and Bruce B. Raeburn, Curator.

Jimmy Noone, Jr., for all his input and information.

Table of Contents

Chapter One
Clarinet

There was the Apex Club, where Jimmie Noone and that great piano man, Hines, started all this fine stuff your 'yars listen to nowadays. They made history right there in the Apex. The tune, Sweet Lorraine, used to gas everybody there nightly.

Louis Armstrong (Hear Me Talkin' To Ya)[1]

James (Jimmie) Fleming Noone was born on April 23, 1895 in the city of New Orleans, Louisiana.

His mother, Lucinda Fleming, was the daughter of a former African slave. Lucinda was an Octoroon (one-eighth Negro), due to her ancestor's miscegenation. Lucinda was never told who her father was, except that he was a full-blooded white man. Lucinda lived at the Stanton Plantation, with her mother and sisters as free negroes.

James John Noone (Jimmie's father) was called Johnny. He was a full-blooded Irishman, who had been born in County Cork, Ireland. After Johnny's mother had died in Ireland, he migrated to New Orleans, and set up a barber shop that he owned and operated by himself, and which was quite profitable.

Lucinda Fleming and Johnny Noone had a short courtship in 1894. As was the custom then, all well-to-do young men of the city, they set up house with young pretty Creole girl's, and provided them with a home, living expenses, and all things imperative to her wishes and needs. Lucinda became Johnny's concubine. Due to various laws in New Orleans, Johnny had the option of staying with her, until he married a European, but if he did marry, he would have to keep his relationship with Lucinda quiet (From a jealous wife) yet provide for any children that they might have.

When their son, James, was born the following year, the midwife announced that the child obviously had a heart problem. She announced, "The child's heartbeat is somewhat irregular, and an authorized medical practitioner, will have to further investigate the child's condition."

James Junior was named after his father, and his middle name, Fleming, was taken from his mother's maiden name. Thus, he was named James Fleming Noone.

The Noone family later moved to Hammond, which was a rural town, for a few years, which was out from New Orleans, and the next town was Covington.

Hammond was where Lucinda's mother lived, along with his half-sister, who was called "Lil." Her younger sister, Elizabeth, was called "Lottie," for short. She was a beautiful girl with bright red hair, and "Ninta," who looked rather on the Spanish side, had long straight black hair.

While there, James attended Hammond Grammar School, where he was daily called a "Passabonne," by the other children. (Passabonne is a Creole word used for quadroons, or fair-skinned negroes, who could pass for white.) While attending elementary school, his mother, Lucinda, insisted on his physical activities be restricted. However, numerous doctors agreed that he had only a slight heart murmur.

To slow down his activities to a minimum, his father provided James with a guitar that he began playing at home and during school recess. It was while he was in grammar school that his parents began calling him Jimmie. His father had all four children instructed in music, and although the girls had learned instruments, they enjoyed singing the blues together, more than playing instruments.

Jimmie's first music instructor taught him the popular songs of the day, such as Polkas, Creole and French tunes, Quadrilles, Ragtime, and the Blues. He was also being instructed in classical music. While his grandmother and mother insisted on the children singing spiritual music for church services.

Jimmie spent his summer vacations at Mandeville, which was a summer resort on Lake Pontchartrain, where he'd go and sit by the lake and listen to the bands play. He had mastered the guitar quite well, and he was able to follow the bands with his guitar.

Jimmie was ten years old in 1905; all the songs that he was playing were Blues, Marches, folk songs, minstrel music, and a ragged type of music that the cakewalk and jig could be danced to.

When Jimmie and his mother, made a short visit to New Orleans to shop, he became exposed to a new music everyone called "Jazz." He wanted to know more about this style of music, so he'd follow the big bands down the streets as they played. He followed the Olympia Jazz orchestra around the French Quarter, as they played for a parade, and second-lined. Second lining allowed him to meet the musicians, carry their instrument cases, and following the musicians he so idolized.

Jimmie was a cute little Creole boy. He was short for his age, had a chunky built, and a near-white complexion. His nose was pug, his hair was black and curly, and he wore short pants. He didn't just second-line with one musician, as some of the greatest players were in the Olympia, such as, comet player, Freddie Keppard, Joe 'King' Oliver, Alphonse Picou, Sidney Bechet and Clarence Williams.

Playing beyond the Olympia Band was the Excelsior Brass Band and the Onward Brass Band. The Onward Band had sixteen pieces playing that day. Their caps looked like something a captain of a ship would wear. However, there was a torch stitched on it. The band took on the appearance of a military band in their uniform.

Manuel Perez, the leader of the Onward, lifted his trumpet to play a tune, and the crowd went crazy hollering his name. Manuel was very popular due to his successful dance jazz orchestra and his marching band.

The Excelsior Brass Band was led by Theogene Baquet, who had started playing an adopted popular jazz tune. Achille Baquet was the son of Theogene, and he was widely known as a teacher and instrumentalist. Achille also had a brother named George, whom Jimmie had heard rumored that George could become one of the greatest New Orleans jazz clarinetist.

The band members in all the bands didn't just march, they carried a carefree type of a strut with a shuffle, dressed in white shirts, with dark ties and slacks. Jimmie noticed a few trombones, an alto sax, a tenor sax, a large sousaphone, and on their drums the printed block letters of the bands, along with one cymbal mounted onto it. The streets were lined with women that carried parasols, that were covered with sequins, trim, fringe or feathers.

The clarinetists are what Jimmie was most interested in, hoping that something in their technique might rub off He watched Sidney Bechet play for such a long time that after the parade, he was invited over to the Bechet's home for a cool drink.

The Bechet's home was located in the Creole section of New Orleans (Downtown.) Sidney Bechet was one of seven children who all played instruments. Sidney had been playing the clarinet since he was six and had received music lessons from Louis 'Big Eye' Nelson, Alphonse Picou and Lorenzo Tio Jr.

The Bechet kids and Jimmie played outside on the Bechet's front gallery (Creole for porch) as they played their music, other kids in the neighborhood, stood on the bamboula (sidewalk,) and danced to their songs. The Bechet children were already involved in playing in local parades and they often created pickup bands for their own fun.

When Jimmie left the Bechet's to walk back home, he remembered seeing an Eb clarinet that had a sound he liked. Listening to its sound, he knew it was an essential part of the traditional jazz ensemble. He wondered if his father would let him learn how to play such an instrument.

Jimmie's father consented to buying him a clarinet, because he felt that his absence from Lucinda, due to his new marriage, could have an effect on his son. He loved Lucinda and had decided that he did not want to give her up. And he did not give her up. So when he married his white wife, he managed to keep his illegitimate Negro family's life a secret, while supporting them. He continued to spend several nights a week with his Creole family.

During the first few years of his marriage, he sent Lucinda and the children to live in Mandeville for the summers, and during school breaks. It was during this time that Jimmie became ardent by his love for music and spent all his free time practicing the clarinet and guitar. He had been trained in the European classical tradition.

When Jimmie Noone was fifteen years old, in the year of 1910, Sidney Bechet had been playing the clarinet in the great Olympia Band, which worked a lot outside the city of New Orleans. It was a summer trip to Mandeville, where the band was playing, that Sidney meet Jimmie again.

Mandeville Swells Hall, located at 2405 Chartres, was sponsoring a rural dance. Jimmie Noone was playing on the back of the stage platform. He was playing along with the musicians, using a clarinet that had been discarded by a family member. As he didn't want the clarinet, his father had given him to leave the house.

When Freddie Keppard heard the sounds of another clarinet being played, he jumped out of his seat and talked to the musician behind the stage. After realizing that it was Jimmie whom he knew, as he was courting Jimmie's sister, turned and then introduced Sidney Bechet to Jimmie, not aware that they had met before.

Sidney told Jimmie, "I can help you play that clarinet the next time that you visit New Orleans. Just look me up."

Jimmie replied, "When summer's over, we're moving back to New Orleans to permanently live. Thanks."

When summertime ended, and school was about to start, Jimmie and his mother moved back to New Orleans, while his sister's decided to stay with their grandmother in Hammond. That same year, when he was fifteen, he took up Sidney Bechet's offer, and received music assistance from him. Later Jimmie Noone said that, "Sidney Bechet gave me instructions that were priceless, and that he showed him the ropes around the district."

Music lessons also came from Lorenzo Tio, Jr., who was a member of another Creole musical family. There was Sr. Luis 'Papa' Tio, born about 1863, who played in the Excelsior Brass Band. Papa believed in teaching others the New Orleans style of jazz and constantly taught many musicians. He played with Manuel Perez and A.J. Piron orchestra.

Because Jimmie's father was well-to-do, he was also able to obtain lessons from 'Big Eye' Louis Nelson and Alphonse Picou. Because of these numerous teachers, Jimmie Noone said later, that he realized, "Control of the clarinet was simply coordination."

Jimmie learned also that bis fingers had to be taught to never flex the outer two joints in his fingers, as it created his integral tone, and the usage of the full range on the clarinet.

With these techniques in mind, and from his music teachings, he was able to learn how to play both high and low registers. On the clarinet, this is something that is rather difficult to do, but it was easy for him, as he had learned how to cover a range of nearly four octaves.

Chapter Two
Storyville

The brass bands had created a completely new sound. It was new, and it was different. The city of New Orleans, had always been quaint, and so was the music. It now consisted of a strong African influence (which preserved it), combined with a little European music; and some spirituals blended into that. This music had now all been fused into the creation of jazz.[2]

In 1897, the tenderloin district of New Orleans was an area that the city council roped off for licensed prostitution. The intent was to control and confine gambling, drugs, and other vices to one specific area.

City councilman, Sidney Story, had become outraged as houses of prostitution were operating in the French Quarter. Story introduced to his council a control ordinance, which forbade the practice of prostitution, anywhere except in the areas bounded by Basin, Iberville, North Robertson, and St. Louis Streets. However, this ordinance did not legitimatize prostitution.

These bounded streets became the tenderloin district of New Orleans, and prostitution became its main income. And within these areas, music became a necessity, and provided many musicians a greater income.

Hundreds of black and white prostitutes had established themselves in the district, along with the madams, gamblers and pimps. To Sidney Story's distress, the area became known as Storyville. Musicians called the area "The district."

Parlor houses totaled about two hundred. There were about one-thousand cat houses that kept the district open twenty-four hours a day.

Storyville did not start jazz. What it did do was to accelerate the progression or awareness of a new style of music. It helped break down the prejudice between the Uptown dark-skinned Negro and the Downtown, light-skinned Creole Negro.

Downtown musicians were taught the traditional music reading abilities, while the Uptown music was the slave work song, the spiritual, and the field holler. When these two styles blended together in Storyville, a Quadrille became Tiger Rag.

The '21' originally was an old whorehouse that had been made into a palace. It was located at 21 South Basin, and Hattie Hamilton was the Madame. It was a moneymaker that attracted the very rich, and the well-to-do.

Bands that played at the 21, got large tips, and never had to spend their pay, which was about $1.50 to $2.50 per gig. In the district, musicians earned $9.00 per week, and this was considered good pay, considering a steak cost ten cents, and a loaf of bread was five cents.

Another Madame that became quite famous was Lula White, who owned Mahogany Hall. It was the largest and most luxurious cabaret on Basin Street. Lulu was called the "Diamond Queen," as she boarded only the fairest and most beautiful Octoroon girls. Lulu had paid $30,000 to elaborately furnish the hall, which was a four story brothel.

Storyville became also known as where the greatest pianists played. As the brothels and bars, demanded piano playing at all times. A fine piano player by the name of Clarence Williams played at Mahogany Hall.

The night that Jimmie Noone met Clarence Williams was when he was visiting Lulu White. Jimmie had stopped wearing knickers, and now wore black trousers. As a young man, he could have passed for white, had he not been in New Orleans, where many Creoles looked like him. Jimmie's big brown eyes seemed to smile.

From his father's Irish race, he had small lips, a somewhat pug nose. His curly hair was now combed straight toward the back of his head. His height still remain somewhat short, a five feet, eight inches in height, and his body was still stocky. He had matured into a handsome man. And since his heart had never given him any trouble, he had developed an attitude that he really was healthy and that his mother was just overprotective.

Clarence Williams and Jimmie played "Alexander's Ragtime Band," and that lead to other songs, as their adaptability of playing together had become quite easy. Clarence invited Jimmie if he'd like to go to Lala's cabaret. There Joseph 'King' Oliver's band appeared.

And Lala's was an after-hours meeting place for musicians, plus a landmark for all tourists that came to visit Storyville. Large crowds of tourists came to see the show on the comer of Marais and Iberville Streets. The music in Lala's was called "Low gully," as it included blues and stomps, that refined people acknowledge they hated so much. However, these tourists changed their minds, as they stomped their feet, and drank many drinks.

About 4:00 AM, band members gathered at Lala's after work. Also converging to meet their pimps were ladies of the evening, hookers, and the girls that worked the sporting houses. It was an exciting place to meet, as the group sang, danced the cakewalk (a high-spirited strutting step) while the musicians got the opportunity to play new music, or whatever they wanted.

That morning, Jimmie met Bunk Johnson, Buddy Petit, Johnny Dodds, 'Pops' Foster, Frank Duson, Lorenzo Staulz, and Tony Jackson, who was famous in Storyville. Everyone got out their instruments including Jimmie, who took out his B-flat clarinet, and they played such tunes as, *Shadow Rag*, *Maple Leaf Rag*, *Number Two Rag*, and *Meat Ball*.

'Tiger Rag' was called number two and 'Sensation' was called "Meatballs," which was the same popular songs played by many bands, so different names were used by bands.

When Jimmie left Lala's, it was 7:00 AM., and although he was exhausted, he carried out his usual routine of practicing on his clarinet. Holding his mouthpiece, he fixed the reed to begin playing. His clarinet was a B-flat, and he used the Albert System mostly, but he also knew and used the Boehm System. Jimmie remembered that morning as, "The day that I knew for sure that I wanted to become a musician, more than anything else in the world. My ambition is to go beyond playing in the district, parades and on picnics. I wanted to become the best clarinet player in New Orleans."

The tradition of the marching bands was widely prominent, causing steady employment for musicians. Clarinet players were in demand also for holidays, funeral processions, and picnics out at Lake Pontchartrain.

The clarinet became the leading instrument because of its high register; it counterbalanced with the comet and trombone. It was capable of harmonizing with the main melody in a style that had become rooted in New Orleans. The clarinet was a necessary instrument for the traditional jazz harmony, and all the great clarinetists were using a more prominent, embellished counter melody (obbligato).

Jimmie said, "Within a year, I was playing the Bb, A, C, and Eb clarinet. I knew them all, because in the brass band, you had to be able to play four different clarinets."

…, Edmond Hall also remarked about having four clarinets, "The reason for that was when there was something to play in the key of E-flat, we would pick up the E-flat clarinet, and the same thing when there was something in the key of A, et cetera. That shows you how much music advances. Today you can take one clarinet and play everything on it. But the fact is that when we had to know all four the standards of musicianship in the brass bands were pretty high—"[3]

The sound and tone that Jimmie Noone was now capable of creating was perfect.

His technique was fast and he played with the greatest perfection, especially his rapid staccato phrases.

Storyville's environment helped ragtime to emerge. There was also a need for piano players to play for the silent films, the vaudeville, the sporting houses, nightclubs, cabarets, public dances, and theaters.

Ragtime was a piano music that lasted from 1896 to 1917. It heralded the arrival of jazz. Following the publication of the first instrumental rag, two black composers, Tom Turpin and Scott Joplin, produced rags that incorporated certain characteristics that governed the style throughout its history. Among these were the familiar multi-theme structure, key change, and the familiar rhythm of two strong beats per measure underlying simple syncopation.[4]

At first called "Rag," it was a form that developed gradually from minstrel music, and later became "Ragtime," when music had been written down in books using various parts of the band. Then practically every song that was written bore the ragtime title, such as Scott Joplin's first ragtime piece entitled, "Harlem Rag."

Jimmie played "Maple Leaf Rag," all over his clarinet, as he played the upper and lower register with expertise. He was capable of playing a typical New Orleans counterpoint.

Aaron Copland is the author of that best describes in his book how to understand the clarinet sound and tone. "The clarinet has a smooth, open, almost hollow sound. It is a cooler, more even-sounding instrument that the oboe, being also more brilliant. In its lower octave it possesses a unique tone color of a deeply haunting effect. Its dynamic range is more remarkable than that of any other woodwind, extending from a mere whisper to the most brilliant fortissimo."[5]

Chapter Three
Jazz

Noone's first job was serving as Bechet's 'understudy' in Cornetist Freddie Keppard's group (ca. 1913).[6]

The music that had been heard up until 1910 to a great part was music that was on the edge of becoming, to some extent, what was called "Jass," and then later "Jazz," Music now combined the structure of the call and response, along with the Rags, the Blues, and the Spirituals. Jazz had arrived, and when the New Orleans sound combined with it, this helped to create the improvised solo parts. The spectrum of music had made a gigantic leap!

Cut Off, Louisiana, was a small city that was between the cities of Larose and Galliano. Many referred to Cut Off as "Over the River." The Sam Ross Orchestra (1910–1921) was a band that began growing in popularity when Jimmie Noone joined their group.

Jimmie started his musical career playing with Sam Ross, the leader, who also played clarinet. Other band members included, Milton Martin (tb), Jackson Butler (b), Skeeter Jackson (g), and Sonny Hampton (d), none of these musicians ended up making music their career. Jimmie was also playing at funerals, church affairs, and entering contest's that were held for teens at the Elk's Club.

Bechet also continued to play dates with Freddie Keppard, and the Famous Eagle Band. For a performance, he asked Jimmie Noone to loan him a clarinet. Noon dutifully turned up with the instrument, but Bechet failed to arrive. Noone filled in for him, working alongside Keppard, Zue Robertson (trombone), Richard M. Jones (piano) and Jean Vigne (drums). It was Noone's first engagement, but he played so well he was offered the job permanently, and remained in the band until Keppard moved to California in the spring of 1914.[7]

Sidney Bechet was also employed with the 'Kid' Ory Band, and they were keeping busy constantly. Jimmie was also working with Kid Ory and trumpeter 'Papa' Celestin.

Ferdinand Joseph La Mente, which is 'Jelly Roll' Morton's birth name, was now considered a genius on the piano. As a teenager, he played Rags, Quadrilles, and popular songs, and he worked in the cabarets and brothels, where he would also sing.

On the piano Morton was a master of form and theory. Yet he ran around with the pimps, he was a pool shark, a con-man and a gambler. Morton's idol was Tony Jackson. Morton earned a large pay check working in the 'sporting houses' of the red-light district. His early composition during this period included 'King Porter Stomp' in 1902.

Walking into his house later and up the staircase, Jimmie hears his mother, Lucinda, call his name. "Is that you, Jimmie?" he called out.

"Yes. I'm going upstairs to read the paper."

The first thing that caught his eye on the front page was an article about the Magnolia Orchestra Jazz Band. It listed the musicians as, Emile Bigard, Joe Oliver, Lorenzo Tio, Sr., George Baquet, Honore Dutrey, Louis Keppard, Johnny St. Cyr, Pops Foster, Happy Goldston, and many others.

The newspaper showed the band playing at the Funky Butt Hall, on Perido Street, between Liberty and Franklin Streets. (Funky Butt Hall was also Kenna Hall)

Turning the page, Jimmie read an advertisement for the few clothes cabaret over on Basin Street, listing the Superior Orchestra. The admission was thirty cents.

Then Jimmie seen an advertisement for the Eagle Band. Everyone knew that the Eagle Band usually played at the Eagle Saloon, on South Rampart and Perdido Street. The saloon had become their headquarters, and from where their name derived.

Danny Barker describes this era perfectly in his book, *Bourbon Street Black*, when he said, "Jazz was in a real sense, born on the street bands of New Orleans, and partially reared in the brothels of Storyville, the Crescent City's legendary red-light district."[8]

The man who inherited Bolden's title of "King," was Freddie Keppard, a cornet player. Then, from Freddie Keppard, the title moved to Joe Oliver. Oliver had learned to compose jazz around work songs, spirituals and rough blues as a youngster. He was unique in his ability to hold his notes for long periods of time.

Louis Armstrong was seen as a young boy in the district selling coal at Pete Lala's. He also stole newspapers from white boys on the streetcars. Since newspapers were only sold by whites, he was arrested immediately and sent back to the Waif's Home.

About 1910, Bill Johnson, a bassist, or Freddie Keppard, organized "The Original Creole Band." (There remains a dispute as to which musician started up the group by jazz historians.) But Bill Johnson did go to California, and within two years sent for musicians, and he put Freddie in charge as the leader. Keppard left New Orleans, but played on transcontinental tours, and to the rest of the nation, played Ragtime and jazz.

Jimmie Noone teamed up with Buddy Petit to form the *Young Olympia Band*. Buddy Petit's real name was Joseph Crawford. They became co-leaders of this band.

"Buddy Petit is a man they've never written much about. He kind of what you call set a pace around New Orleans. He was a real leader and he set the pace around New Orleans. He was a real leader and set the pace for a lot of other bands. I mean these other bands would hear Buddy play something and they would all want to play it. If Buddy had left New Orleans to go to Chicago when a lot of the other men left, I'm positive he would have had a reputation equal to what the others got—"[9]

In Chicago, the great migration had started. By the turn of the century, the black population had become concentrated along Chicago's State Street, on the South side.

Also, a need for theater bands, cabarets, sporting houses, and dancing schools grew. By 1914, Chicago had a wide variety of job opportunities for musicians.

Freddie Keppard notified Jimmie Noone in New Orleans that he was needed for the Original Creole Orchestra, which was an Orpheum Circuit traveling band. Jimmie left his family in New Orleans, and traveled to Detroit, where he met Keppard.

Jimmie was seventeen when he traveled to Detroit and met Keppard. Upon his arrival, the band traveled and played in various cities for six months, with the tour ending in Chicago. Freddie Keppard, the leader and cornetist of the

Original Creole Orchestra (1913–1917), also had musicians, George Baquet, 'Big Eye' Louis Nelson, and Dink Johnson, playing with him.

In 1914, the Creole Band was the biggest hit at the Winter Gardens and other places in New York. They had also received a Victor offer, but did not accept it, as musicians at the time were afraid of being copied by other bands.

The Creole Band took a new form of music out into the world and became the first good Negro band to make tours out of town. This band opened all the doors for other bands to do road tours.

When the band stopped in Chicago, he was totally amazed to see stockyards and all the railroads the city had. And the wind and cold weather was also something that he was not used to. Never before had he seen so much smoke coming out of the buildings, or so many people in one city. These people were desperately waiting to hear this new music called jazz.

Jimmie Noone returned back to New Orleans after the Creole Band finished their tour, and he was able to obtain work in the district (Storyville) immediately.

Jimmie was doing quite well with the Noone-Petit Orchestra, that had formed in 1916. Also, Buddy Petit played with the Eagle Band, along with Joe 'King' Oliver.

Jimmie was also performing with the Original Creole Orchestra. The band that Noone and Petit had co-directed was called the Young Olympia Band.

In 1917, the Young Olympia Band dissolved in order for Buddy Petit to go to Los Angeles, California, for a short visit to join 'Jelly Roll' Morton. Jelly Roll had already recorded his original *Jelly Roll Blues* in 1915, which was his first published song. At the time, he was living in California, and gambling had become his main source of income, not music.

Joe Oliver had told 'Kid' *Ory* when they were discussing his leaving New Orleans, that he could recommend a trumpet player to take his place. But Kid *Ory* told him that he had already chosen someone to replace him.

'Kid' Ory realized that there were many good and experienced trumpet players in New Orleans, but he selected Louis Armstrong. *Ory* went and visited Armstrong, and told him that if he got himself a pair of long trousers, he'd give him a job. And within two hours Louis had arrived at Ory's home, ready to play.

Ory was doing one-nighters all over the city, he worked at yacht clubs, country clubs, and promoted his dances at Pete Lala's Hall on Sundays, and the Cooperative Hall on Mondays. *Ory* was doing top jobs and receiving top pay. Because Armstrong could not read at the time, tunes were usually played once, hummed or whistled one time, and he'd never forget the tune. Joe 'King' Oliver's protégé was, Louis Armstrong. He paid Armstrong with trumpet lessons in exchange for him doing errands for Stella Oliver (Joe's wife) and Oliver had also given Louis one of his older comet's to replace his secondhand one.

Jazz had been born. It had taken a quantum leap, and the abrupt transition had taken its dramatic advance in Storyville. The interactions of the Downtown Creole and the Uptown Negro had blended its European Classical, Spirituals, Blues, and Ragtime into one style. Which allowed musicians to improvise, compose, and arrange their new style of music to take place.

This element of individuality is then another African characteristic carried over into jazz. It is so strong in quality that it has survived despite the fact that jazz developed almost entirely on instruments that came out of the tradition of European art music. This is one of the miracles of jazz, and it is never sufficiently emphasized.[10]

Before the originators of jazz had migrated to Chicago, the music had been heard and duplicated. The early facsimile was first made by young white musicians, such as *The Chicago Rhythm Kings, The Friars Society, The Wolverines*, and numerous other bands. This migration of New Orleans music soon became known as "Chicago jazz."[11]

These white musicians played and duplicated the emerging black music, and eventually a group called "The Famous Original Dixieland Jazz Band" (ODJB) recorded on the Victor Talking Machine Company. Their rendition of "Livery Stable Blues," and Dixieland Jazz Band One-Step (later called Original Dixieland One-Step) in 1917, became the first jazz phonograph record to be issued.

Jimmie Noone had contempt for the music of the Original Dixieland Jazz Band. As he remembered Nick La Rocca (Leader of the ODJB) hanging around and getting lots of ideas from Joe 'King' Oliver. And La Rocca's father owned a Negro saloon, and from the Negro bands playing there, young Nick would ask the clarinetists to teach him some licks. Some, later, would regret that they had taught him so well.

The United States Navy was pressuring the city government about closing the district, while a local business slump was occurring, Storyville the famous red-light district was ordered closed in 1917, by the Navy Department of the Federal Government. At the sporting houses, prostitutes moved out from the streets of St. Louis, Basin, Franklin, Iberville, and Bienville. Belongings and possessions were carried out on two-wheel carts, or by wheelbarrows. Madames and Queens of the once notorious red-light district had gone, and Storyville later became history.

The closing of Storyville is seen historically as the time that jazz was forced out of New Orleans, but it may have been more coincidental than casual as it is likely that the new music would have spread anyway to other cities; but certainly many of the New Orleans musicians went to Chicago and elsewhere round about that time.[12]

With the closing of Storyville, the gradual shift up north to Chicago and its migration was because of the difference in pay and the opportunities. Music was now all about jazz and improvisation.

Now that Storyville had closed, Jimmie Noone and Joe 'King' Oliver, traveled by railroad to Chicago to join up with Freddie Keppard and his Original Creole Orchestra. It was 1917, and the band had an engagement that opened at the Royal Gardens.

Louis Armstrong had replaced Joe Oliver in the Kid Ory Band, and he already knew the repertory by heart, so they continued to receive many jobs. Armstrong, however, was still using his coal wagon for extra money.

The clarinet technique that Jimmie Noone developed was precise, incredibly fast, while he maintained quick staccato phrases. His tone delivered a full and rich quality, possibly because of his body and chest size, which allowed the full volume to be heard. He had developed a New Orleans style of jazz.

New Orleans jazz is described as a "Style we generally understand, a small group, with comet or trumpet leading the ensemble and making the initial statement of the theme tenor role; the trombone playing and underlying counterpoint bass role; the clarinet playing a decorative ad lib high register part."

"Each of the solo instruments takes it in tum to assume the lead, the others generally continuing to play in improvised counterpoint or riffs. The front line instruments are backed by a rhythm section—a drummer with an elementary kit keeping a steady beat going; a banjo or guitar chording in a matching relentless way; and a wind-bass, tuba or bass-saxophone, later a string bass."[13]

"Oliver had moved to Chicago from New Orleans, ostensibly to join the band that brass player Bill Johnson was organizing for the Royal Gardens, a dance hall and barroom. Oliver was not Bill Johnson's first choice; the brass player had originally wired an offer to Buddy Petit, who failed to answer. Johnson then tried Oliver, who accepted, as did clarinetist Jimmie Noone."

The Gardens were also a well-frequented dance hall for jazz listeners and dancers. Jimmie Noone worked at the Royal from 1917 until 1919. And that the *Original Royal Garden Blues* had been written by him and Joe Oliver for the band to play, as a remembrance of the cafe. They later sold it to Clarence Williams for a small amount, and Williams published it himself.

It was in 1917 that Paramount Recording Company was owned by a furniture store called the Wisconsin Chair Company. Paramount was producing phonographs, and decided to get into the recording business, when they realized the addition profit. As a consequence, they entered into the neglected needs of the Negro market. Their reward was an increase in their financial position.

Jimmie was now twenty years old, the year was 1917. He looked suave and dignified wearing his best suit jacket, with matching trousers, and a soft straw Panama hat. And inside his pocket was a chain-watch, along with advance money that Bill Johnson had sent him to get to Chicago.

And then he heard an announcement, "Chicago, Illinois. Five minutes, all aboard."

With tickets now in hand, and ready to board the train, they heard a voice and turned around. It was Jimmie's mother, Lucinda, running toward them. With tears streaming down her smooth clear skin, she took out her handkerchief to dry her face, and grabbed her son. "When will I see you again?"

Jimmie replied, "Mother, I will return soon."

But Lucinda knew that her son was now a man reaching out for success, and that perhaps this would be the last time she would hug him. She handed him a sack full of French bread, cheese and fruit.

Jimmie asked, "Mother, where is father?" She replied sadly, "He left early this morning, without talking to me first. He did leave me a note. It said, 'Now that the United States has declared war on Germany, he was going to sign up to fight a battle in World War 1. He left us $20,000 in the bank to take care of our living expenses'." Lucinda hugged him, then left weeping.

Jimmie took one last look at his Crescent City. It was a hot, humid day, with temperatures reaching about 85 degrees. Joe Oliver told Jimmie, "Remember how the city looks, 'cause it could be a long time before we return back here. But there's one good thing about leaving New Orleans as a musician, we'll always know that you'll be welcomed back. It's all part of a musician's code."

Boarding the train, Oliver mentioned, "I almost forgot that the railroad has started the practice of using passenger cars for long distance traveling. Especially on the Chicago line, which will provide us with sleeping-cars."

Jimmie replied, "I hear that they've been very successful."

As the train's engine roared, a Pullman walked them to their sleeping compartments. When Jimmie and Oliver entered the small area that contained his bunk, he stopped first to place his instruments down, then his luggage, as Oliver who had decided to take the bottom bunk, did the same. Joe Oliver noticed a sign advertising a menu.

He told Jimmie, "Well, it looks like that large appetite you have will be taken care of in the train compartment set up for dining."

As he pointed to the sign, Jimmie remarked, "What are we waiting for? Let's go."

As they headed for the dining car, a conductor standing near their window yelled, "Last call for Chicago!"

While another conductor walked toward them yelling, "Tickets! Tickets!" The train slowly moved away from the station.

Entering the dining car, a handsome Creole waiter met them at the door and seated them. He said, "It will be a pleasure serving you both. I can't believe that the famous Joe 'King' Oliver, and Jimmie Noone are traveling on my train."

He instantly bowed, handed them a written menu and the Chicago Defender. It was a Negro newspaper that had been printed a week ago, and was dated April 3, 1917. The courteous Porter mentioned, "You might be interested in this article. I'll be back with coffee." He left to wait on the other passengers.

The article was read by Joe Oliver to Jimmie: "Negroes are rushing to the recruiting stations to volunteer for the first World War. Enlistment is opened to all able-bodied Americans between the ages of twenty-one and extended to thirty-one."

While eating in the diner, Joe and Jimmie talked about the war, and what they expected when they reached Chicago, and their musical careers. After eating, Joe Oliver wanted to smoke a cigar, so they entered the smoking car. Where a group of Negro soldiers, obviously drunk, were holding each other up as they sang a military song. It reminded them both of the article that they had just read.

After a long trip of traveling through many states, and days of sleeping in their compartment, Joe Oliver and Jimmie Noone were anxiously waiting to arrive. They had played their instruments daily, in order not to become bored. They had entertained both white and Negro passengers, but at separate times, since neither race could still not eat or sleep among each other.

The train had entered the Prairie State of Illinois. Joe and Jimmie went to their assigned sleeping car, and finished packing. It was early in the morning when they arrived in Chicago, as it was so windy, they both put on their overcoats, hats, and gloves. Remarking how they already missed New Orleans and its weather.

Chapter Four
Chicago

The migration of New Orleans musicians to Chicago, Illinois, involved Joe 'King' Oliver, Freddie Keppard, Tommy Ladnier, Louis Armstrong, Jimmie Noone, and 'Jelly Roll' Morton. The 'New Orleans Jazz style' was copied and adapted by young white musicians in Chicago, and was now known specifically as the, 'Chicago Jazz Style'.[14]

Jimmie and Joe stepped off the train and entered the biggest railroad depot that Chicago was so proud of. They noticed signs for the taxi's, which read, "Twenty cents for the first one-third mile, ten cents for each additional two-thirds mile, and five cents for each additional passenger."

Lawrence Duhe, who was from La Place, Louisiana, had arrived just weeks before in Chicago with his own band. Later he would add pianist, Lil Hardin, from Memphis, Tennessee. "Duhe, learning of Oliver's impending arrival, made plans to entice the cornetists into his band. In order to do this, he asked Sidney Bechet to accompany him to the railway station, to meet the morning train (Knowing of Sidney's unpunctuality Duhe made *him* stay the night at his apartment). Oliver listened to Duhe's offer, then decided to have the best of both worlds by doubling between the Royal Gardens and the Dreamland Cafe."[15]

Duhe and Bechet however, did not arrive at the train station on time, as the train arrived thirty minutes early, and Jimmie and Joe caught a Checker taxi immediately to the Royal Gardens, they then missed Bechet and Duhe.

Jimmie and Joe sat in the taxi, as the driver got friendly and talked about Chicago. "Yeah, the demand for labor is so great that the Negro areas are very crowded. The south-side is where most of our people live." He took a deep breath, then continued, "There is only one hotel here that will rent rooms out, or you'll need a relative or friend to stay at. It's prejudice here, and there're Germans, Irish, Swede's, Russian's, Polish, French and French-Canadians."

Arriving at the club, he continued talking as they paid him, and thanked him for all the tourists information. As they looked at the outside of the building, a large sign read, "The Royal Garden Band."

Entering, they were surprised at the extremely large dance floor.

The band members were all inside the hall, and included Paul Barbarin (from New Orleans), Lottie Taylor (from Nashville), and Freddie Keppard. The organizers of the club, Eddie Vincent and Bill Johnson, had not arrived yet.

The musicians informed Joe Oliver and Jimmie Noone that they would be joining the local musicians' union, that was called Local 208. It was also called, "The Colored Branch of the American Federation of Musicians," and that white musicians belonged to Local 10, Chicago segregated union. (It was not until the 1960s that the two unions joined together.)

While Bill Johnson had been waiting for replies from New Orleans, he had utilized the services of his longtime colleague cornetist Freddie Keppard. Both Johnson and Keppard were in Chicago because the Original Creole Orchestra's trombonist, Eddie Vincent, had been forced to quit that group unexpectedly to undergo an appendectomy.

It so happened that all three of these musicians found the Chicago atmosphere congenial, and they never went back on the road again as a unit.[16]

Lawrence Duhe asked Freddie Keppard to join his band. Keppard was proud and did not want to be anybody's second choice, so he demanded a pay of $50 per week, and he received it, allowing him to be paid more than Joe Oliver.

When Oliver doubled with another group at the Dreamland Cafe, its leader was Duhe, and featured trombonist Roy Palmer, Sidney Bechet, clarinetist, drummer, Minor Hall, and Wellman Braud, bassist.

At the same time, Johnny Dodds had joined up with the trumpeter, Mutt Carey's four-piece ensemble, the "Mack Merrymakers," which was touring as a vaudeville group. When Carey got to Chicago, he left the group and stayed in Chicago. Johnny Dodds rejoined Kid Ory in New Orleans.

Tony Jackson, a piano player, that had started his musical career in Lulu whites Mahogany Hall in Storyville. Now in Chicago, he often he sold his written musical compositions for five dollars. He was working at The Elite No.

I club, it was a famous cabaret. Jackson was also with 'Jelly Roll' Morton playing in bars along State Street.

Morton was on his first trip to Chicago, and was traveling between New York and California.

"The Royal Gardens, the most striking thing that hit your eye, once you got into the hall was a big crystal ball that was made of small pieces of reflecting glass and hung over the center of the dance floor. A couple of spotlights shone on the big ball as it turned and threw reflected spots of light all over the room and the dancers."

"Usually, they'd dance the bunny hug to slow blues like *London Blues*, or some other tune in a slow-blues tempo, and how the dancers would grin away. The ceiling of the place was made lower than it actually was by chicken wire that was stretched out and over the wire were spread great bunches of artificial maple leaves. I'll guarantee that chicken wire was the only artificial thing in the place."[17]

Now that all the musicians for the Royal Band had arrived, Bill Johnson, told them that additional jobs would be at the Lexington opera House and The Columbia Theater.

Jimmie was able to locate tenement housing over on the south-side of Chicago, where the negroes lived. This was an area that extended the length of the north half of the South side west of the lake shore communities; it was called, "The Black Belt." The Black Belt area, also went by the name of "Bronzeville." It was a narrow rectangle for about 16th Street. Eventually, negroes from the north end of the belt and spread southward.

In the late nineteenth century, traveling for musicians for more than a few miles was difficult. Horse-drawn wagons and buggies were used for casual travel, but musicians were limited until Henry Ford's Model T appeared. Now the automobile was cheaper than a horse and faster. The only problem Negro musicians faced traveling was where they would spend the night and eat. Although they could afford to stay at the white hotel, they were not invited to stay.

The South side had slaughter houses and stockyards, all along the Chicago River. Because of the packing industries rapid growth, and the development of the refrigerator train car. The tenement housing he lived in, is where Jimmie made an eating friend by the name of John Jackson. His nickname was "Black

John," and he was rightfully called that. He had a jet-black complexion, and Jimmie like John because they both liked to eat.

When Jimmie went to the slaughterhouse one day to meet John, he thought he would become sick. The stench was overwhelming. There stood Black John with a large instrument in his hands, and as the cattle came through the gate, his job was to hit the cattle with his hammer, with the hardest blow he could aim.

Black John never missed. As the cattle approached, he'd spread his feet apart very wide, he'd lift his hammer, take aim, and with all his might, he swung his final blow. Jimmie was surprised when he seen the head of the cattle swing up in the air, and the brains of the animal flew every which-way.

Lunch break for Jimmie and Black John was a ritual. They'd eat at a little place next to the slaughterhouse called "The Pig Pin." The cook, Mama Jane, served soul food and Creole food. Jimmie had now become overweight.

Chapter Five
Pre-1920s

Employment for Chicago musicians meant working two jobs per day, and possibly seven days a week. Jimmie Noone was playing at the Royal Garden's Cafe on Chicago's South side, and leading his own band at the Edelweiss, with Glover Compton.

Lil Harden, a pianist (who later married Louis Armstrong), joined the New Orleans Creole Band at the Royal Gardens, with such men as Freddie Keppard, Ed Garland, Paul Barbarin, Jimmie Noone and Eddie Vincent. Her salary went from three dollars a week to fifty-five dollars per week.

"Among the great pianists of Chicago was a man named Glover Compton, who always played with a big cigar in his mouth. At the Panama, on Thirty-sixth and State Street, Glover was playing piano there also. Everyone knew Glover Compton. He was doing the stuff that Willie 'The Lion' Smith did later on, you know, the big fat cigar hangin' out of the comer of his mouth and sittin' sideways at the piano talking to the people. Glover was great."[18]

Virgil Williams, operated the Royal Gardens. Musicians played from 9:00 PM until 4:00 AM nightly. The musicians were Joe 'King' Oliver, Jimmie Noone, Eddie Venson, Bill Johnson, and Lottie Taylor, on piano. They were great playing together, and the long lines to get into the club were great advertisement and money for the club. Salary for musicians had become about twenty-five dollars a week. Compared to the one dollar a night made in New Orleans.

Jimmie Noone and his new eating friend, Black John, had decided together to enlist in the Army. They went to Scott Field near Belleville for their medical examination. This was where squadrons were trained before being sent to France. World War 1 was in its third year. The Yanks had descended on Europe, and the battlefields of France had become bloody.

Black John had passed his examination and had been scheduled to report for active duty. When Jimmie was examined, the doctor immediately asked him, "Have you had problems with your heart?"

Jimmie answered, "Many doctors have tested me. They said that it's a palpitation of irregular heartbeats."

After another doctor checked him, they declared that he was exempt from military service, as his heart was too weak for combat duty. Jimmie left the dispensary, determined to lead a normal life as fully as he could, because nothing medically could be done. Years later, Jimmie stated that he had never heard what happened to his friend, Black John.

Riding back to Chicago, Jimmie decided that if music was to become his career, and be taken seriously, that he needed additional lessons. And that to learn the correct way, his music teacher had to be the best clarinet teacher that he could find.

The teacher that Jimmie Noone selected was Franz Schoepp, a symphonic clarinetist, who taught the very young Benny Goodman.

Benny Goodman was a white Chicago ghetto kid, the eighth of twelve. His father was a poor Russian immigrant who worked in a factory. There wasn't any musical background in the family. It was through a local neighborhood synagogue, that assisted immigrants, and sent them to a local settlement house, to become familiar and adjust to a large city. The Hull House sent Benny Goodman to Franz Schoepp and sponsored payment of his lessons.

Jimmie Noone, later told his family that, "The Goodman's lived in a ghetto area for Russian's, and I lived in the Negro ghetto area, we lived close to each other, so we traveled together to old man Schoepp's house. I took my music lessons first, and Schoepp allowed Goodman to watch." At first, I was developing skills in classical music, then it tum to what I'd like to call, "my style."

"Sitting there, Benny Goodman was able to see my technique and hear the music I played. It's very obvious that Goodman was able to recall and translate later what I had played at those lessons. That's why Goodman was able to become a professional by the age of fifteen. Goodman used no restraints, he took the origin and roots of jazz, and my soul."

"The diaspora from New Orleans swelled from 1917 on. By 1920, there were so many jazzmen in Chicago, most of them black, that the center of jazz had shifted. As many as forty outstanding exiles were playing at the Royal Gardens, Dreamland Cafe, De Luxe Cabaret, Red Mill Cafe, The Pekin, and the Vendome Theater, where Erskin Tate led a band of New Orleans luminaries from 1918, to the end of the twenties."[19]

Jazz was traveling to all the states. The New Orleans Rhythm Kings (NORK), which was led by Paul Mares, on trumpet, and featured Leon Rappolo, on clarinet. They were playing at The Friars Inn, on the north side of Chicago. In Los Angeles, cometist Mutt Carey, and trombonist Edward 'Kid' Ory were featured. In New York, migrated musicians were Sidney Bechet, clarinetist. and cometists, Oscar Celestin.

"From the beginning, the biggest problem the whites were faced with in dealing with jazz was figuring out how that 'Swing', which they could feel in the music of the New Orleans players, was produced. For most, it took several years to get the hang of it, and in the meantime, as the early records show, their playing suffered from that ragtime stiffness of which the New Orleans players had already divested themselves."[20]

Sidney Bechet had been working with Freddie Keppard, and them with pianist, Tony Jackson. He then taught himself how to play the soprano sax. Later, he moved to his new home, Europe.

By the year 1920, the Negro population in Chicago had increased greatly. Also, the phonograph record had become a craze, and helped jazz develop. This, in turn, created the dance boom. The recording companies realized that people could now dance at home to their favorite records. In the year 1914, over twenty million records were sold.

In 1919, the Andrew Joseph Volstead's National Prohibition Enforcement Act was passed. It banned the sale of alcohol in Chicago, and this in tum had a financial effect on musicians, and the success of jazz. Jazz musicians were now controlled by gangsters such as Torrio, the O'Bamopms, the Gennas, the Aiellos, and Capone.

Prohibition took effect in 1920. It was now illegal for anyone to manufacture or drink alcohol. Gangsters and bootleggers and the owners of the speakeasy's were able to make a tremendous profit. In Brownville, what was called 'Nigger gin' could be purchased for fifteen cents a drink. It was a low-grade, terrible tasting moonshine booze.

Young women during World War 1 begin to take freedom from conventional living. They sought retaliation and freedom that men had been enjoying all their lives as they stayed home. The new 'Flapper' had emerged. Women went to saloons, cocktail bars, cut their hair into bobs, wore short dresses, became looser, and began to flap her wings.

Prohibition had caused a great demand for jazz, and black market booze. This period became especially important to musicians. Muggsy Spanier, who was fourteen at the time, and allowed by the owner of the Dreamland to sit in a dark comer of the balcony and listen to music, had this to say, "The band played from about nine thirty to one AM., and after hours they played at the Pekin Cafe, one of the worst gangster hang outs in Chicago. Sometimes the goings-on would get rough inside, the music would stop and you'd hear the flash of forty-five caliber revolvers trying to fire with a beat."[21]

Jimmie Noone used to talk about the times he worked at the Dreamland and the Pekin, and what went on with the gangsters. "Alphonse Capone (AKA scareface), had bodyguards at both clubs, they always had hiding places, or sometimes they just stood around the club while having a drink."

Noone's favorite story about gangsters and prohibition is about the time that he was working at the Dreamland and he needed his clarinet case, that he had left behind the stage curtain.

"When our intermission came, I pulled the heavy draped curtains back, and was looking eye to eye with about ten of Capone's men. They yelled, 'Get out of the way', as I viewed wide eyed ten big Thompson submachine guns staring me in the face. Right after that, I ducked out of the way, as gunfire was being aimed toward a man sitting out in the audience. He was shot dead within a few seconds, possibly by every bodyguard that was hiding behind that curtain."

Jimmie Noone told more about the Prohibition era, "Chicago had become a wicked city. Prohibition of alcohol brought about greed between the bootleggers, the gangsters, and the owners of the speakeasy's."

"Automobile producers were Chrysler, General Motors, the Pierce-Arrow, Chalmers by Chrysler, and the Ajaz by Nash, and production of over six million cars were muse."

"Americans became greedy for jazz, causing the originators and creators of the music to be unable to record before white musicians had stripped away our music. The only good that came about at this time, was the development of jazz musicians in New York, Chicago, St. Louis, and New Orleans.

Musicians in every state were awaiting the arrival of the 1920s, to further and maintain their creative powers."

Chapter Six
The Jazz Age

The first World War had ended in 1918. About ten million men died from 1914 to 1918. A generation of men had died for their country.

From 1917 until 1929, there was a period that has been called, "The Jazz Age," "The Roaring 20s," and, "The Post War." And most importantly, it brought about the fusion of Negro and white music together.

What set off the Jazz Age, was the disillusionment of the war, and a large number of men that had died, which caused a rebellion among the young toward the older generation.

The Roaring 20s became associated with a dance called the, "Charleston," which was named after James P. Johnson, who wrote a song for the city of Charleston, South Carolina, in 1923. It was an instant hit with the Negro. Popular dances included the "black bottom," the "quickstep" the "foxtrot," the "two-step," and the "bunny hug."

With a new decade, the young had experienced Prohibition, and homemade bootlegging bad booze, and women and men had become used to drinking in bars. Gangsters, mobs, and violence were everyday headlines in the Chicago newspapers, and in the Fox Movieton Newsreels.

Women and morality became a thing of the past. Women were doing men's jobs during the war, they took off their corsets, wore lipstick, earned their own pay, bobbed their hair, wore rolled stockings, and some went bare legged.

Along with the rebellious morality, and disregard of former living customs, having fun, included sex, liquor, and enjoying a new music craze. It meant listing to a new sound of jazz, and enjoying the pleasure of listening to both white and Negro jazz bands.

For the first time, Americans had more leisure time. The work week had decreased from twelve hours daily to eight. Technology had now furnished automobiles, radios, and the movie theater.

A middle-class society became interested in fads, fashion, baseball, lawn tennis, and the introduction of golf. Which, in tum, created municipal golf courses, baseball stadium's, the purchasing of golf balls and equipment, along with various golf fees.

Golf had originally been played by aristocrats as their pastime, until Walter Hagen and Bobby Jones showed that it was an exciting sport, and these two men helped to stir enthusiasm for the game.

Jimmie Noone had taken up the hobby of playing golf, as it was a sedate type of sport, and less strenuous, especially since he had been gaining weight. When he finished an engagement, it would be about 7:00 AM, as he usually played at two nightclubs per night. The golf clubs were designed by hand to suit his individual style of playing.

His appearance for golf was a wool felt cap with a short brim, his shirt was white with a brown tie, and he wore a V-neck sweater. His pants were knickerbockers that gathered at the knee with elastic. He wore argyle socks, with shoes that wcrc multicolor brown and white. He carried a neat and handsome appearance, and he was still single, at the age of twenty-five.

As he turned to leave the golf course that day, a young Negro woman passed by him. He looked up to see what he would later call his "Sweet Lorraine."

Jimmie said, "She was beautiful. It was love at first sight for me! The red dress she wore that day was something that complemented her. It created a look that said—I'm available. Before I could speak to her, a young man ran behind her yelling, 'Lorraine, wait for me!' She smiled in passing, but I swear my heart must of skipped many beats, as I remember feeling engulfed in her presence. Although I only seen her for a few seconds, I knew that one day I'd see her again. And that is what I waited for."

Leaving the golf course that day, Jimmie walked several blocks to catch the El, as he hummed a popular song that was called, *The St. Louis Blues*. This song had been written by W.C. Handy and had been published in 1914. It was the first blues that had become commercialized. Its success came about from singer Ethel Waters, and in 1920 she became the first popular Negro singer to record jazz and was also being called, "Hot music," and the size of a band had changed from four or five musicians, to a larger scale. The music became more serious, and the big band sound was emerging.

Possibly the best description of the ending of the Jazz Age, is told by Arnold Shaw in his epilogue, "Numerous hits became million-copy sellers, enriching an expanding group of popular music publishers and songwriters."

Apex Blues 40

The nation danced to the music of a thousand bands. Black creativity made Harlem a center of New York life and introduced novel dances, tempos, and sounds to the musical theater and the hit parade.

With the infiltration of blues and jazz—the syncopated rhythms, new tonalities, fresh, off-beat harmonies, and improvisation—popular music acquired a unique American sound.[22]

The 'Jazz Age' had ended, and with it numerous hits became million-copy sellers, which contributed to music publishers and songwriters economy. The nation danced, and sang to blues, syncopated rhythms, popular music, and improvisation of music was now accepted as a unique American sound.

The speakeasy world of the twenties may have been rowdy, boisterous, extravagant, cynical, and violent, but it produced Show Boat, Bix, Tea For Two, Duke Ellington, Bessie Smith, Rhapsody In Blue, Louis Armstrong, and Star Dust.[23]

After Jimmie Noone had arrived at home that day, he practiced for several hours, and upon looking up at the clock, he noticed that it was almost noon, and he had not yet gone to bed. He then heard a knock on his front door.

A voice outside was calling out, "Western Union," opening the door, Jimmie accepted the wire, and gave the messenger a tip. The telegram read:
Jimmie Noone
25th & State Street Chicago, Illinois
Dear son, you father died from a heart attack.
It is imperative that you return home immediately. Love, Mother.
APEX BLUES 41

Chapter Seven
The Twenties

Noone's earliest recordings made with Oliver in 1923 and Doc Cook in 1924 show him to be already an adept clarinetist in either an ensemble or solo context. His playing is already superbly controlled in respect to tone, rhythm, and musical ideas.[24]

Jimmie Noone sat on the edge of his bed, as he read the telegram that he had received for the third time. With tears streaming down his cheeks, and raging anger, he yelled out, "NO." He called out in a loud voice, "Oh father. You died before I could tell you how much I loved you. And, you never got to hear how improved my playing is. Oh God. Now you'll never know."

Jimmie immediately wired his mother back. He packed for the trip and went to the Royal Gardens to deliver the news.

Bill Johnson at the Royal Gardens was informed by Jimmie, that he needed time off. He was given ten days to travel home for the funeral. He quickly caught the train leaving Chicago for New Orleans. It had been two years since his return home.

Arriving in New Orleans, all he could think about was his father. Walking into his home, he was greeted by his mother and a Mr. Charles McIntosh. He was Johnnie Noone's lawyer, someone that his father had trusted to handle his estate.

The lawyer read the will to them both. Lucinda had been left an inheritance, by Jimmie's father, and Mr. McIntosh, stated that he would be releasing a check to her monthly to handle her household needs.

Mr. McIntosh then told them, "Johnnie has been taking care of two families. He has allowed Lucinda to receive a total of $50,000. Upon his death, however, it is with the speculation that his white family never be approached, and that his Negro family not attend his funeral. If your family can agree to that, Lucinda, then I will bring back papers for you to sign. Just let me know." He shook their hands and walked out the front door.

Jimmie caressed his mother tightly, like he did as a child. Lucinda fell onto her son's shoulders, while crying and shaking. He knew that her mother needed consoling when he said, "Mother. We knew Dad had another family. He never kept any secrets from us. You must remember that you were his first and only love. We can't allow ourselves to get upset that we can't go to the funeral. It is not our place to be with his white family."

Jimmie continued to hold his mother, and they rocked each other back and forth in comfort.

While visiting his mother, Jimmie was able to visit his grandmother that was still alive, and his sisters. Nita had married into the Barbarin family. His sister Lil was engaged to marry Charlie Dags, while Elizabeth, known as "Lottie," was still single.

Jimmie paid a visit to Kid Ory, and ran into Johnny Dodds, who was working for Ory at the time. Dodds was the older brother of 'Baby' Dodds, a drummer. Johnny Dodds, a clarinetist, lacked the technique that Jimmie Noone had, but was considered extraordinary for his blues renditions.

Johnny Dodds told Jimmie, "You know Sidney Bechet is my idol."

Jimmie replied, "Mine too toilet."

Dodds was called "Toilet," by fellow New Orleans jazz musicians, because of the style of his blue clarinet playing. Johnny continued while smiling proudly, "Have you heard the news? Joe Oliver has sent for me to work with him at the Dreamland. I ain't got no music case, guess just some old newspaper or bag will have to do. Yeah, I'm going north." They shook hands, then Jimmie left.

Jimmie then went over to Chartres Street, where the Mandeville Swells Hall was, and had a drink with some of the musicians still in the city. Seeing the door open, he walked inside, but no one was there. He sat down on a stool, and remembered the night of 1910, when Sidney Bechet was playing the clarinet in the great Olympia Band.

It was his friend, Freddie Keppard, that jumped out of his seat to introduce him to Sidney, but Jimmie knew that he had to, because Freddie was dating his sister.

When he left the hall, he told this story: "I heard some birds chirping a thin sharp sound that reminded me of a walling songbird. When I looked up toward the electrical lines, birds sat perching there on the magnolia trees. They might have been rare species, or maybe they had just learned how to make unusual noises."

"I then heard their walling clearer. I started humming it and whistling that over and over, as I returned back to my mother's home. As I entered the door humming, my mother said, 'That sounds like a nice tune, I don't believe I've heard it before'. Jimmie began running to his room to get his clarinet, while telling his mother, 'I'm going to practice for a while'."

"I then unpacked my clarinet while humming, then I began slowly to try and reproduce what I had heard from the birds. What developed were notes played quite fast, producing many loud tremendous vibrating notes."

"I had learned to play what I called 'The Trill' I later learned that the sound was what birds make when they are mating. It's all part of the nature thing. As a consequence it would become the foremost developing style in how I played the clarinet."

The following day, Jimmie left New Orleans. He had stayed to help settle financial matters. And, with the advice from Attorney Charles McIntosh, the family's inheritance had been invested in stocks and bonds. Mr. Mc Intosh assured the family that the bank would give them good dividends from their investment.

When Jimmie had started playing at the Royal Gardens, his style of playing seemed to be influenced by his early teacher, Sidney Bechet. But, within two years, and studying under the influence of Franz Schoeppe, and playing the "Trill," he had hit on the creative beginning stages in developing his own distinguished style of playing, that he would become famous for. It would be a style that would be recognized, after hearing only a few notes from his clarinet.

Freddie Keppard met Jimmie at the train depot. They headed straight to the Royal Gardens and grabbed a bite to eat. They talked about how Joe Oliver who was with the Original Creoles, and was now doubling gigs with Lawrence Duhe's Orchestra at Bill Bottom's Dreamland Cafe.

The Dreamland opened its doors in 1917, over on State Street and 35th. Nearly from its creation, it attracted nothing but the best of jazz bands. Many black musicians bragged, "That because it was located over on the south-side of Chicago, only the best of jazz could be heard."

Apex Blues 45

The Dreamland Cafe was where jazz singer, Alberta Hunter performed. She spoke of how hard musicians had to work, "That Dreamland was some place. It was big and always packed. And you had to be a singer then—there were no microphones and those bands were marvelous."

"King Oliver's band was there when I started (Louis wasn't with him yet), and I'm telling you, you could sing one chorus or sixty choruses and that band would never be a beat away. And they'd always end on the same note and at the same time the singer did."[25]

Freddie also talked to Jimmie about the possibility of him replacing the bandleader at the Royal Gardens, who at that time was Joe 'King' Oliver. Oliver, he told Jimmie, was also working at the Pekin Cafe. Freddie then remarked, "Man, they packin' people up in the Dreamland, and at the Pekin Cafe, people are being turned away. People here are going crazy for jazz."

As Jimmie and Joe Oliver were talking, Charlie "Doc," Cook walked in to the Royal Gardens. He had a group in Detroit that was called "Cookie and his Ginger Snaps."

Jimmie Noone once remarked that Charles Cooke began composing music when he was about eight years old. Cook knew the piano, organ, arrangements, and was the first black to receive a doctorate from the American Conservatory.

Charlie shook hands with Jimmie and Joe and sat down. Doc had black hair that was combed straight back and slicked down. He was a nice-looking guy, that wore eyeglasses, many talked of his handsome features. Cook talked fast and excited.

--

"Listen Jimmie, I need you. I'm starting up a new group here in Chicago, I've got a mind to call it, 'Charlie Cook And His Fourteen Doctors of Syncopation'. My new band must include you and Freddie Keppard, and I've also got William Dawson, that will join us. What do you say?" Jimmie instantly accepted the offer, thanking that he needed to keep busy and get back to work.

Joe Oliver remarked, "Man, every place that I go, I see advertising posters all over the El trains."

Jimmie, Oliver, and Doc continue to talk music while having another drink. Doc told them that John Hammond, who had become owner of the famous "Dreamland Casino and Ballroom," promised to come and hear them play. They talked about how he was a descendant of the Vanderbilts, and had become involved in Columbia Records, and how he was becoming involved with everything involving jazz, from the band leaders, nightclub owners, and recordings.

What became known as one of Chicago's best known bands, were the "Cook Orchestra." They played at a club called, "White City," it was located on 63 and Stony Island Avenue.

Then Charles Cook, played at the Riverview Club Dance Hall. He then moved into the soon to be famous, Harmon's Dreamland Casino and Ballroom.

By 1920, with Edison's invention of the phonograph, numerous records had been recorded, but only of white musicians, except some minstrels. Race records (Race meant the Negro race) took off when the General Phonograph Company, issued a record on OKEH, by a Negro composer named Perry Bradord, entitled, *That Thing Called Love*, and *You Can't Keep A Good Man Down*, by vocalists, Mamie Smith.

While in New York, Fletcher Henderson, an unemployed chemist, began working for a record company. It was owned by W.C. Handy, and Harry Pace. In 1921, with Handy, and pace, they organized a recording company called, "Black Swan Recording Company," which sold to the race market.

Mamie Smith's recording of *Crazy Blues* in the 20s took Blues that was called, "Trashy and Rough," by some, and brought it out of the Southern states. This started the Blues craze and started the recording companies to record Blues.

Jimmie Noone had said that in the early 20s, "Negroes were separated from the white race. whites worshipped in their own churches, ate at their own restaurants, listened only to white bands, and purchased only records played by white musicians. This caused a creation of a new style of jazz. And also left the black musicians with little recording abilities."

Johnny Dodds, a clarinetist, arrived in Chicago, from New Orleans, with his instrument wrapped in newspaper, just as he had told Jimmie Noone, he would do. When Joe Oliver got his job at the Dreamland, he had sent for Johnny.

Johnny Dodds, lacked the technique of his contemporary Jimmie Noone, but he rendered the blues with extraordinary passion. (In this he was equaled only by Sidney Bechet.) Despite similarities in the two men's biographies, Dodds's hard-driving flights were the antithesis of Noone's more flowing approach.[26]

In New Orleans, Louis Armstrong, was still picking up charcoal scraps, when he wasn't working with Kid Ory at the Economy Hall, or across the river in Gretna, near Algiers. He also was working with Oscar Celestine's Tuxedo Brass Band.

Louis Armstrong met and fell in love with a girl named Daisy Parker. She was twenty-one and he was eighteen when they married. The relationship quickly became turbulent.

Armstrong, later received a permanent job from Fate Marable in St. Louis, to play on the Streckfus Riverboats. There he played with Baby Dodds, Pops Foster and Johnny St. Cyr. It was Fate Marable that assisted Louis Armstrong in reading music.

In 1921, in New Orleans, Louis Armstrong and Warren 'Baby' Dodds left Fate Marable to play at Tom Anderson's The Real Thing Club, that was over on Rampart Street. They also played a trio gig at Zutty Singleton at Butchy Fernandez's place. Fletcher Henderson had offered Louis Armstrong a job to accompany singer Ethel Waters, but he refused unless Zutty was part of the deal. Henderson turned Armstrong down, and Armstrong went on to play with the Tuxedo Brass Band.

Arthur James Singleton received his nickname as an infant. Zutty (Creole name for cute) best friend to Louis Armstrong, followed him with Fate Marable's riverboat band. As a drummer, Zutty learned the drum roll using either hand. He also made an important stylistic discovery by using brushes. The story about Zutty's brushes is that Manuel Perez, a cornetist, had gone to Chicago and given them to Louis Armstrong.

Louis didn't want them, and gave them to Zutty.

Most drummers at the time were playing on cow bells, temple blocks, wood, triangles, gongs and chimes. However, Zutty hated using all that stuff. Instead, he used a bass drum, a snare, two tom-toms, woodblock, and three cymbals. And neither did he use the familiar two cymbals with a foot pedal.

The musicians that had now moved to California, included, Kid Ory, Jelly Roll Morton (known as, "The Roll") Buddy Petit, clarinetitst, Wade Whaley, and trombonist, Frankie Dusen.

Ory was employed at the Cadillac on Central Avenue and Fifth Street in Los Angeles, and Jelly Roll Morton was at the Penny Dance Hall. Jelly Morton was known then as "The Roll."

Jimmie Noone knew that Chicago life in the 20s meant that if he was to make a living playing jazz, that he had to work for the hoodlums, which included Al Capone and Dion O'Bannion. Crime in Chicago included racketeers, kidnappers, extortionists, illegal liquor selling, gambling, prostitution, labor unions, loan sharks, and owning nightclubs and cabarets.

Sidney Bechet had went over to Europe with Will Marion Cook, with a group they called the "Southern Syncopated Orchestra," a thirty-six-piece orchestra, where he became the featured soloist. While in London, Sidney passed J.F. Lafleur's Music Shop, and seen a soprano saxophone in the window. He had the salesman add a double-octave key to the instrument. The sax that he purchased changed his life completely and awakened the world to the saxophone.

Lil Hardin, who later married Louis Armstrong, started off demonstrating piano music at Jones Music Store in Chicago. She was being paid three dollars a week. Then Lil joined the New Orleans Creole Band, that consisted of Freddie Keppard, Ed Garland, Paul Barbarin, Eddie Vincent and Jimmie Noone, where she was paid fifty-five dollars a week.

In 1921, Jimmie Noone played with Joe 'King' Oliver, Pops Foster and Freddie Keppard, at the De Luxe Cafe with Lil Hardin, pianists.

Freddie Keppard, Jimmie Noone, and Paul Barbarin were playing together with the Creole Band. Keppard was the bandleader and wanted to have Barbarin leave the group. However, Noone would not play without his brother-in-law (Barbarin), so they both quit Keppard with Noone joining Doc Cook's band at the Dreamland Cafe. Paul Barbarin went back home to New Orleans, and Bill Johnson went with Joe King Oliver.

"Noone, unlike his contemporary Johnny Dodds, who grew up exposed to the black folk tradition, Noone was a Creole whose background favored the European classical tradition. As a result, Noone was one of the best formally trained jazzmen of the 1920s. His fluid style and proficiency influenced the next generation of clarinetists, including Omer Simeon, Barney Bigard, Benny Goodman, and Pee Wee Russell."[27]

Joe Oliver was also doubling at the Pekin Cafe. The Pekin was a remodeled theater house that also featured boxing events, and like gigs that Noone had, it was operated by gangsters. Oliver worked there from 1:00 AM to 6:00 AM, with Johnny Dodds, Honore Dutrey, Lil Hardin, Ed Garland, and Minor Hall.

Chicago musicians' work was hard, but life was full of prosperity. The music that was being played was still somewhat original New Orleans jazz. But, the distinctive New Orleans style in its purest manner did not survive the 1920s.

In New York, big bands were starting up. Playing in ballrooms such as the Roseland and the Savoy. And Harlem had the famous Cotton Club.

In New Orleans, the musicians that were able to preserve New Orleans jazz were Alphonse Picou, Oscar Celestin, A.J. Piron, and Chris Kelly.

Noone, unlike his contemporary Johnny Dodds, who grew up exposed to the black folk tradition, Noone was a Creole whose background favored the European classical tradition. As a result, Noone was one of the best formally trained jazzmen of the 1920s. His fluid style and proficiency influenced the next generation of clarinetists, including Omer Simeon, Barney Bigard, Benny Goodman, and Pee Wee Russell.[28]

Chapter Eight
The Dreamland Ballroom

At the Dreamland. *Each entertainer had what was called an 'up', when they would go out and perform. And believe me, there was always something going on. There were no such things as intermissions and there was never a quiet moment. When you worked at the Dreamland, you worked from about seven thirty in the evening to three or four in the morning-and you didn't move out of there.*[29]

Chicago was passionately in love with jazz. World War 1, or the "Great War," as it was first called, had ended. Prohibition was in full swing. Recordings were finally being made by Negro musicians, who were constantly employed.

The New Orleans Jazz style that Jimmie Noone, King Oliver, Freddie Keppard and other Creole musician's transported to Chicago, had now been cloned, by young white musicians from the Chicago area, and became known as, "Chicago style jazz," or "Chicago jazz."

"Black players did use these strings of even eighth notes, especially the ones who came from the more European Creole tradition, like Jimmie Noone. But in their runs, the black players and the Creoles usually accented the second note of a pair. It was not until the mid-or late 1920s, that white jazz players generally got the feel of this practice. In sum, the improvising of whites was tied more closely to the beat, in the ragtime manner, than it was among blacks."[30]

Jimmie Noone had said, "The reason that the New Orleans Jazz style was first created was to rid themselves from the music that was referred to as, 'Dixieland'. Dixieland was a commercial name used by whites in the South and Chicago. The Negro race wanted to have something that they could call their own. And it worked to a certain extent. Oh sure, many musicians could play jazz and became excellent at it, but not many could duplicate the difficult New Orleans style."

The teachings from Noone's former instructors, seemed to reveal themselves. His playing style was a combination of Sidney Bechet, Franz Schoepp, and Lorenzo Tio, Jr., all wrapped up together in his clarinetists package.

Jimmie Noone had ended his two-year stay at the Royal Gardens Café (1917–1919).

The Royal Gardens Cafe was a place that was always packed. "People belonging to all classes of society attended (doctors, lawyers, students, entertainment people, musicians, people of all colors were found there). The Royal Gardens could contain a thousand people. If business there was excellent it was also due to the fact that besides an orchestra without rival the Royal Gardens presented sensational attractions."[31]

"The original cafe was commemorated in Spencer and Clarence Williams' Royal Garden Blues (1920). Jimmie Noone later claimed that he and Oliver wrote the original Royal Garden Blues for the band to play and then sold the title to Clarence Williams who published it as his own."[32]

By 1921, Tommy Ladnier (from Louisiana), had become a great blues trumpet player. Muggsy Spanier recalls when he first met Ladnier, "I was playing in back rooms along North Clark Street in Chicago. Tommy was playing in some hole-in-the-wall out on Thirty-ninth and State. Whenever I wasn't working at night, I was out listening to Tommy, and, on his nights off, I generally managed to get him to come to whatever joint I was playing at."

"I was in seventh heaven when he sat down to play beside me! If you're not familiar with his work, get hold of Noble Sissie's old Brunswick records like 'Basement Blues' (Tommy's chorus is right after Sidney Bechet's) or the Rosetta Crawford records on Decca, or those old Orleans Feet-warmer sides. Take it from me, when old Gabe blows that horn one of these days, he'll probably use the fingering that Tommy Ladnier taught him."[33]

In 1922, Joe Oliver returned from San Francisco's Pergola Dancing Pavilion, to Chicago, and began playing at the Lincoln Gardens (formerly Royal Gardens), where his Creole Jazz Band helped to influence white jazz musicians. Joe Oliver had wired Louis Armstrong to join him. When Armstrong received the telegram from his "Papa Joe," as he called him, he took the next train out of New Orleans and traveled to the Windy City.

Armstrong had already received the nickname, "Dippermouth." With Louis Armstrong playing second trumpet, he created a sound that no one in Chicago had ever heard.

Oliver's group became possibly the most influential group in the 1920s.

"A crude attempt at swinging was made by another famous early orchestra, King Oliver's Jazz Band, which appeared at Chicago's Lincoln Gardens between 1921 and 1923. During its heyday, the band consisted of not the usual five but seven musicians, trombonist Honore Dutrey, clarinetist, Johnny Dodds, pianist Lil Hardin, banjoist Bill Johnson, drummer Warren 'Baby' Dodds, and two cornetists, Oliver and young Louis Armstrong."[34]

The Lincoln Gardens was a cafe and a dance hall. The outside of the building had a sign that advertised King Oliver and his Creole Jazz Band. Inside the dance hall, was a large crystal ball that hung over the dance floor. Spotlights on the ball reflected beams of light on the dancers.

Joe Oliver, Jimmie Noone, Pops Foster, and Freddie Keppard, used to eat lunch or breakfast together, depending on their schedules. Freddie Keppard, was becoming a heavy drinker, while Joe Oliver and Jimmie Noone became overeaters.

Noone and Oliver, would later tell the story of how white musicians came to listen and steal their music and riffs. Noone often spoke of how he'd been stage, and he watch musicians writing down his music on their bar napkins, or shirt sleeves. Joe Oliver often called these type of men, "Alligators," because they'd snatch up every note the band played.

"Indeed, it was claimed that French composer Maurice Ravel once notated a solo by Noone, but was told by the first clarinetist of a symphony orchestra that parts of it were impossible to play!"[35]

Pops Foster said, "Yes, I remember King Oliver. He was a happy-go-lucky guy. He liked to play pool all day long, and baseball. He would eat a lot. We would order one or two hamburger sandwiches, and he would eat a dozen at a time, and a quart of milk."[36]

In 1923, a new dance called the 'Charleston' was introduced. This dance required loose limbs. It was a dance for the young adult, and proved rather difficult. Arthur Murray had opened numerous dance studios, where a standardized five basic steps could be learned.

The Charleston created a greater need for more dance halls, ballrooms, and larger nightclubs. This demand created more jobs for musicians and was the beginning of large, big bands.

On March 2, 1923, before he was to tum twenty-eight years old, he played at the Paradise Gardens, appearing with Ollie Powers, comedian and vocalists, along with Freddie Keppard on cornet, who had been the bandleader of the Original Creole Band. Jimmie had said, "Ollie Powers had a sweet voice."

Louis Armstrong had said, "Ollie Powers had one of those high, sweet singing voices, and when he would sing songs like 'What'll I Do?' he would really rock the whole house."[37]

When Noone began recording with Joe Oliver, he was in great demand. And his recording with Oliver became memorable. Recording for Columbia Records, he replaced Oliver's regular clarinet player, Mitchell Slocum.

September 1923 is when Jimmie Noone made his first appearance on a recording, with Ollie Power's Harmony Syncopators, in Chicago, in September 1923. The band included, Ollie Powers (d, l), Alex Calimese (first cnt), Tommy Ladnier (second cnt), Eddie Vincent (tbn), Horace Diemer (alto), Grover Compton (pno), John Basley (bjo), Jimmie Noone (cl), and William 'Bass' Moore (tu, bb). Five different masters were made of "Play That Thing."

In Down Beat Magazine in the November 23, 1961 issue, the well-known jazz critic, Leonard Feather called Noone, "The first real clarinet giant, and Jimmie was doubtlessly the first clarinet virtuoso playing jazz with an exceptionally beautiful tone though still deeply rooted in the blues idiom. An early example is his solo on the various takes of 'Play That Thing' with the Ollie Powers Band."

October 15, 1923, was the recording date for Joe King Oliver's Jazz Band. The talented musicians used for this recording included, King Oliver, Louis Armstrong (comets), Eddie Atkins (trombone), Jimmie Noone (clarinet), Lil Hardin (piano), Johnny St. Cyr (banjo), and Baby Dodds (drums).

The three songs recorded were: *Chattanooga Stomp* (composed by Joe Oliver, and Alphonse Picou), *Junk Man Blues* (composed by Joe Oliver), and *London (Cafe) Blues* (composed by Joe Oliver), and *London (Cafe) Blues* (composed by Ferd Morton, or better known as 'Jelly Roll' Morton).

"In the early twenties Noone sometimes shaped his phrases in even eighth notes that were excessively stiff. This is a vestige of the pure New Orleans ensemble style, and all the New Orleans clarinet players of that period frequently fell prey to this rhythmic tendency (as in the case of Noone on London Cafe Blues, with Oliver and even as late as Here Comes The Hot Tamale Man, recorded in 1926 by Cookie's Gingersnaps)."[38]

Joe King Oliver's band was also playing at the Royal Gardens, and this is when he was considered at his peak, with Johnny Dodds on clarinet, Baby Dodds, on drums, Honore Dutrey on trombone, Bill Johnson on bass, and Lil Hardin on the piano.

"Noone learned very early to fill in his breaks and linking phrases with arpeggio figures. But unlike Bechet's arpeggio passages, Noone's never became an integral part of the stylistic melodic fabric; they always remained secondary. His break on Oliver's London Cafe Blues, is a fine example, and shows the kind of fluency Dodds, for example, did not have."[39]

The following month, October 1923, Jimmie Noone recorded with Ollie Powers Harmony Syncopators (with the same musicians, as the previous month), a popular song, entitled, *Jazzabo*, on the Paramount Recording Label. The Harmograph Label was titled as, "Clarence Young's Harmony Syncopators."

Ollie Powers Hannony Syncopators consisted of: Ajex Calamese, Tommy Ladnier (cnts), Eddic Vincent (tba), Jimmie Noone (clt), Horace Diemer (alto), Glover Compton (pno), John Basley (bjo), Bass Moore (bbs), and Ollie Powers on (dms, vcl).

The Ollie Powers Hannony Syncopators recordings in October 1923 were erroneously released under the name of 'Powers' and still remains that way. It should have read Ollie Powell's Harmony Syncopators. Ollie Powers was directing an eight-piece band at the Dreamland Cafe in 1923.

Earl Kenneth Hines had begun learning classical piano at nine years of age and had played the trumpet when he was eight. By thirteen he was working in clubs around Pittsburgh, we he dropped out of school. Lois Depee offered Hines a job, while he was *I* still wearing short pants, and while he still had to ask his parents' permission to play. But in 1923, he had recorded two records with the group.

In that same year, he moved to Chicago and worked at a cafe that had a piano on casters, that enabled him to move from table to table and play. Within two years, he had a style that was so rhythmically powerful, and he later played with Erskin Tate, Carroll Dickerson, Jimmie Noone, and Louis Armstrong. Many jazz critics later were to call his style of playing the, "Trumpet style right hand." It meant that his right hand seemed to invent the same lines as a trumpet player would play, and many believed that his style was based from the older blues tradition.

"The style bridging the gap between Jelly Roll Morton and Earl Hines was called 'Stride', and was immediately influential. Stride was a style in which the left hand, though basically a timekeeper, alternated strong, 'walking' bass notes with triad chords while the right improvised freely. Left-hand octave jumps were frequently used as well. Hines, though initially influenced by stride, broke from its mold by avoiding constant chording and by playing the left hand closer to mid-keyboard."[40]

"Hines, then was playing a modified stride piano, which mingled stride with the primitive blues tradition. It gave him a style that was rhythmically powerful, with a preference for single lines of notes in the right hand, or characteristically, simple rhythmic figures spelled out with a hard attack in octaves."[41]

Jimmie Noone was in great demand for recording sessions in 1923. The recording of what was considered a "memorable," recording session for Columbia Records. On this recording, he replaced Oliver's regular clarinet player, Mitchell Slocum.

On October 15, 1923 in Chicago, Noone recorded on a Monday morning with the King Oliver Jazz Band, which included: Joe King Oliver, Louis Armstrong (comets), Eddie Atkins (trombone), Jimmie Noone (clarinet), Lil Hardin (piano), Johnny St. Cyr (banjo), and Baby Dodds (drums).

This recording date they used three songs, entitled, *Chattanooga Stomp* (composed by Oliver and Picou), *Junk Man Blues* (composed by Oliver), and *London Cafe Blues* (composed by Joe Oliver), and *London (Cafe) Blues* (composed by Ferd Morton 'Jelly Roll' Morton).

It was on Tuesday (the following day), October 16, 1923, when Noone recorded with King Oliver Jazz Band on Columbia Records, for the second time in a week.

Musicians recording with him were Louis Armstrong, Eddie Atkins, Lil Hardin, Johnny St. Cyr, and Baby Dodds. The songs recorded were *London (Cafe) Blues*, *Camp Meeting Blues*, and *New Orleans Stomp*.

Gunther Schuller, in his book Early Jazz, does an excellent evaluation of this recording. "Consider Noone's solo on *Camp Meeting Blues*" (with Oliver in 1923). The control of his intonation, the precise way in which he colors the melodic thirds slightly flat, and the controlled manner in which his rhythms are stated without sounding stiff or 'Legitimate' are marks of a unique talent.

"The anticipated E-flat and g are part of a planned syncopation pattern, one very rarely heard in early jazz. The entire performance shows to what extent Benny Goodman learned from Noone, and who phrases and the special inflection Noone's tone and legato gave them can be heard to this day in Goodman's playing."[42]

Before the end of 1923, Jimmie Noone and Freddie Keppard, had hooked up an engagement at the Dreamland Ballroom, under the leadership of Charles L. 'Doc' Cook. The popularity of the band created large crowds Chicago jazz was jumping during this time, and the south-side provided many clubs to party at. Across the street from The Dreamland Cafe was the Deluxe Cafe. Many jazz enthusiasts hopped bars to take in the full array of jazz musicians.

Jimmie Noone's engagement at the Dreamland Cafe ended at midnight, which allowed him one hour to grab a quick sandwich, before he started another gig at 1:00 AM. His next gig was with Ollie Powell, a drummer and singer, and Glover Compton, as pianists. He also was playing at "The Oriental," "The Panama," and "Paradise Gardens."

The Dreamland Cafe and Ballroom, was located at 3520 State Street. It prided itself on presenting nothing but the finest talented jazz musicians. The orchestra there was considered unusual at that time, with a four-piece rhythm section. A piano, banjo or guitar, tuba and drums. What made it unusual was that the alto saxophone played the lead, while the clarinet played in the New Orleans style and added harmony melody as an accompaniment to the lead.

Patty Harmon, an Irishman, was the owner of the Dreamland. He liked music that had a sweet sound. He also invented the Harmon mute, that soften the sound of brass instruments. (It was a plumber's plunger that produced a 'Wah' sound. Miles Davis later became a master of Harmon's mute.)

During a cold winter in Chicago that year, Noone ran into the girl he had seen on the golf course once before. Little is known of the girl called "Lorraine." The known facts are that she was a Professional Golfer, and that she was beautiful. They met when the very popular song *Sweet Lorraine* was recorded.

However, what is typical of records regarding black history is that no records were kept regarding her maiden name, her family's background, or even what their courtship was like.

What also is known about Lorraine is that she and Jimmie did play golf together, about 4:00 AM or 5:00 AM, after the clubs closed for the night. It was the only time that negroes at the time could play golf at the resorts. Only whites were allowed to play during the day.

Also, there are no records presently found regarding her being a golf pro, as negroes were not playing with the white players. Golf was a very segregated sport then.

It has been confirmed by the Noone family now living, that Jimmie Noone did in fact marry his 'Sweet Lorraine' about 1924. What is not known is if they had any children together? As of this writing, there are no known children that the Noone family knows of. Noone married Lorraine when he was twenty-nine.

"1924 was an interesting year for jazz. The ODJB, having broken up and begun to fade from memory, was 'saluted' in Aeolian Hall, New York (a venue then considered as prestigious as Carnegie), as 'the wild, untamed beginnings of jazz' by popular bandleader Paul Whiteman. The previous year, Fletcher Henderson had formed an all-black popular dance band that slowly but surely worked its way toward jazz greatness."[43]

In 1924, Louis Armstrong, married his second wife, pianist, Lillian Hardin. Lil contributed to teaching him how to read music better, and about a year later, talked Louis into leaving Oliver at the Dreamland Cafe. Several months later, Fletcher Henderson asked Armstrong to join his band.

Armstrong had left Joe Oliver's band and joined Ollie Powell and his Harmony Syncopators.

Joe 'King' Oliver's Band was having competition with the orchestra of Doc Cooke.

"Among those who did record during the twenties, Jimmie Noone displayed as unprecedented rhythmic versatility on most of his recordings. llis fluid staccato runs exuberant stop-choruses, and interweaving counter-themes, characterize his style, requiring a very firm embouchure and accomplished technique on the instrument."[44]

Oliver Gennett, who was the owner of Gennett Records, had made a recording proposal with Doc Cook, and his Dreamland Orchestra, to be in Richmond, Indiana, on January 21, 1924. Jimmie Noone said the paying salary was $50.00 per musician. The band traveled by train for the recording engagement, and plans were made to return that evening in time for their show at the Dreamland.

Before leaving for Richmond that morning, Jimmie Noone, Freddie Keppard, and Joe Poston met at Sadie's Cafe for breakfast. Sadie's was over on the south-side of Chicago. Jimmie remembered, "The weather was eighteen degrees, it was snowing, and the wind was a monster that day."

Jimmie and Freddie ate their large breakfast, which consisted of a large order of hotcakes, eggs, bacon, potatoes and toast. Joe Poston was a light eater. However, Jimmie had gained a lot of weight since arriving in Chicago. His stomach was beginning to bulge.

Jimmie said, "There was excitement as we boarded the train to Richmond. Upon arrival at the Gennett Studio, we set up our instruments, and tuned them, in preparation for the session. Keppard made many jokes and kept everyone laughing."

Doc Cook and his Dreamland Orchestra, in Richmond Indiana, January 21, 1924, recorded with eleven musicians that were called Cook's Dreamland Orchestra.

Musicians included: Freddie Keppard, Elwood Graham (cots), Fred Garland (tbn), Jimmie Noone (cit), Clifford King, Joe Poston (alto), Jerome Pasquall (ts), Jimmy Bell (vln), Anthony Spaulding (pno), Stanley Wilson (bjo), Bill Newton (bbs), and Bert Greene (dms).

The following six songs were recorded that day: *Scissor Grinder Joe* (written by Gillespie-Stocco); *Lonely Little Wallflower* (written by Kahn-Simons); *So This Is Venice* (written by Clark-Leslie-Warren); *Moanful Man* (written by Gillespie-Baker-Cook); *My Daddy Rocks Me*; *The Memphis Maybe Man* (written by Gillespie-Cook-Moll); *The One I Love (Belongs To Somebody Else)* (written by Jones-Kohn).

Charles 'Doc' Cook was a musician, bandleader, and an agent. He worked with bands such as, Erskin Tate, Dave Peyton, Sammy Stewart, and Hugh Swift. During the '20s, he was very active, and was able to assist the large orchestras with his scoring abilities for the theater and dance bands. Cook is possibly best remembered by jazz historians today, as the bandleader of Hamon's Dreamland Orchestra, where he was employed for nearly six years, and where Cook and Noone made jazz history books.

On June 15, 1926, Jimmie Noone recorded with Lillie Delk Christian, contralto vocalist, and Johnny St. Cyr, banjo player. They recorded *Lonesome And Sorry* and *Baby O'Mine*.

From 1926 to 1928, Cook recorded fourteen records for the American Columbia Label, recording on June 22, 1926, titled *Jazz Odyssey Volume 1*, the Sound of New Orleans 1917–1947, with Chicago's Cookie's Gingersnaps.

The recording personnel included Freddie Keppard, William Dawson, Jimmie Noone, Joe Poston, Sterling Todd, and Johnny St. Cyr. The following songs were recorded: *Messin' Around* (written by Cooke-St. Cyr), *High Fever* (written by Sanders), *Here Comes The Hot Tamale Man* (written by Rose-Harrison), *Love Found You For Me* (written by Williams-Cook).

"Because of his technical proficiency, Noone was able to take advantage of the natural fluidity of the clarinet; he played with an easy grace rare in jazz of any time."

"In a music where so much playing borders on panic, his is never frantic."

"Characteristically, he starts a line high on the instrument and works his way easily downward in stages, sometimes in long arpeggios, sometimes in the saw-toothed runs that the clarinet lends itself to."[45]

The last Dreamland Orchestra recording that included Jimmie Noone, was recorded on July 10, 1926, and entitled *Cook and His Dreamland Orchestra*. Musicians used for this recording were: Charles Doc Cook (dir), Freddie Keppard, Elwood Graham (c), Fred Garland (tb), Jimmie Noone (cl), Joe Poston, Clifford King (cl, as), Jerome Pasquall (cl/ts), Kenneth Anderson (pno), Robert Shelly, Johnny St. Cyr (bjo), Rudolph 'Sudie' Reynaud (bb), Bert Greene or Andrew Hilaire (d, v).

The recorded songs on Columbia Records was: *Here Comes The Hot Tamale Man*, *Brown Sugar*, *High Fever*, and *Spanish Mama*. Noone had remained with the Charles 'Doc' Cook Orchestra, until he realized it was now time to branch out on his own, and become more creative. Upon leaving the Dreamland in 1926, Jimmie Noone had played with such musicians as Lorenzo Tio Sr., and Jr., Sidney Bechet, Freddie Keppard, Papa Celestin, Kid Ory, Louis Armstrong, Lil Armstrong, Doc Cook, and numerous others.
Jimmie Noone's next gig would take place at the famous "Apex Club." His small ensemble would soon feature Earl 'Fatha' Hines. This ensemble would comprise a wind section, which was a saxophone, clarinet, and the magical fingers of Earl Hines.

Chapter Nine
The Late Twenties

Chicago's late twenties were pleasurable and exciting. The south-side of Chicago had their share of speakeasies (a place where alcohol was sold illegally). The speakeasies had gambling, drinking, or whatever your pleasure might be. Dancing consisted of the bunny hug, Texas Tommy, foxtrot, the hug-me-tight, or the sea-gull swoop, the camel walk, or the skunk waltz.

The honky-tonks (a nightclub or dance hall) is where Jimmie Noone mostly played for the Negro population, on the south-side of Chicago (Where he liked to play/the most for two nightclubs daily). The city had received his style of music with open arms. The transformation of his New Orleans style of playing was still preserved. However, his choppy phrasing of notes had been replaced with a more polished, distinctive Chicago sound.

Jimmie Noone, now over thirty years old, had taken on the appearance of an Italian opera tenor, with the typical stocky built. He was indeed handsome, with his straight black curly hair combed neatly back away from his round face. He had the beginnings of a second chin and was a man of medium height. His disposition was good, he always remained calm and pleasant. He was married to Lorraine, and by all accounts was very happy.

Leon Scott, a trumpet player, was one of Jimmie Noone's close friend. He knew Lorraine Noone well. "I first met Jimmie in 1924. I was working as a pharmacy apprentice in a drugstore just around the comer from where Jimmie lived, and his wife shopped there. She was a beautiful Creole girl and her name was Loretta. Jimmie never told me this, but I believe she was his inspiration when he recorded the ever popular number *Sweet Lorraine* because he played it so beautifully."[46]

In Chicago, Kid Ory had recorded with Louis Armstrong's Hot Five, when they recorded their classic jazz record for Okeh, that included *Heebie Jeebies*. This song is when Armstrong indulges in what later was called *Scattin'*.

In New York, jazz musicians played most in Harlem, when a Negro district opened up, due to white Landlords new practice of renting their apartments to negroes. This occurred about the time when the West Side of New York started becoming overcrowded.

Harlem had the Apollo Theater, at 253 West 125th Street. The Cotton Club was called "The Place." It was located at 644 Lenox Avenue, and at first opened under the name of the Club Deluxe.

In 1926, the Cotton Club, due to Prohibition laws. When a new house band was sought, someone suggested Duke Ellington's Orchestra, but new management asked Joe Oliver for the job. When Oliver rejected the offer, Ellington accepted. Ellington stayed at the Cotton Club until the 30s.

The Savoy Ballroom, which was located at 596 Lenox Avenue, became famous for the jazz musicians that played there. The Savoy covered the length of a block, and had a large dance area, a double bandstand, allowing two bands alternated music playing.

The Savoy's marble staircase led to the second floor of the building, that was billed as, "The world's most beautiful ballroom."

Jimmie Noone said, "The Savoy about 1927 featured what they called a 'Battle of the bands', that featured Fletcher Henderson and Chick Webb, to represent New York, and they played against King Oliver and Fess Williams, to represent Chicago. The crowd that gathered was tremendous, and a riot squad had to be called out to control the people."

It is said that Armstrong dropped his sheet of lyrics while he was singing, and he simply substituted rhythmic syllables for the words. However, Lil Armstrong and her husband, Louis Armstrong, composed a song titled *Skit-Dat-De-Dat*, which was just scat written down.

The recording Noone did on December 12, 1927, with Lillie Delk Christian, was performed with the absence of a piano and drums. But it seemed unimportant with Johnny St. Cyr, playing the guitar, along with Noone's fine clarinet playing.

The technique that Noone used on his B-flat Albert System clarinet is a pleasing combination of qualities. His low register and fluid passages create a musical composition that is extremely pleasing to listen to.

On December 12, 1927, the Okeh recording had two songs recorded. *My Blue Heaven* (written by Whiting-Donaldson) and *Who's Wonderful! Who's Marvelous? Miss Annabelle Lee* (written by Clare-Pollack). These songs were reissued on the Historical Record Company, titled "Hot Clarinets."

Noone still held down music engagements for the gangsters and hoods in Chicago, because without their employment, there would be no work for a musician. Al Capone owned practically everything in *Chi* Town. Jimmie said that "When Capone's hunch men pulled out their machine guns, he became very agreeable to their request."

Earl Hines was playing at the Grand Terrace, when he witnessed Capone, "A frequent visitor to the Grand Terrace was the big man himself, Al Capone, who went around town in a seven-ton armored limousine. He like to come into a club with his henchmen, order all the doors closed, and have the band play *his* requests. He was free with hundred dollar tips."[47]

"Another band leader who had considerable contact with the Capone group in those days was Lucky Millinder, who worked for Ralph Capone in a spot controlled by the syndicate in Cicero, headquarters of the Capone gang. Others who held jobs in Capone-controlled clubs were the late Tiny Parham and the late Jimmie Noone, one of the greatest of all jazz clarinetists."[48]

Noone said that, "During Prohibition big time gangsters were making large fortunes of money with bootleg whiskey, due to a monopolized control on nightclubs and speakeasies. And that admission into a speakeasy required knocking on the door, where someone would either look through a peek hole or slide back a wooden slat. And if you passed the test, and did not look like a cop, or a Prohibition Agent, you were admitted in."

The song "Sweet Lorraine," by Mitchell Parrish, who wrote the lyrics, and Cliff Burwell, who composed the music, had become quite popular. It was Rudy Vallee's favorite and became a popular jazz tune by Jimmie Noone's. Jimmie added a version with his clarinet that many clarinetists today listen to and study. Noone's interpretations reveal his New Orleans training, with his high register and sweet tones.

One evening when Jimmie Noone and Freddie Keppard, were having dinner in a restaurant, they heard an Announcer's voice introduce Leon Rapollo's newly recorded record. Rapollo played Dixieland clarinet style for a while with the New Orleans Rhythm Kings (NORK).

When the radio Announcer said, "This record's hot," and the tune played, Jimmie jumped right out of his chair screaming loudly, "Hear that Freddie! That's Rapollo playing my style. How dare him! He's copying me!"

Keppard started yelling also, upon listening more to the song being played, and stated, "Son-of-a-Bitch! That's your shit!" Noone was so pissed, he started pounding his fist on the restaurant table. He was steaming with pent-up anger. His whole musical career was on the line.

White musicians had continually taken away, the God-given talent that he alone possessed, and recorded it, plus reaped the monetary rewards. Finally, a waitress had to walk over to Keppard and Noone, and ask them to leave, as they were causing a disturbance. Keppard and Noone were so angry that they immediately went to a speakeasy and indulged in several drinks.

"Rappolo plays an easy, graceful, and technically sound clarinet that is far in advance of the playing of Larry Shields of the Original Dixieland Jazz Band. In fact, it sounds as if he had been listening carefully to Dodds of the Oliver's Band and probably to Jimmie Noone, as well."[49]

"This band came to be the primary influence on the Midwesterners. To be sure, by 1925 they were also listening to Oliver, Armstrong, Morton, and other black players. Muggsy Spanier, followed Oliver all of his life; Morton was drawn to Armstrong; Benny Goodman appears to have listened to Noone for a time; Krupa to Baby Dodds."[50]

Before the twenties had ended, a succession of clarinetists had passed on their knowledge to a new generation. From New Orleans, the first generation included, Lorenzo Tio, George Baquet, and Alphonse Picou.

The second generation of clarinetists were, Sidney Bechet, 'Big Eye' Louis Nelson, Johnny Dodds, Jimmie Noone, and Barney Bigard.

The new featured clarinetists to come along with a new generation were, Omer Simeon, Edmond Hall, Albert Nicholas, Larry Shields, Leon Rappolo, Benny Goodman, and Woody Herman.

Coleman Hawkins, a saxophonist, whose early nickname was "Bean," then later in life was called "Hawk," was able to bring the rating of the saxophone into a new classification before the end of the twenties. The sax became known as a serious reed.

Hawkins style of playing became known as "Vertical improvising," and his recorded tune *Body And Soul* is a perfect example of his style that Sonny Rollins, and later, John Coltraine followed.

Another saxophonist that made their entrance before the end of the twenties was both alto and soprano sax player, Johnny Hodges. Hodges was also known as "Jeep" and "Rabbit," among musicians. He started playing with Bobby Sawyer, then Lloyd Scott, in 1926, and then with Chick Webb's band, and in 1928, with Duke Ellington.

One of the most exciting singers of this period was Billie Holiday, or "Lady Day." There was also Gene Krupa, a talented drummer, who by 1927 was playing with Mezz Mezzrow, Jimmy Mc Partland, Frank Teschemacher, and by 1929, his move to New York, gave him the opportunity to work with Gershwin.

The late twenties revealed Barney Bigard, also known as Leon Albany Bigard, a clarinetist, for his exciting solos with Duke's orchestra. It was Wellman Braud, a bassist, that helped in bringing Bigard to the Ellington band before they entered the Cotton Club. Bigard had studied with Lorenzo Tio, Jr., and then worked with Joe King Oliver.

Noone as early as 1927 was phrasing in a manner that stood in a halfway house between the New Orleans style and swing. Thus, because he was a fine technician, an inventive improviser, and a leader of the jazz vanguard, he was widely emulated.[51]

The late twenties had many honky-tonks and nightclubs that were patronized by both negroes and whites on the south-side. They were: The Black Hawk, Bridewell Prison, Lincoln Gardens, The Panama Club, The Royal Gardens, Dreamland Cafe, The Grand Terrace, The Deluxe Cafe, The Savoy Ballroom, The Sunset Cafe, and Kelly's Stables.

These nightclubs had top-rate entertainment, along with big-band orchestras, and they featured stage acts. As far as big bands were classified, if there was more than one instrument in any category, then it was looked upon as a big band, which could consist of up to fifteen instruments.

Jimmie Noone had nightly doubled or tripled jobs because of the need, and the fact that musicians made very little money. His employment at the Nest Club started in the early morning hours, as it was an after-hours club.

The Nest Club in Chicago was to become the home of the Jimmie Noone Orchestra in the late twenties. Previous to this, Noone had developed a reputation, while with Joe King Oliver, and Doc Cook's Dreamland Orchestra. Noone continued to play in the traditional New Orleans style.

The Nest, was located at the corner of 35th and Prairie, in Chicago. This nightclub was not the typical bucket of blood. It was an establishment, that had become quite fashionable during the late twenties. It was located in the downtown section of Chicago, on the south-side of the city. Its main attraction, was the quite popular, Jimmie Noone Orchestra, that was featured.

Noone's drummer, Walter Johnson, used the hi-hat-cymbals. This technique had a great influence on other drummers in the usage of either brushes or sticks on the hi-hat.

"In company with Hines and the obscure but excellent alto saxist Joe Poston, Noone explored the facets of his art that made him a legend (as well as an influence on Benny Goodman): the fluent, well-practiced runs, the elegant phrasing, and the occasional unexpected break."[52]

The Apex Club—had Zutty Singleton and Earl Hines. Then after Noone played with Doc Cook Orchestra, he also played evenings with Cook, Singleton, and pianists Jerome Carrington, as a trio at the Nest. At the Nest Club was sometimes Mezz Mezzrow, Louis Armstrong, and Joe Oliver.

Zutty Singleton, Earl Hines and Jimmie Noone, were the best of friends while performing in a club, or in their personal lives. Margie Singleton (Zutty's wife) was a gracious woman, who welcomed other musicians into her home. Hines and Noone were able to eat there, play music, drink beer, and they felt quite at home with Margie.

"Zutty's earliest important job in Chicago had also been the result of doubling. He was the first drummer with Charles 'Doc' Cook-Doc Cook and his Seventeen Interns was the billing then, believe it or not."

"It was the Cook that cornetist Freddie Keppard made most of the few records he made, and Jimmy Noone was Cook's featured clarinetist. But following their evenings with Cook, Singleton and Noone, with a pianist named Jerome Carrington, became members of a trio at the Nest, and after-hours club where the music began at 1 AM."[53]

"Jimmie Noone represents the other side of the Creole style. He was more a product of classical European influence, blessed with a superb technique. He was a pupil and friend of Bechet, and really took off in Chicago, first with Freddy Keppard, then above all by becoming the star of the 'Apex Club' with Earl Hines (1926)."[54]

When Noone took his band into the Nest Club, he had Joe Poston, Bud Scott, Walter Johnson, Freddie Keppard, Arthur Campbell, and Ollie Powell.

"Unlike his contemporary Dodds, Noone developed a sweet, liquid, even sensuous tone. In fact, it was claimed he didn't use a brass team in his Apex Club band so his sweet sound would not be overpowered (although in at least one session he did use cornetist George Mitchell, and trombonist Fayette Williams was a regular)."[55]

In the late twenties, when Jimmie Noone left the secured and guaranteed income of 'Doc' Cook, and ventured forth on his own to the Nest Club, he had taken a chance and gambled that he could secure the bandleader title.

Jimmie took a financial risk also, to seek the numerous opportunities available for being his own boss, and being able to play the music he loved the best, and sounded the best playing.

Noone's later recording of *Apex Blues* showed that he was finished with competing with fellow clarinet musicians, and now he was the new champion of the clarinet. The evidence presented itself, on *Apex Blues*, with his clarinet licks, as being a dominating factor, making this twelve-bar blues, a classical recording performance.

Jimmie Noone should have been declared the ruler of the clarinet by the late twenties, and his sovereign should have ruled with him becoming either a Duke, King, or perhaps a Regal Prince. The staff or scepter that he carried was his clarinet. And his authority to carry such a scepter was his ability to play in the high register, and the low register, in the New Orleans traditional style of jazz.

Chapter Ten
Apex Blues

The Apex Blues story should be retold, about jazz played long—long ago. Jimmie Noone blew his clarinet allegretto's Bud Scott played his banjo, While Earl Hines redefined his piano style, At their workplace—The Apex Club. Noone's dame was Sweet Lorraine There was Sachmo & His Hot Four, And Joe Poston's alto sax The Apex Blues story is about jazz played long—long ago.

C. Picou

The Nest Club it was called. It was just a regular nightclub were numerous musicians had entered to hear the now famous Jimmie Noone that people were talking about.

Customers had lined up outside the door, waiting to hear his music, it was not so much as a dancing club, its purpose at the time was to listen to and enjoy Chicago jazz music, with a New Orleans traditional sound.

A typical Saturday night might include Mezz Mezzrow, who was a regular fan of Noone's. And friends such as Louis Armstrong and Joe Oliver, sneaking in to hear a few bars, before they had to appear at their own gig.

Noone had said, "That one night's audience included Gene Krupa, the new drummer that people were whispering about, or perhaps, Benny Goodman, Thomas Dorsey, or Fletcher Henderson, who sometimes came with Zutty Singleton."

The band at the Nest consisted of Joe Poston, a clarinet and alto saxophone player, along with Bud Scott, a banjo player, and Walter Johnson, on piano. Also playing were Freddie Keppard, Arthur Campbell, and Ollie Powell.

Dave Nelson, who played trumpet, piano, and was a music arranger, replaced Jimmie Noone for a short time at the Nest Club. Nelson was also Joe

'King' Oliver's nephew and had recorded numerous songs on the Victor Label, which had been arranged and written by Nelson.

This replacement was made possible, so that Noone could rejoin Cook's Band for a short period. Toward the end of the year of 1927, the Nest Club closed for remodeling. This is within the same time period that Noone was playing with Cook. The club was not satisfied with their appearance because of the status of the customers they were now serving.

The Nest Club was on the south-side of Chicago, and previously their clientele consisted with about ninety-five percent minorities. Now that Jimmie Noone had become the house band, the clientele was now made up of fine playing musicians and well-to-do whites.

After the face lifting of the Nest Club, and renovation, it opened up under a completely new name. The Nest Club had been renamed "The Apex Club." Noone had said that it "Bore the correct name, as Apex meant the uppermost or the highest, and indeed it was just that. Music flowed out of that club, onto the gates of heaven, right where it had originated from."

-

After the Apex Club reopened, one of Jimmie's closest and best friends, Ollie Armstrong, at the Dreamland Cafe for three months, was a featured vocalist.

Jimmie Noone had played for years with Powell, and while he had doubled jobs with Cook in 1923, he had been playing at the Midnight club with Ollie Powell. Powell and Noone had recorded on the Paramount Label for the songs, *Jazzbo Jenkins* and *Play That Thing*. After Ollie Powell had passed away, is really when Jimmie Noone received the leadership of the band.

Joe 'Doc' Poston, who played the alto saxophone, clarinet, and was a good vocalist, had been playing in the Cook Orchestra, left Cook, to be with his good friend Noone, at the Apex. The Poston-Noone relationship became almost more like a partnership that was to last well into the early 1930s, Poston, had received his nickname, 'Doc' due to his knowledge of theory and harmony, which most 'Doc's' in jazz are named after.

A magazine article by Bob Garrison, in the band leaders of 1944, had this to say about Jimmie Noone, "I quizzed Mezz Mezzrow about Noone: 'Top man on technique. You can't compare him with anyone else; you can't appreciate his difficult style. His drive on the clarinet is beautiful to hear. And he was a wonderful guy, personally. He was an easygoing guy'."

Mezzrow, also told Bob Garrison, "Yes, a swell fellow. Besides that, I don't suppose you know he'd play that sensational stick all night and shoot a darn good game of golf the following morning? A great, all-around genius."

When Jimmie Noone needed a replacement for Walter Johnson, his pianist, at the Apex, he was able to obtain, the great Earl Hines. Louis Armstrong and Zutty Singleton, also wanted Earl Hines, for their band, but Hines went with Noone. He stayed until the end of December 1928, before his opening at the Grand Terrace.

William 'Red' Mc Kenzie, vocalists, who had formerly played with Condon Chicagoan's, and who had recorded *I'm Nobody's Sweetheart Now* was able to assist Noone through the Vocalion Label. Jimmie Noone's band of the Apex Club was able to record for the first time, with the first session starting on May 16, 1928.

It should be noted that there were exactly twelve sides that were recorded during the dates of May 16, 1928 until November 26, 1929. Jimmie Noone's Apex Club Orchestra, recorded during that time, some of the most pleasing combinations of quality jazz songs ever recorded.

The selection of tunes recorded included: *Sweet Sue, Four or Five Times, I Know That You Know, Forevermore, Ready For The River, Every Evening, Apex Blues, Sweet Lorraine, Blues, Oh, Sister, Ain't That Hot, A Monday Date,* and *King Joe.*

The musicians that recorded with the Apex Band were the finest and cream-of-the crop. Such as Joe Poston (alto sax), Earl Hines (piano), Bud Scott (guitar), Johnny Wells (drums), and Lawson Buford on tuba.

The first song recorded on the Vocation Recordings is *I Know That You Know.* It was written by Vincent Youmans, songwriter and musical director. This was a popular song of the time, and it is clever, cute and fast.

The song recorded *Every Evening I Miss You* on Vocation is quite upbeat.

Bud Scott's banjo playing, along with the hand clapping to the beat done by Noone, when Hines plays his beautiful solo, is handled quite well. This song was ideal for the Apex Club, where patrons would kick up their heels and dance the Black Bottom.

Jimmie Noone performs what could be called a rating of A+, if he was to be graded. His playing is masterful, unique and expertise, and when this song comes to an end, it becomes very obvious.

Earl Hines backs Jimmie up with his piano sounds that are just fabulous, with his incredible left hand, that he became famous for. When Joe Poston's saxophone combines with Jimmie's clarinet, things happen—like putting on a pair of gloves—they just fit perfect.

Jimmie Noone said that Joe Poston "knew how to fit his alto sax into their improvised ensembles, that's why he had earned the nickname of Doc. Credit was never really paid to Doc and he endured playing with me until around April or May 1930."

He could read, play the alto sax and clarinet, he was a real reed man.

Doc was a good-looking man. He was of medium height, a light-skinned Creole, like me, with hair that was slicked back, and he occasionally wore glasses. Women would swoon over him, so much that when he entered a room, or stood on stage, the ladies thought that he was devastating.

Noone plays his trills and climbs up and down that clarinet, without missing one single note. It's the creation of a good rendition of *I Know That You Know* with its bounce, kick, and jump sound, and dancing the Charleston to this song, is highly recommended.

I Know That You Know was first recorded on Vocalion, then Jazz Society (French), made a reissue, along with Brunswick, the 80000 series American (Collectors Series) on the black and gold label.

Sweet Sue was written by Wynonie Harris, composer and James 'Trummy' Young, trombone player, vocalists, and composer. It was recorded with the Vocalion series, and reissued through Brunswick, 80000 series.

This is a beautiful ballad, meant for lovers to listen to, as it's so romantic.

Jimmie Noone's clarinet takes you back to the South, down the Mississippi River to New Orleans. It has the taste of sweet magnolia trees, and when the beat quickens just a little, the smooth clarinet sound delivers a gentle tone. Earl Hines piano solo is just what it should be —beautiful and gracious.

Four or Five Times written by Marco H. Hellman, and Byron Gay, was recorded two different times on Vocalion Records, was one of Noone's favorite recorded songs. It later was reissued on Meltone (American), Brunswick 80000 series (American CoHectors Series), black and gold label, on two occasions, and then on Vocalion (British).

"By 1927 and 1928 when his famous Apex Club Orchestra began to be recorded, Noone articulated a thoroughly advanced rhythmic inflection. It fluctuated, depending on the tempo, between swinging eights (at very fast tempos) and lazy, relaxed triplets (on slow tempos)—a rhythmic conception still in use in the bop period and modem jazz three decades later. In essence, Noone had the same catalyst relationship to Dodds and some of the slightly older New Orleans clarinetists as Waller had to James P. Johnson."[56]

"How Noone could use the full range of the clarinet can be heard in his playing on *Four or Five Times* (1928) or the May Alix vocal of *My Daddy Rocks Me* (1929)."

"The former title also shows how well Noone and his alto saxophone player Joe Poston had worked out the problem of fitting the saxophone into improvised ensembles. The ease with which Poston and Noone intertwine their melodic lines or, if demanded, stay out of each other's way, is just short of miraculous."[57]

"For a man of his reputation Noone recorded surprisingly infrequently. There are a few sides accompanying blues players, a somewhat larger number with pickup blues bands, and a couple with Oliver. The major body of his work is with a group under his leadership generally called Jimmie Noone and His Apex Club Orchestra, after a club where he worked for a long time. The Apex sides were made with a group consisting of Noone, alto saxophonist Joe 'Doc' Poston, and various rhythm sections."[58]

From May 19, 1928, until November 26, 1929, Noone recorded his Apex Club Orchestra, on the Vocalion Label. This recording had two different takes of the song *Every Evening*. The same musicians were used for both recordings, but they are two different renditions of the same song.

Jimmie Noone had purchased himself a new B-flat Albert System clarinet, along with an alto saxophone and a soprano saxophone. The money that he used came from his mother, Lucinda, who still lived in New Orleans. She had wired it from some of the proceeds from his deceased father's estate.

Jimmie had said that, "After someone masters the difficulty in playing the clarinet, all other reeds instruments are usually a breeze to learn, for example, the saxophone, rather it be an alto or soprano."

According to all the jazz records Jimmie Noone had made, he never once recorded his playing of the alto or soprano saxophone. It's possible that the recording studios only wanted his clarinet to be used. But it is known, that he did play both sax's along with his clarinet, in all the nightclubs he appeared at. on June 4, 1928, Noone recorded with the Apex Club Orchestra on Vocalion Records. Only two songs were recorded, which were *Ready For The River* (Gus Kahn-Neil Moret) and *Forevermore* (Gotthelf-Burnett). Both songs were reissued by Jazz Society (French).

Ready For The River, the vocal duet is by Jimmie Noone and Joe Poston, this was a reissue by Decca Records, a division of MCA Inc. On Ready For The River, Noone has successfully created a link with New Orleans and the Chicago style together musically.

The song, *Forevermore*, is by Manfred Gotthelf, Helen Burnett and Allan Lewis. The musicians change up a little bit on this song, with Joe Poston playing alto sax and clarinet, and Bud Scott playing banjo and guitar.

Forevermore, that was reissued by Decca has linear notes by Hugues Panassie, along with Stanley Dance as collator, had this to say about the song, "In *Forevermore*, 'Doc' Poston puts his alto sax aside during the first chorus and plays the second clarinet part to Noone's soulful statement of the theme, while Earl Hine's right hand traces some real swinging phrases; and then Earl launches into a terrific solo."

Hugues Panassie, also had this to say about Earl Hines, "Now, with the great Earl Hines on piano, there was a kind of third voice to be heard. Hines did not confine himself to comping and soloing; he would often play with his right hand, especially in the 'ride out' choruses, a beautiful and incisive melodic line which added a lot to the frontline work."

Twelve days after recording *Ready For The River* and *Forevermore*, Noone entered a different studio, by the name of Okeh (American).

On June 26, 1928, Noone recorded on Okeh, with Lillie Delk Christian (vocalists); Louis Armstrong (trumpet), and His Hot Four. Earl Hines played the piano, along with Maney Cara on guitar. This recording became a reissue under Temple (American).

The songs recorded on the Okeh Label were: *You're A Real Sweetheart* (Coslow-Spier-Britt); *Last Night I Dreamed You Kissed Me* (Kahn-Lombardo). The Temple recordings were titled as Louis Armstrong and His Hot Four.

The recordings that Noone did with Lillie Delk Christian and Louis Armstrong's Hot Four did not do well, as did some of his other recordings.

The following month, on July 2, 1928, Noone recorded Jimmie Noone Apex Club Orchestra, and this recorded of three songs were rejected due to the vocals, being a problem. This recorded had the addition of Lawson Buford on bass.

During this early jazz period, many records were rejected for various reasons.

Once a record was made, the recording company could not correct any type of mistakes, the record itself simply had to be made over.

The three songs that recorded in July were: *Apex Blues, Oh! Sister Ain't That Hot!, Blues (My Naughty Sweetie Gives To Me)*.

On the same recording date of July 2, 1928, a novelty type recording was made with Jimmie Noone, and Stovepipe Johnson. This was made with four musicians: Stovepipe Johnson (vcl), Jimmie Noone (clt), Earl Hines (pno), and Budd Scott (gtr).

This was a vocal with piano, guitar and clarinet. The first song recorded was *I ain't Got Nobody* (Williams-Graham) and on the reverse is *Don't Let Your Mouth Start Nothing, Your Head Won't Stand*, also with Stovepipe, and with unknown piano accompaniment.

Four days later, the Jimmie Noone Apex Club Orchestra returned for another recording session of three songs on July 6, 1928. Unfortunately, the vocals were rejected again on *Sweet Lorraine, King Joe*, and *Monday Date*. Tests may still be extant on these recordings.

Approximately one and a half months later, in Chicago, on August 23, 1928, Noone recorded The Apex Orchestra in Chicago with four songs. What was extremely fortunate was that *Apex Blues* was a successful recording, and was recorded two times on the Vocalion Label with reissues by Brunswick.

The featured musicians on *Apex Blues* were Bud Scott, playing both the banjo and the guitar, along with Noone, Hines and Poston. There is so much that can be said about *Apex Blues* that one hardly knows where to start.

But for Jimmie Noone, Apex Blues was his style of music, and it could have easily become his theme song at the Apex, as he played it so well. *Apex Blues* could be compared to Alphonse Picou, playing *High Society*, or Doc Cook, playing *Blame It On The Blues*.

Certain techniques played by Noone on *Apex Blues* in the recording of 1928, is still being heard by clarinet players today. This twelve-bar blues has become a 'classic' due to Noone's solo performance. Every musician has one song that he excels at, and for Noone, it was *Apex Blues*.

On *Apex Blues*, Lawson Buford added his tuba playing, to make this a sextet, and this changes the performance quite a bit. One cannot help but notice how the opening and closing of the song is played in unison. This helps to set up the solo by Earl Hines, and also several exalted choruses by Jimmie Noone.

"*Apex Blues* is especially interesting because we can see in it Noone's rather conscious approach to the blues. His solo is made up of a simple, touching figure filled with blues notes; but, played with ease and a clean tone, it lacks the passion we expect to find in the blues of a player from a more purely black tradition. And yet it is a rewarding record."[59]

"The obscure Joe Poston makes an excellent foil for Noone. His improvising lacks imagination, but he is technically proficient and his timing is excellent, so his statement of the leads around which Noone winds his runs glides easily through the music."

"Hines was at the top of his powers. All together, these records constitute one of the most satisfactory small bodies of work in early jazz, and are as fresh today as the day they were made. A student interested in early jazz could do worse than start here."[60]

The next recording the Jimmie Noone Apex Club Orchestra recorded was on August 23, 1928, at the Vocalion Recording Studios. The songs recorded were *Apex Blues, A Monday Date*, and *Blues My Naughty Sweetie Gives To Me*.

"When Jimmie Noone takes a solo chorus—as he does on *Monday Date* and *Ready For The River*—he sticks to the melody as if intending that all through a number the melody should never be left out of sight."[61]

The last song recorded on the August 1928 date, *Blues* (*My Naughty Sweetie Give To Me*) (Swanstone McCarrin Morgan), recorded on the Vocalion Label, then reissued on the Brunswick Label 80000 series.

Again on this song, Noone shows a full, clear tone, enduring stacatto inspired techniques, all that flow without any effort. Earl Hines has an important part of all the Vocalion Recordings with Noone, mainly because of the choruses he played which contained a melodic line, which contributed to the brilliance of their recorded music.

Two days later, on August 25, 1928, the Jimmie Noone Apex Club Orchestra entered the Vocation Recording Studios again, and recorded *Oh!*

Sister, Ain't That Hot! which was two takes (Will Donaldson-Harry White), *King Joe* (Arthur Scott), and *Sweet Lorraine*, which was also two takes (Cliff Burwell, Mitchell Parish).

The first take of *Oh! Sister, Ain't That Hot!* recorded on Vocalion, the second take was also recorded on Vacalion and also on Association Francaise Des Collectionneures De Disque Du Jazz (AFCDJ), French.

King Joe (Arthur Scott) was recorded on Vocalion, and on AFCDJ, and Hot Record Society (American) (HRS), and Decatur.

Sweet Lorraine that recorded on Vocation and also Brunswich 80000 series, under the name of Jimmie Noone, and His Club Ambassadors (Collectors Series), black and gold label, and under Brunswich 500000 series (French).

"King Joe," was written by Bud Scott. Scott played the violin, guitar, banjo, and was also a vocalist. King Joe was Scott's dedication to the great Joe 'King' Oliver, with whom he recorded with for several years. In the book *Early Jazz*, Gunther Schuller stated that Bud Scott was no doubt the great guitarist. Jimmie Noone said that "Scott was a qualified guitarist whom he loved playing with."

The two takes of *Sweet Lorraine* are not exactly played alike, but they vary greatly in the solo performed by Earl Hines. There is no doubt the reason became the theme song for Jimmie Noone, because of his love for Lorraine, his wife, but the fact that playing this song came so easily to him.

Sweet Lorraine is a song as beautiful as heaven probably is, or maybe even better. Besides it being a romantic love song, Earl Hines plays his piano that simply blows your mind away. With the combined melody that Jimmie Noone plays along with the harmony, everything done on this song is just plain great. Noone created a song that jazz history will never forget.

"Noone's recordings with the Apex Club Orchestra, whose wind section was no more than a saxophone and clarinet, from the bulk of his recorded work (Jimmie Noone/Earl Hines at the Apex Club, MCA)."[62]

"Jimmie Noone's lightly tongued, arpeggiated counter-melodies reveal his New Orleans background, but his smearing high register climaxes and relaxed rhythmic feeling foreshadow the swing era. 'Sweet Lorraine' is a showcase for Noone's sweet tone."[63]

The Apex Club Orchestra was being listened to by Frenchman, Maurice Ravel, who was a modern classical composer, as well as Debussy and

Stravinsky. Others that listened and visited the club after hours that started at 1:00 AM, where attentive patrons such as the young Benny Goodman and Artie Shaw. Opportunist, Goodman, Shaw and Ravel all sat together with their mouths opened while exploiting Noone's clarinet playing.

Jazz historians have retold how Ravel wrote out a few solos of Noone's, and then later delivered them to a classical clarinetist, who could not read the notes. Another reported story is that Ravel brought into the Apex Club a classical composer, he used his white shirt cuff to jot down the notes of Noone. He was unsuccessful also, of being able to interpret or construe his own hand-written notes.

This is what Jimmie Noone said about Benny Goodman, Artie Shaw, and Maurice (Ravel, "These three musicians did write down hand-written notes. Ravel was a talented classical musician, and recognized that I also knew classical, and that it showed in my clarinet playing techniques."

"Ravel's visit to the Apex Club proved to be successful, if anyone who listens to his recorded composing called 'Balero'. He discovered a different harmonic but classical sound. It was the placing of classical and jazz together, and making it all an orderly jazz connection. It was also the adding of instruments, and the building up of sound, causing a roar, much of which happens in Bolero."

When Maurice Ravel left the Apex Club, he had told Noone, "That's a nice piano player that you have in your orchestra." And then later, of course, he denied ever seeing Noone at the club, or even being there. He had taken advantage of a musician, and this time in front of Noone's face, the music was written down a note for note.

The contents that makes 'Bolero' so unique, is how it starts off in a calm matter, then slowly builds up to something quite like a march. The march takes off in sound, almost close to the New Orleans style of the marching band.

However, 'Bolero' embraces similarities to the whistles that young Negro children did in the sixth and eight wards in New Orleans during the early 1900s. Every ward or parish had its own whistle. That way, everyone in the neighborhood knew if someone from another ward was in their district. Kids nowadays do similar things with their gangs in the big cities. They have some type of warning or code to show outsiders are in their neighborhood.

These whistles were simple trills or short notes, all having their unique sound.

However, if a musician remembering his young days, combined these sounds together, he would have created a similar diatonic second part that Jimmie Noone had become famous for playing in the high and low registers.

Jazz critics have often described Noone's clarinet playing while he was at the Apex Club as "Lyrical." The music that Noone created cannot be compared to what jazz musicians are doing today, because they lack the classical background that Noone's Creole upbringing brought to him.

It is so obvious that Noone was a brilliant performer, if a classical composer such as Ravel, would enter the much feared south-side of Chicago, while fearing the Negro, and be bold enough to jot down his classical and jazz notes.

Jimmie Noone's outlook on what Ravel did was this, "First, I took it as a nice compliment that other musicians were excited about my music, but when they take your complete style of playing and use all of it, not just a few staccato like movements, then it becomes more of a theft."

On December 6, 1928, Noone recorded the Jimmie Noone Apex Club Orchestra, on the Vocalion Studios Label, this recording was with Joe Poston. It had been four months since the last recording. This is when the first change in band personnel had taken place.

Joe Poston was playing alto sax. Earl Hines had been replaced with Alex Hill on piano, Junie Cobb, had replaced Bud Scott, along with Bill Newton, replacing Lawson Buford, on brass bass. Johnny Wells did remain on drums.

The orchestra recorded a song entitled *Some Rainy Day*. Also, *Some Rainy Day* is the well-known, but slightly altered song entitled, "Someday Sweetheart," by the Spike brothers.

Many jazz historians have asked the question, "Why did Earl Hines and Jimmie Noone make a split in 1928?"

There was speculation that it was a personality dispute, which was not the case. They both loved working together, and they loved each other dearly. Jimmie Noone and Earl Hines were leaders and masters in music, and they both needed their space, and both wanted to branch out and reap some rewards from music.

So in essence the Noone-Hines spit was actually based on financial reasons, and the fact that they both were in heavy demand and wanted to take full advantage of it. All musicians know about lean times, and that they can rise up at any day, month, or year.

They both felt that the decision to split was happening at a good time, as they were gaining popularity, selling records, and playing at all the 'Hot' nightclubs. Also, Hines had accepted an offer to go into the Grand Terrace Ballroom as leader of his own band.

The Noone-Hines breakup, however, left them both feeling lost for the other. The recordings that Noone made after 1928 never prospered quite the same as when he had Hines. This is a fact that even Noone did not deny, as his style of playing demanded a high caliber piano player such as Hines.

The Grand Terrace Ballroom was located on the south-side of Chicago, and was formerly a movie house that had been rejuvenated into a luxurious nightclub. Hines opened there on his twenty-third birthday, on December 28, 1928. He fell into the same situation that Noone had succumbed to—the Alphonse Capone Gang—and their control on nightclubs. For this reason, Hines stayed at the Grand until 1939, when the club folded, some twenty years later.

The day after Jimmie Noone had recorded *Some Rainy Day* (December 6th), Earl Hines, recorded on December 7, 1928, with his new band for QRS Records, with a series of piano solos.

In 1928, Louis Armstrong was playing at the Savoy Ballroom, and had begun broadcasting on the radio regularly, and his income was about $200 a week. Louis 'Pops' Armstrong, from 1926 to 1928, cut his most influential records with various groups known as the Hot Five and Hot Seven Bands (The genius of Louis Armstrong, Vol. I, Columbia).

These bands included Baby Dodds, Johnny Dodds, Earl 'Fatha' Hines, and Singleton (Louis Armstong and Earl Hines—1928, Smithsonian Collection).[64]

On December 12, 1928, Okeh Records recorded Noone and Lillie Delk Christian, with Louis Armstrong and His Hot Four. The Hot Four included Armstrong, Noone, Earl Hines, and Maney Cara.

The records made were two songs entitled *I Can't Give You Anything But Love* (Fields-McHugh) and *Baby* (Fields-McHugh). Both were recorded on OKEH, however *Baby* was reissued on Parlophone (British) (Race Series No.16) as Lillie Delk Christian with Orchestra On December 27, 1928, the Apex Club Orchestra recorded on Vocalion.

Fifteen days later, Jimmie Noone took his Apex Club Orchestra into the recording studios of Vocalion. His musicians were: George Mitchess (cnt), probably Kid Ory (tbn), Joe Poston (alto, clt, vol), Alex Hill (pno), Junie Cobb (bjo), Bill Newton (bbs), and Johnny Wells (dms).

The orchestra recorded two takes of *It's Tight Like That* (Dorsey-Whittaker), two takes of *Let's Sow A Wild Oat* (Gay), and one take of *She's Funny That Way* (Whiting-Moret).

On *She's Funny That Way* the complete title is, "She's Funny That Way (I Got A Woman, Crazy About Me)." And Joe Poston plays clarinet behind Noone's vocal. *It's Tight Like That* was a song that could be classified as a cutesy popular song of the day. The sayings of the 1920s, or the slang used for a tight situation was *It's Tight Like That*. Besides the recording for Okeh Records, it was reissued for the Jazz Record Society (French).

The second recording of *Ifs Tight Like That* was first recorded by Vocalion Records. The song featured Noone on clarinet, Joe Poston on alto saxophone, and Noone and Poston handled the vocals. The first reissue was done with Vocalion (British), then on Decca (British export only).

Let's Sow A Wild Oat was recorded two times. The reissue was made from the second take, through the Jazz Record Society (French). Vocals again were performed by Noone and Poston.

This recording date of December 27, 1928, became the last recording date that the Apex Orchestra did while Noone was still employed with the Apex Club.

Prohibition by the year 1929 had become a billion dollars a year business, and alcohol had been taken away from the small breweries and distilleries, and was now controlled by crooks.

"Even a prominent figure like Armstrong had at one time to go around with bodyguards, as he was under threat from a gang trying to get him to move to their territory. Many of the musicians themselves carried guns."[65]

Gangsters were providing protection to businessmen. Big-city crime wars were led by Al 'Scar Face' Capone, in Chicago. But Prohibition helped establish the change from saloons to speakeasies. In the city of New York, there were over 32,000 speakeasies. The restaurants or cabarets were replaced with nightclubs, and the cost of drinks badly risen up to ten times more.

Jimmie Noone was affected with the Mafia in Chicago, as he was told very early upon his arrival in Chicago, that he would not be allowed to leave the city.

Unfortunately, his music was well loved by Capone, and because of that, he was limited in his recordings, if it required travel.

The majority of nightclubs that he was hired at, in some way were controlled by the hoodlums. Jimmie often talked to his family about the Apex Club, and the gangsters that just hung out there nightly. They carried guns in their shoulder straps and always kept machine guns under the bar counter and backstage.

After Jimmie Noone had recorded *Apex Blues*, there was no stopping his musical talent. It was unfortunate for him financially that so many others were able to use him, the way they did. The stealing of music happened when musicians had no legal rights or laws to protect them.

And although Noone recorded monthly starting with his *Apex Blues* by the end of 1928, he was still a broke, struggling musician. The recordings he had during his career only paid a straight working fee, royalties, or any incentives.

All in all, the 1920s could be classified as being successful for Jimmie Noone, as the Apex Club Orchestra had been extremely popular. Noone's recordings with Vocalion Records had been selling well.

Even today, *Apex Blues* is still considered one of the great twelve-bar blues that has ever been recorded. Noone's solo choruses prove his musical capabilities.

Listening to *Apex Blues,* it becomes very easy to know why this song is now a "classic." It would have to be called a classic, especially since every lick—and note for note—is being reproduced by clarinetists today.

At thirty-three years of age, Noone's appearance had taken on the look of a Jewish opera singer. His stomach was no longer flat, but rather plump for a man of his age. The black tuxedo that he wore at the Apex, matched his black hair, his brown eyes, smiled constantly. Although he had gained weight, he was quite a handsome Creole.

When Noone sang in his tenor voice, it was done forcefully and energetically. The singing of *Sweet Lorraine* brought traces of tears to his face. After many hard working years at the Apex Club, his last night there was filed with a large crowd.

Patrons of the Apex Club, jammed into the club for his last song of *Sweet Lorraine.*

I've just found joy
I am as happy as a baby boy that has found a brand new cho-cho toy
Since I've found my sweet Lorraine.
She's got a pair of eyes
That are bluer than the summer skies
When you see them you will realize
Why I love my Sweet Lorraine.
When it's raining, I don't miss the sun
Cause it's my sweetie's smile
Just to think that I am the lucky one who will take her down the aisle.
Each night I pray that nobody steals her heart away
I can't wait until that lucky day
When I marry my Sweet Lorraine.

After Jimmie Noone sang this last song at the Apex Club, he said to his audience, "We will not say farewell, but good night." Tears ran down his face, his blew his nose with his handkerchief, picked up his clarinet, and played the melody to another wonderful song that had made him so popular *Apex Blues*.

Chapter Eleven
The Depression

The United States Stock Market prices had collapsed. This created the first phase of the Depression, and a world economic crisis. This was in 1929. The poorest of the poor—The Negro suffered extreme poverty.

The "Great War," or as it was later called, "World War l," had ended in 1918.

The troops had returned home from war, while the economy prospered.

In 1919, territorial changes were happening in Germany and Russia. In 1924, Lenin had died, while Stalin had become the Soviet Dictator. Economy in Germany had collapsed.

The war had started in Europe, and the stock market in 1929 had done what was considered impossible, it collapsed. It the United States, the collapsed totaled twenty-six billion dollars. This was to mark the first phrase of the economic crisis and the Depression. It also created a new poor white society in the U.S.

It had a tremendous effect upon musicians, and not just the black artist, all the races suffered in their own way, but it was the black musician that really felt the pinch. Some black musicians were just reaching their popularity and fame, with the ability to be able to record, or to have their music transmitted on the radio waves.

"Not many jazzmen became wealthy by music alone. The remarkable genius of Goodman earned him top billing as 'Ben Goodwin, the eleven-year-old clarinet wizard', and ten dollars nightly for several years. Oliver and Noone were leaders doubling on early- and late-hour jobs to earn independence; neither did."[66]

On February 26, 1929, Jimmie Noone's Apex Club Orchestra recorded for Vocalion Studio's, two songs: *The St. Louis Blues* (Handy) and *Chicago Rhythm* (Groslsman-Kanter).

St. Louis Blues was recorded for Vocalion, and reissued by Swaggie (Jazz Collector Society), and "Chicago Rhythm," was recorded on Vocalion, and reissued by the label of Association Francaise Des Collectionneurs De Bisque Du Jazz (French).

The song *Chicago Rhythm* was recorded while Joe Poston was still in the band. Although its recording is somewhat on the commercial side, but done well.

Joe 'Doc' Poston, is attributed by most jazz critics as setting the groundwork for all jazz alto saxophone players. And his recordings that he made with Noone's Apex Club Orchestra, proved his capabilities.

On March 2, 1929, less than a week since their recording with Vocalion, the Jimmie Noone Apex Club Orchestra was recording with the previous personnel. Joe Poston (alto), Alex Hill (pno), Junie Cobb (bjo), Bill Newton (bbs), Johnny Wells (drns). Only one song was recorded, which was titled *I Got A Misery,* in which Joe Poston joins Noone on vocals and clarinet.

On April 27, 1929, the Jimmie Noone Apex Club Orchestra, recorded two songs for Vocalion, *Wake Up! Chill' Un, Wake Up!* (Trent-Robison), and it was reissued on Supertone (American).

The second song recorded was *Love Me Or Leave Me* (Kahn-Donaldson), which was also on Vocalion, and reissued on Supertone (American).

From 1929, Jimmie Noone made quite a few recordings for Vocalion, and many of these recordings were on the commercial style of playing. He did have numerous musicians change in his Apex Club personal, which created poor vocal or poor recordings, which resulted in a few rejected recordings.

When Jimmie Noone recorded songs such as, *Let's Sow A Wild Oat* and *Chicago Rhythm,* he enjoyed having fun by adding in words that were the craze at that time, such as 'Dadaism'.

"The word, 'Dadaism', was the greatest literary craze of the Roaring Twenties, and since the band played before a public often mainly consisting of artists and young writers it was no mere accident that this game with fancy words found its way into Noone's music on *Let's Sow A Wild Oat.*"

"The two takes of this title reveal that those 'Dada' lyrics were spontaneously invented by the singer (Noone). They are entirely different, and with such fantastic word creations like, 'Meeossuezy', or 'Reebalshuegare galutsseyerre', most funny, indeed."[67]

In May 1929, Jimmie Noone closed at the Apex Club and moved to the Club Ambassador. The laws of Prohibition had closed down the Apex Club, when a Prohibition Officer visited the club and ordered a drink with the waitress, and she served him alcohol. The Prohibition Amendment was not repealed until December 5, 1933.

"The Apex Club closed down in the spring of 1929, and Jimmie's band moved to the Club Ambassador, on Ontario Street, a fact documented on the original race."

"Brunswick Label of 7096 reading, "The Club Ambassadors." (But hereafter Jimmie maintained his previous band title on records up until 1931.) Zinky Cohn, another pianist of the Earl Hines school, replaced Alex Hill and stayed with the band for almost two years."[68]

On June 21, 1929, Jimmie Noone's Apex Club Orchestra, recorded for Vocalion Studio, a song entitled *Anything You Want*. The title is actually St. Louis Blues, a fact which may account for the company's rejecting the recording of the correct title of February 26th, and there is no composer credit for this song on the label.

Three days later, on June 24, 1929, Jimmie Noone's Apex Club Orchestra, recorded two additional songs, *Someone's Falling in Love* and *Serenading The Moon*, both songs were rejected for the vocals. The only difference in the musician personnel was Kid Ory (trombone), and George Mittchell (cnt), "Little Mitch."

Mezz Mezzrow, remembers the June 24th recording, "Jimmy Noone's band was too much. Playing with him then were Teddy Weatherford on piano, Tubby Hall on drums, Johnny St. Cyr on guitar and banjo, Little Mitch (George Mitchell) on trumpet and Kid Ory on trombone; and what Jimmy didn't do with that clarinet on his, weaving in and through and all around those cats like an expert hackie in heavy traffic, just ain't been invented yet."

On July 1929 Jimmie Noone Apex Club recorded for Vocalion Studios, the band consisted of an entirely new personnel: George Mitchell (cnt), Kid Ory (tbn), Joe Poston (alto), Zinky Cohn (pno), Wilbur Gorham (bjo), Bill Newton (bbs), Johnny Wells (dms), and May Alix on vocals.

The four sound made in the recording studio in July will be listed with the label number, as there are numerous reissues and under numerous labels.

Birmingham Bertha (Clarke-Akst) #1296 for Vocation, and *Am I Blue?* (Clarke-Akst), label of Vocalion reads, "May Alex." The third song, *My Daddy*

Rocks Me (With One Steady Roll) (Barbour), which features Mitchell, Noone and Alix, was reissued for Brunswick#7096 and 4966, and Brunswick A#500196 (German, also for the French export market), British Record Society #1008, Vocalion (British) #1007 and Decca (British export only) #31024. Vocation #2779 was labeled as Jimmie Noone and Orchestra, Brunswick #7096, and #4966, as the Club Ambassadors.

The fourth and final song is *Apex Blues*, Brunswick #7096, #7966, Brunswick (French), Vocation #2779, and British Record Society #1008. Brunswick #7096 is the original issue, and Vocalion #2779 was released as late as 1934 and is the first reissue.

The Apex Club Orchestra played at various nightclubs, such as Detroit Michigan's Graystone Ballroom, where it became so crowded nightly that even the balcony was jammed packed. The Club Ambassador was another nightclub that was usually sold old, then late 1929 the band opened at the El Rado Cafe, which was located over on 55th and Prairie.

After the band's recording session, July 1929, Jimmie Noone took the El car to the south-side, also called the "Black belt area." This was also his neighborhood, as he lived at 3520 State Street, in Chicago. He walked toward the Club Ambassador when he ran into Joe Poston. Jimmie had been thinking about how sickly the Doc had been looking, but didn't mention it.

Joe walked with Jimmie to the Ambassador, and spoke sort of soft, "Jimmie, I've got to talk to you after work tonight. Something important has come up."

Jimmie replied, "Sure. We could grab a bite to eat, maybe have a stack of cakes, some bacon and eggs, besides we seem to eat well together."

After the Ambassador closed that morning, Noone and Poston went over to Emma's Coffee Shop. After they had ordered, with Noone ordering a double meal, they talked about how crowded the club had been, even with the owner presenting two nightly shows.

Poston then spoke to Noone, "I've been carrying around a heavy burden for some time, and I've got to get it off my chest. You see, I'm—"

And then, two young boys from the local college came over and interrupted their conversation before Poston could finish his sentence. They asked, "Can we have your autographs?"

Poston told Noone, "We'll talk later."

The Depression had ceased the carefree spending of money, and the good life which included going to nightclubs. Jazz had been flourishing, but now was starting to slow down for musicians.

The whole nation was grabbing tightly onto their purse, jobs were scarce, bands were losing their main players, or in many bands, they were breaking up all together.

Before long, rental of apartments had doubled in price, along with food, transportation, and entertainment. But in Chicago, and New York's Harlem, and in many other large cities, something new called the "House rent parties," had become established.

It had started slowly with local churches selling dinners, to aid church members in need of financial help. It aided plenty of broke musicians, as their fee was $8 to $10.00. They'd provide music, and also have a home cooked meal. If a musician got lucky, he could play at three or four rent parties in one day.

"House rent parties were a facet of Harlem life even before the Depression. Neighbors brought all kinds of food—fried chicken, baked ham, pig's feet, pork chops, gumbo, potato salad, and more—to which a supply of bootleg liquor was added."[69]

"It has been suggested that the house rent party grew in popularity as a reaction of blacks to their exclusion from Harlem clubs like the Cotton, Connie's Inn, Smalls' Paradise, etc. There was dancing—the bump, grind, and monkey hunch."[70]

Ellington once recalled how James P. Johnson, Willie 'The Lion' Smith and Fats Waller became such great favorites at rent parties. "For ten bucks a shot, they somehow made appearances at three or four different rent parties on a good Saturday night, which did not end until sometime on Sunday."[71]

1929 was a good year for popular music, dance bands, and great for songwriters.

And it was the first year for a screen musical.

"In major cities like New York, Chicago, and Los Angeles, these hotel bands, especially those heard over the radio, became the focus of the music business, with publishers and songwriters turning to them for plugs and hit-making. The number of dance bands increased tremendously around the country so that by 1929 Variety carried the routes of over seven hundred bands, noting whether they were playing ballrooms, cafes, dance halls, hotels, parks, restaurants, or theaters."[72]

Jimmie Noone and His Apex Club Orchestra recorded for Vocalion on July 18, 1929. Three songs were recorded with the same personnel, except the comet player identification is unknown, and could possibly be Preston Jackson. The songs recorded were, *Ain't Misbehavin'*, *That Rhythm Man* (Razaf-Waller-Brooks), arid *Off-Time* (Razaf-Waller-Brooks).

Andy Razaf, wrote the lyrics for *Ain't Misbehavin'* tells how the song was written in record time. "I remember one day, going to Fat's house on 133rd Street to finish up a number based on a little strain he had thought up. The whole show was complete, but they needed an extra number for a theme, and this had to be it. Fats worked on it for about forty-five minutes and there it was—*Ain't Misbehavin'*."[73]

The song, *Ain't Misbehavin'* became Fats Waller's theme song.

Razaf and Waller, had written the floor show that went on to Broadway, called *Hot Chocolates*. The hits from this show was *Ain't Misbehavin'*, *Black and Blue*, *That Rhythm Man*, and *Can't We Get Together*.

September 24, 1929, the Apex Club Orchestra, recorded another two popular songs. *S'Posin'* and *True Blue Lou*, both songs were vocalized by Elmo Tanner. Joe Poston plays the first clarinet on *S'Posin'*, but the obligation behind Tanner is by Noone. *S'Posin'* was sung by Rudy Vallee in 1929, and he helped make it a hit.

Two days later, on September 26, 1929, the Apex Club Orchestra recorded two additional songs for Vocalion. Elmo Tanner sang on both vocals, *Through! (How Can You Say We're Through?)* (McCarthy-Monaco) and *Satisfied* (Caesar-Friend). Jimmie Noone said, "Me and Poston, had previously made plans, that after our recording session, on Thursday, September 26th, we'd meet up on the golf course, and have a talk in private. Poston had said that we needed to talk."

"Anyway, Thursday was always our day to play golf. And depending upon which musicians were in town, or available, I'd play with Louis Armstrong, Zutty Singleton, Joe Poston, Joe Oliver, and Paul Barbarin."

"Traveling to the golf course that day was myself, Joe Oliver, you know—The King—and Joe, the Doc Poston. Me and Doc had planned to play a match together, while the King decided he wanted to practice teeing off My wife Loretta, was at the golf course that day, and she yelled out to us while she was working as a golf instructor, *I'll see everyone tonight.* Loretta had become a golf instructor, but she was also a pro-golfer, that could not find work because of her race. A Negro pro-golfer was unheard of in the late twenties."

"When the Doc went to use his iron, he took a clump of turf out of the grass with his golf club, and he told me, 'Jimmie, man, I can't seem to do anything right these days, I'm so upset'."

"We started walking together, to the next hole, when I told him, I think it's time you told, we what's bothering you, as you know that I love you like my brother."

"Before I could say another word, Doc dropped his clubs onto the grass and placed his hands over his face. It was obvious that he was about to cry, and was trying to hold it back. And then he said softly, 'I don't know what to do man, but I've got to tell you that I will be leaving Chicago soon. You see, I— oh, I have—Oh damn it to hell! I have Syphilis. There, I've finally said it'."

"Doc collapsed onto the ground, as if finally relieved to tell his best friend, so I slid down on the grass next to him. I placed my arms around him to try and console him, and found myself crying. I told him I loved him and asked if there was anything that I could do to help him."

"Doc told me, 'When I first developed a chancre hard red sores, I went to the doctor, and he said it was an early indication of the disease—Syphilis. He said it was chronic and also contagious. I'm in stage two, and my doctor recommended that I enjoy myself before I die'."

"We sat on the grass, holding each other, and cried for quite some time. That's when I really realized how much I really loved him. I kissed Doc on the cheek and asked him when he would be leaving."

"We plotted what we would do and say to our fellow musicians and friends. We came to the explanation that Doc would be traveling to California because of his arthritic problems, and that we'd start looking for a replacement alto player for the band."

"I remember that me and the Doc discussed the remaining five recording sessions we had lined up with Vocalion until the end of the year. We had four dates in October, and one in December. I asked Doc if he could hang around until then, and he told me, 'I'll stay until December, unless my health gets worse, or you tell me to leave'."

"I'll never forget that Thursday. The Doc played with me on those recording dates, and at nightclubs, until the end of 1930. I never told a so what Doc's aliment was, or why he left the band, but I felt lost without his music."

Later, it was recorded in jazz history books that Doc Poston just disappeared from the music scene and the Chicago area.

"The very moving way Jimmie plays the melody in harmony with Joe Poston's alto sax, in most of these Vocalion Records, is also a joy for the ear. Incidentally, I don't remember having seen printed before what a marvelous alto player this Joe Poston was; his tempo was absolutely impeccable, and he knew how to phrase a melody in the clearest and most rhythmic way."[74]

The Apex Club Orchestra recorded two songs on October 15, 1929, and the vocalists on both songs was Helen Savage. Vocation taped, *I'm Doing What I'm Doing For Love* (Yollen-Ager) and *He's A Good Man To Have Around* (Yollen-Ager).

Joe Poston, Noone's alto sax partner, became a straight man, "A kind of a lot ego," against which Noone could bounce his own dexterity, wit and bustling energy. Poston usually played a very decorous, unjazzy' lead/obliggato.[75]

October 21, 1929, the Apex Club Orchestra recorded two songs under the Brunswick Label as the Savannah Syncopation. The name change is due to recording contracts Jimmie Noone had with Vocation.

They recorded *After Your Gone* (Creamer-Layton), with vocals by Helen Savage, and *My Melancholy Baby* (Norton-Burnett). Reissues were made through Brunswick (French) Label.

Black Thursday, October 24th and black Tuesday, October 29, 1929, were not the two days that started the Wall Street Crash. The rolling slide had started for several weeks, but the 29th is the day when over sixteen million shares changed hands.

A newly inaugurated president, Herbert Hoover advised Americans to buy Liberty Bonds and to continue to invest in stocks and bonds of their employers.

Millions of people were reducing their savings accounts to speculate into gambling ventures.

The outcome of the Wall Street Crash caused hysteria and panic for Americans.

The result is thousands upon thousands of people suffered from malnutrition due to a decline in consumption of milk, eggs, fruit and vegetables. Their diet changed to bread, potatoes and beans.

It became common to see men, women and children digging with sticks in the garbage and trash, looking for bits of food. Some restaurants provided stale bread and leftovers, while vegetable dealers gave away overripe produce.

Jimmie Noone had received a telegram from his mother, Lucinda, notifying him that the Wall Street Crash had taken all their savings. Her telegram read:

Jimmie: The money your father left us is lost. The crash has left us penniless. All our savings are gone. Lawyer, Charles McIntosh, invested all our money in stocks and bonds. Notify me regarding what to do?

Your Mother.

Jimmie read the wire several times, unable to believe what he had just read. The Depression had just started, and his dear mother was without a cent to her name. He did not care about his money, which he had spent about $1,000 investing in new instruments, but what was he to do about his mother?

Johnny Noone, Jimmie's father, had originally left his mother enough to live off of until she was elderly, now she had nothing. Jimmie called his mother and talked to her, she was worried and upset. He told her, "As soon as I can get time off, I'll come home, and we'll solve the problem. I'm sending you some money today for expenses."

Jimmie remembered that he was due to go into the recording studio in a few days, and that would bring in additional income, but not much. The recording cost for the studios ran from $300 to $500.00, but he and his musicians *only* got paid anywhere from $12 to $16.00 for the entire recording.

Jimmie walked over to the El Rado Cafe, on the Southwest Comer of Garfield Boulevard and Prairie Avenue, located at 231 East Garfield. The Garfield Hotel had a basement that was called "The El Rado Cafe," where Noone led his Apex Club Orchestra as bandleader. After talking to the manager of the club, it was agreed he could take some personal time off.

The El Rado wasn't just another nightclub on the south-side, it drew hundreds of night life people. In the Garfield Hotel, there was a barber shop, with a poolroom in the back section. It was also a hangout and attraction for all the Negro musicians, as it stayed open all night.

The barber shop in the Garfield was owned by Charlie Farrell. Noone went to Farrell's place to get a haircut before he left Chicago. Then he walked down the street to Dave's Cafe for a bite to eat, and when he opened the door of the Cafe, he saw one of his best friends, Johnny Dodds.

Jimmie yelled out, "Johnny."

Dodds jumped up from his table, hugged Jimmie real tight as he asked him, "Man, where have you been? It's been a while since I've seen you."

Jimmie replied, "I've been busy recording. I hear you're still at Kelly's Stable."

"It's been five years now. Things are really slowing down with this damn Depression. Have a seat and order something."

Dodds patted Jimmie's stomach and said with a smile, "Looks like you've gained some weight, hugh?"

After Jimmie had ordered a large meal, Dodds told him, "I've been recording also with The Jimmy Blythe's Washboard Band, The New Orleans Wanderers, and with The New Orleans Bootblacks. Man, I've been hustling up jobs in clubs. You know, I'm just trying to make a living as a musician."

While eating their meal, Johnny Dodds continued, "Jimmie man, Kelly's Stable, is just a converted damn barn. You know it's over on the north-side of town. I know that you remember those black walls and the horse stalls. I do declare, it even smells to this day of horses sweat, even with that damn sawdust on the floor." They both laughed so hard and loud, people in the Cafe could hear them.

While waiting for their bill, Johnny mentioned, "I've been buying rental property for the last few years, with the idea of having additional income at retirement."

Jimmie replied, "Man, that's great. I'm taking the next train out of Chicago to visit my mom back home. She's lost everything in that damn stock crash. I'll try to catch up with you when I get back."

Dodds added, "Don't take the L & N train, it stops via Mississippi and Alabama, and I've been hearing about how rough going through can be, and how many negroes are being hanged. Listen, we should talk. Everyone's comparing our style of playing. I'd like to know your thoughts on that."

Noone answered, "There's nothing to say, man. We both play good. We both got our own style of playing and that's it." They shook hands and left the cafe, promising to get together soon.

"Unquestionably the best known of Dodd's work are some four dozen sides he made as a member of Armstrong's Hot Five and Hot Seven recordings bands. One of the finest examples of his work is on the tune made as both *Gully Low Blues* and *S.O.L. Blues*."

"The piece opens with an up-tempo passage based on the cord changes of *Sister Kate*. Dodd's plays a strong driving solo here, and then brings the tempo down for a typically passionate blues chorus. It is a prime example of New Orleans clarinet playing at its best."

"Dodd's, however was not as technically skilled as others among the early clarinetists. His tone often grew shrill in the upper register, and he frequently fumbled notes in quick passages. But he was, we must remember, one of the inventors of the art."[76]

Jimmie caught the El Train to the railroad station. At the ticket window he asked the clerk, "I'd like a round-trip ticket to New Orleans, and nonstop on the Illinois Central Railroad, not the L & N."

Aboard the train, Jimmie watched some little kids running up and down the aisle, and memories of New Orleans drifted into his thoughts. He could almost smell his mother's cooking of Creole cabbage, sweet potato pies and lemon pies. And her alligator's tails, stuffed with crab and her Creole praline candy.

Riding on the train had made Jimmie restless and sleepy, so he went to the cafe train, where a posted sign read, "whites only." A porter passed by, and recognized his dilemma, and pointed in the opposite direction as he said, "We gotta go to the back."

After purchasing some chicory coffee in the Negro section, he sat in the cafe and listened to the movement of the train, which reminded him of a certain song he had heard on the radio, and the lyrics had stuck in his head.

Hop down front and then you doddle back,
Mooch to the left and then you, mooch to the right,
Hands on your hips and do the Mess Around,
Break a leg until you're near the ground.
Now that's the Old Black Bottom Dance!

A porter walked through the cafe calling out, "New Orleans, coming up in five minutes." Jimmie finished up his coffee, went into the washroom and freshened up a bit, and was ready to depart when the train entered the station.

Looking out the train window, he expected to see his mother waiting for the train's arrival, but as he departed from the train with his suitcase, she was nowhere to be found.

The smell of New Orleans was so different from Chicago. The air was clean and clear, yet warm. As passengers and residents passed him, they smiled and greeted each other. And the politeness reminded him that he had arrived home.

As he rode a cab to his mother's home, he had the taxi driver stop so he could watch a marching band parade down St. Claude Street, as they advertised a dance, and attempted to play *High Society*. This brought back memories of The Onward Brass Band. (Danny Barker wrote in his book, *A Life In Jazz*, "That this band was the greatest in the city, and highly respected.")

The driver continued driving at Jimmie's signal, as he thought about how Alphonse Picou had played High Society with the Manuel Perez Band, at Mahogany Hall. Alphonse had taken that piccolo part and transposed it into a unique clarinet solo—and Jimmie could hardly wait to challenge him on the tune. He patted his clarinet case that had been placed on the seat next to him.

Jimmie realized he was in a daydreaming state, when the taxi driver remarked, "Sir. Ah sir, this is your street."

Jimmie read the meter, then remarked, "Here's a dollar, keep the change."

The driver smiled, then remarked, "A twenty-five cent tip ain't so bad during Depression times. Thank you, sir."

Walking up the steps to his mother's house, Jimmie began to feel that maybe something was wrong. Why didn't his mother meet him at the station? And why wasn't she sitting on the porch when he arrived? And as he turned the front doorknob to open the door, it was locked. He questioned why her doors locked in the middle of the day?

Using his skeleton key (that he had kept since living at home) he opened the door, but pushed the doorbell also. Jimmie felt the beginning rush of anxiety sweep through his body, as he wondered if his mom was all right.

The house was very still, he yelled out loud, "Mother, where are you?" He walked into the kitchen, and on top of the stove, water boiled in a large pot. He turned the pot off, after realizing there was little water left.

Jimmie, feeling somewhat apprehensive, yelled out, "Mother, where in the hell are you?" With no answer, he searched the entire house. The only area left was the pantry, and the back porch, and the backyard.

Running into the pantry, and then to the back porch, he noticed the back door was unlocked. He headed to where the swing was outside and almost tripped on his mother's leg. As he jumped to keep from falling over her body, there she was, face down on the ground.

Jimmie fell to his knees screaming, "Mother." He reached for her hand, felt her pulse, and noticed a faint beat. He ran inside and called for an ambulance. Running outside again, he used mouth to mouth recitation on his mother, and after five minutes or so, they arrived.

Jimmie rode in the ambulance with his mother to the hospital. Lucinda opened her eyes, seen her son, and tried to smile, but the pain was too great. Instead, she squeezed his hand. He knew that squeeze, it had all started when he was a kid, when his mother would hold his hand to cross the street, and later, she'd do it to give him confidence.

The hospital rushed Lucinda into the emergency room, while Jimmie signed papers to admit her. He walked to a phone and called his sister's. Paul Barbarin, the drummer, and himself, had married two sisters. While his sister Lil had moved to Chicago to be with her husband, Charlie.

(The Barbarin family was large, it consisted of about twenty musicians, all cousins, uncles, or relations in some way.) The talented Danny Barker's uncle was Paul Barbarin, and it is believed that Alphonse Picou's relatives married into the Barbarin family also. Elizabeth, Jimmic's sister, who was better known as Lottie, was still single and working in New Orleans.

Jimmie couldn't reach Lil in Chicago, so he sent her a Western Union telegram. He did reach Lottie and Nita, who lived in New Orleans, and they were rushing over to the hospital.

Before his sisters arrived, an emergency resident doctor came out and told him, "Mr. Noone, your mother has had a cardiac heart attack. She's in a critical stage, and I do not know if we can save her."

He replied, while holding back the tears, "May I see her?"

The doctor replied, "Yes. But only for a few minutes. The nurse will show you her room."

The hospital room smelled sterilized. The walls, cabinets, towels, and even the bed were white. He noticed the tubes in his mother's nose, and on her arms. Jimmie reached for his mother's hand and squeezed it softly. She opened her eyes while trying to clutch his hand, but she was too weak.

Lucinda spoke softly, "Jimmie, never stop playing music. Nev—e—r." And then her eyes closed, and she was dead.

Jimmie took his mother's death hard. He took care of her funeral arrangements and paid for all expenses. Lucinda was buried at St. Vincent De Paul Cemetery, on Louisa Street, among many relatives and friends.

It was decided among the Noone family that since Lottie was single, she would move into her mother's home and take care of the property, rather than sell it.

Before Jimmie left to go back to Chicago, he told his sisters, "I'm going to see Dad's grave, but I need a plan to get into St. Patrick's Cemetery."

Lil said, "You ain't white forget it." Lottie suggested, "Make yourself look more white. Remember how kids used to call us, 'Pasabonnes'? Mama said it was the Creole word for Quadroon, or a fair-skinned Creole, who in some place other than New Orleans, would pass for a white man. You could do it Jimmie."

Lottie added, "Besides, we're always taken for white."

The next day, Jimmie put on what he called "Standard Clothing," which consisted of a plain suit, he parted his hair down the middle, put on a plaid bow tie, and asked Lottie, "How do I look?"

She replied, "White. Like Johnny Noone. Dad would be proud of you."

The gates to St. Patrick's graveyard were made of cast iron latticework, and attached to the entrance was a sign that read, white cemetery. No negroes allowed. Bravely, Jimmie walked up to a guard at the gate and asked him, "Directions to Johnny Noone's crypt, please, sir?"

The guard replied, "Four lanes down, and second crypt to the right."

As Jimmie walked in, he expected the guard to stop him. And he anticipated the guard to yell out, "Niggers are not allowed in this cemetery," instead the guard smiled at him as if he was a white man.

Jimmie was amazed at the cemetery's upkeep. It was different from where the negroes were buried. All the graves had whitewashed stone crypts, with red brick walkways that were neatly swept.

Reaching his father's crypt, he was amazed by the size. It was a monument; it was a real burial vault, and it was obvious that his father had been a distinguished person in the New Orleans community.

The carved stone read, Johnny O'Nooney, born 12-5-1876, died 3-11-1929, loving father and husband. Jimmie sat down on the lawn and tried to absorb all this information, and then he thought, "O'Nooney would have been my father's full-blooded Irish name. Since he had been born in County Cook, Ireland, he must have shortened it when he came to America."

After Jimmie arrived back home, he told his sisters that were waiting for him, what he had seen, and their father's other name. Lottie said, "O'Nooney was his white family's name, while us negroes had the name of Noone. Maybe Dad did that to keep his from getting hurt, and to protect his other family from learning about us."

Lil added, "Pa was a successful white man. If we revealed what we've learned to anyone, it could ruin his name. Not to mention that we know there's some half-brothers, or half-sisters that live in this city."

Jimmie remarked, "Mom knew everything, and accepted our dad as he was. We must always respect what they attempted to cover up. Tomorrow, me and Lil will be leaving on the train for Chicago. Now Nita and Lottie, you two will have to stick together real close now that Mom is gone. It's gonna be hard living without her," they grabbed onto each other, and cried as they hugged.

Lil and Jimmie arrived back in Chicago. Lil went back to her home and husband, while Jimmie returned back to his flat and music on the El Train. When he got off the train on the south-side, he could see people of color in various shades in the crowd.

There were men and women of chocolate, black, yellow, coal, and yellow complexions. While he walked home, he promised himself to devote all his music to people of all races, and especially his recently deceased mother.

With Noone as bandleader, his famous Apex Club Orchestra was again playing at the El Rado Cafe's basement. It was October 1929 and downstairs the room was jammed packed with jazz enthusiasts waiting for his first set. The entire time that Noone performed at the El Rado, crowds gathered nightly, which created long lines.

There has been much confusion regarding the El Rado Cafe's name. Earlier jazz critics and writers that have written linear notes on Noone, have listed the El Rado Cafe and The Eldorado Club as being two separate nightclubs. However, this is incorrect.

The El Rado and The Eldorado Club, are indeed one and the same club, however as years passed, its nickname became the El Rado. Located on 55th and Garfield, this club became known as the most hippest place to be seen and party at.

Dempsey Travis's great book entitled *The Autobiography of Black Jazz* and mentions when Floyd Campbell, talked to him about the El Rado and its neighborhood.

"I took a cab to the Garfield Hotel, which was the hub of the jazz scene on the south-side. Charlie Farrell's Barber Shop and Poolroom on the ground floor of the hotel stayed open all night."

"There was a Greek restaurant on the Prairie Avenue side of the hotel, and Jimmie Noone was playing in the El Rado Cafe in the basement. Down the street were the Golden Lily and Dave's Cafe."

"I went down to the El Rado that first night. A fellow named Wells was playing the drums. He let me sit in for him and play, and I sang with the band. The cats liked the way I played, and they asked me to stick around and watch the floor show."[77]

Tommy Brookins, who worked at Kelly's Stables on the north-side, recalls the Eldorado Club, "After having worked for a year at Kelly's, I was hired at the Eldorado Club at the corner of fifty-fifth Street and Garfield Boulevard. The Eldorado was in a cellar and Jimmie Noone had the orchestra there. Many musicians and visitors from many countries came to her, his little orchestra at the Eldorado."

"Jimmie Noone was the 'sweetest' clarinet who ever existed. He knew it and he often confined himself to the style to style to which he owned his success. But when Noone let himself go, using the high register of his instrument, his tone lost nothing of its beauty. Jimmie Noone was a calm man. His voice was gentle but he wasn't any less energetic."[78]

Noone had said, "Doc was like my right hand. He was a musical genius. When he left the band, we both cried like babies. Man, I hated to see him go, but his health demand it."

"After the band had gone to the El Rado, in the fall of 1929, Jimmie's group suffered its greatest loss when Joe Poston resigned in the following summer. Eddie Pollack took Poston's chair, and although he played very much in Joe's style the outfit lost something of its former elegance."[79]

October 23, 1929, The Apex Club Orchestra, recorded three songs in Chicago. *Love Me*, which was recorded two times, with vocals by Elmo Tanner. The third song was *Song Of The Sands*, all three songs were never released, as the vocals were rejected.

The three songs were recorded under the name of Jimmie's Blue Melody Boys. The personnel in the band were Joe 'Doc' Poston (alto), Zinky Cohn (pno), Wilbur Gorham (gtr), Bill Newton (bbs), Johnny Wells (dms), and Elmo Tanner (vcl).

The last recording that the Jimmie Noone Apex Club Orchestra recorded in 1929 was on October 23, for Vocalion. The personnel of the band remained the same.

However, Vocalion had two songs that were successfully recorded, *Love* (Goulding-Janis) and *Love Me* (Morse-Aivaz), both songs were sung by Elmo Tanner.

Technically, on November 26, 1929, another recording was done, but on all four songs the vocals were rejected. The titles of these songs were *Zonky, Singin' River*, and *I'll Still Go On Wanting You*.

1929 Jimmie Noone played at Detroit's Graystone Ballroom, where crowds jammed into the balcony, as the main floor was full to capacity. The Graystone was famous for its jam sessions that usually occurred at 2:00 AM.

The Graystone is also remembered when John Nesbitt, trumpet player with the Mc Kinney's Cotton Pickers, assisted in training musicians to read music, by sending them out into the woods for additional practice, this started the term, "Woodshedding."

The year 1929 had seen the Depression, which would continue until 1941. The Depression's effect upon jazz was drastic, and probably will never be forgotten.

This period brought out into the open the Ku Klux Klan, and with them, lynching's that became every day. Negroes that had worked such undesirable jobs as garbage collectors, elevator operators, waiters, street cleaners, and domestic servants were now sought after by whites.

They were the new unemployed. They suffered the greatest mentally and physically, as the Negro had not yet elevated themselves into the middle class. Negroes were still feeling the aftereffects of slavery.

The Negro jazz musician who had become the leaders in their creativity, now were to see that all taken away from them, with the beginnings of the "White Big Bands."

When the El Rado Cafe closed because of the Depression, it left the Apex Club Orchestra without a steady gig. Numerous jazz critics have suggested that this date is when Noone's greatest era had come to a halt.

But this theory is not correct, the closed of the El Rado, provided Noone more time and freedom to perform in other clubs, and he remained steadily employed.

Chapter Twelve
The Thirties

The year 1930 became the era of the big bands and the big ballrooms. The Depression had taken away the majority of jobs for jazz bandleaders with small bands.

Some of the bands there were to become famous included; Jimmy Dorsey, Artie Shaw, Bob Crosby, Guy Lombardo, Woody Herman, Chick Webb, Duke Ellington, Glenn Miller, Count Basie, and Gene Krupa.

Earl Hines, who had played with Noone's Apex Club Orchestra in 1929, had become a bandleader. Hines fulfilled his leader ambitions and went on to form one of the great bands of the thirties.

But Noone was at heart an ensemble player, despite his enormous solo capabilities. He replaced Hines with pianists who obviously worshipped Hines: at first Zinky Cohn, and later the unjustifiably neglected Clarence Browning.

When Alex Hill left the Apex Club Orchestra, he was replaced by the legendary Zinky Cohn in 1929. Cohn sounds so much like Earl Hines that even jazz critics have become confused with trying to recognize the piano player. Cohn stayed with Noone until he left for Europe in 1931.

Noone's band of the early and middle thirties made some concessions to the swing era and the incoming Moten and Basie styles. But in essence he continued with the original format, still intertwining duets with the alto saxophone (now Eddie Pollack) and relishing Browning's Hines re-creations.[80]

By 1930, there were more than a dozen instrumentation bands.

"Calloway had taken over the Missourians, and there were Luis Russell, Charlie, Johnson, Claude Hopkins, Louis Armstrong, Chick Webb, Henderson, Ellington, Cecil Scott, all in New York; Earl Hines and Tiny Parham in Chicago, the Cotton Pickers in Detroit; Benny Moten, Andy Kirk,

The Blue Devils, and Alphonse Trent in the Southwest; Lunceford in Memphis."[81]

"The typical size band of the thirties, were, three trumpets, three trombones, four reeds and four rhythm instruments."[82]

Jimmie Noone was offered a job with Cab Calloway, who had succeeded Duke Ellington into the Cotton Club. Instead of accepting it, he took his own eight-piece band to New York. His band also included Charlie Green on the trombone, who had worked with Bessie Smith. But after several weeks in New York, the Apex club Orchestra returned back to Chicago.

Four months later, on February 3, 1930, the Jimmie Noone Apex Orchestra recorded for Vocalion Label. The orchestra included, Joe Poston (alto), Zinky Cohn (pno), Wilbur Gorham (bjo), Bill Newton (bbs), and Johnny Wells (dms). The two songs recorded were *El Rado Scuffle* (Rose) and *Deep Trouble* (Rose).

On February 6, 1930, Jimmie Noone's Apex Orchestra recorded for the Vocalion Label. The two songs recorded were popular hits, *Crying For The Carolines* (Lewis-Young-Warren) and *Have a Little Faith In Me* (Lewis-Young-Warren). The vocals were performed by Elmo Tanner.

Nightly broadcasting from radio station WSBC became popular. The Cabin Club broadcast had a Frankie Jaxon contingent, and later, Jimmie Noone's Big Band. Noone was then heard from Skoller's Danceland, with the entire set being broadcasted.

On February 18, 1930, the Jimmie Noone's Apex Club Orchestra recorded for Vocalion. Because of the economic times in existence (Depression), recording payments that musicians once made had dropped almost in half. Jimmie Noone received approximately $12–$16.00 per session, and now he was making anywhere from $6–$8.00 per recording session.

Noone had once said that, "Recording session pay was his extra spending money," but now it had become payment toward the rent, grocery store, and other expenses.

The two songs recorded on the old 78 wax record on February 18 were, *Should I* (Freed-Brown), and *I'm Following You!* (Dreyer-MacDonald), both on Vocalion. Both songs featured vocals by Elmo Tanner, and these tunes were popular songs of the 1930s.

Franz Jackson, who played tenor saxophone and clarinet, and who later became an arranger, composer, and bandleader. While he was employed at a mob controlled speakeasy, he talked about musician's salary, "The sidemen in the band were paid four dollars per night, plus a meal. In addition, we picked up sixteen to twenty dollars per man in tips from the big Prohibition spenders. Our nightly tips were equal to the average colored person's salary during that period. That was good money when you consider my weekly room rent was only two dollars and the average meal would cost me about thirty-five cents."[83]

The early thirty years surged and swept forward upon minorities, and salaries from employers became lower than low. The negroes existence became a 'Live for today' attitude.

The minority's only hope centered on belief in their God and church, and from the jazz music being played throughout this era. Besides starvation, negroes had to come to grips with the United States government's denial of freedom and democracy.

On May 16, 1930, a recording on Vocalion was made of two songs, *I Lost My Gal From Memphis* (Tobias-De Rose), which featured Wilbur Gorham on the banjo, and *When You're Smiling* (*The Whole World Smiles With You*) (Fisher-Goodwin-Shay), which featured Wilbur Gorham on guitar, and Georgia White on vocals. Elmo Tanner was not used on this recording for vocals.

Twelve days later, on May 28, 1930, Vocalion recorded *On Revival Day* (Razaf), featuring vocals by Eddie Pollack and Wilbur Gorham, on banjo. Another tune recorded was *I'm Drifting Back To Dreamland* (Charlesworth-Harrison-Sadler) and it featured Wilbur Gorham on the guitar.

These two songs were later reissued through the Supertone Label (British). The reason for the reissue is that *without* the popular vocal singers, the quality of the recording seemed to be more outstanding. When a member of the band, such as Eddie Pollack, provided the vocals, the selling of the song became that much greater.

Jimmie Noone's Apex Club Orchestra recorded on the Vocalion Label on July 1, 1930. The musicians used were Jimmie Noone (clt), Eddie Pollack (alto), Zinky Cohn (pno), Wilbur Gorham (bjo), Bill Newton (bbs), Johnny Wells (dms), Elmo Tanner (vcl).

The songs recorded on July 1 were all popular hits, *Virginia Lee, So Sweet,* and the song, *San,* was recorded two times on Vocalion Label. The song San was recorded as a Vocalion test, then later reissued through Swaggie's Jazz Collector Society, and through Ace of Hearts, as a 12' LP, then later deleted.

On July 29, 1930, the Jimmie Noone Apex Orchestra, recorded on Vocalion, with the same previous musicians from the July 1st recording. This recording was long remembered by the musicians in the band, mainly because they had so much fun recording that day.

Musicians, Pollack, Cohn, Gorham, Newton, and Wells, proved on the two recordings what a delight that day had been. The song *Bring It On Home To Your Grandma* (Theard), features vocals by Eddie Pollack, who delivers the popular song quite well, however, *You Rascal You* (Theard), which features vocals by Noone and Pollack, prove to be one of their best recordings.

The reason *You Rascal You* is rated highly is mainly because it's a cute song, with lyrics such as:

I'll be glad when you're dead-you rascal you,
When you lay six feet deep
No more fried chicken will you eat—

Oh course, *You Rascal You* cannot be compared to the romantic, yet sweet, *Sweet Lorraine* but for a popular song of the thirties, it's good. The vocals of Noone and Pollack hit it off quite well, and the clarinet blends into a perfect routine.

The song *Bring It On Home To Your Grandma* and *You Rascal You* were considered to be issued in the British Vocalion of Jazz Series, but only reached the test pressing stage in 1951.

The next to the last recording for the year 1930 came on August 23, 1930, and was recorded on Vocalion as The Jimmie Noone Apex Orchestra. The male vocal recording done in this session is unknown. The two songs recorded were *Little White Lies* (Donaldson) and *Moonlight on the Colorado* (Moll-King).

The last recording is in October 1930, for Vocalion Records. The two songs recorded were *Something To Remember You By* (Dietz-Schwartz), which featured the vocals of May Alix, and *Three Little Words* (Kalmar-Ruby), which also featured vocals by May Alix.

In Chicago, Negro musicians found steady employment in the Black Belt's night life areas of Thirty-fifth Street, and a half-dozen blocks between State Street, and South Parkway-Wabash, Michigan, Indiana, Prairie, and Calumet Avenues.

In Chicago, white musicians hangout was over on the North-side of Chicago. The Three Deuces Club was a little small joint on State Street. The downstairs room was an ugly place that had no covering on the floor.

The musicians that performed in Kansas city included, Bessie Smith, Alberta Hunter, Lizzie Miles, Ma Rainey, King Oliver, Fletcher Henderson, and Duke Ellington.

In Kansas city, a whole new school of jazz music had been born by Bennie Moten, Count Basie, Walter 'Hot Lips' Page, Andy Kirk and others. Gangsters provided Negro entertainers steady work, at clubs like the Panama, Eblon, or the Lincoln Theaters.

Other nightclubs were The Subway club on Eighteenth and Vine, in its basement, and The Sunset Club, which became famous for its jam sessions.

"When Count Basie played the Reno Club, band members worked from nine in the evening until six in the morning, seven nights a week, and received eighteen dollars a week each. They were grateful for the work and the opportunity to jam."

"After World War II, the jam session became 'Illegal' in the nation's major jazz centers. In an effort to force nightclub operators to share their profits from customers coming to hear jazzmen who jammed free of charge, the Musicians Union prohibited the advertising of such sessions and the jazzmen from participating without pay."[84]

Duke Ellington, Don Redman, Fletcher Henderson, and numerous other bandleaders were slowly increasing their orchestra size, during a period that could be called, "Pre-Swing."

The string bass was gradually replacing the tuba. The loud four-four rhythm of the tuba turned into a gliding one-two-three-four beat. The change in the rhythm section also created a swing base on which the band could play various compositions.

On January 12, 1931, the Jimmie Noone's Apex Club Orchestra, recorded two songs for the Vocalion Label *He's Not Worth Your Tears* (Dixon-Rose-Warren), with vocals by Mildred Bailey.

Also recorded was *Travlin' All Alone* (Johnson), again with vocals by Mildred Bailey. The personnel in the orchestra remained the same as earlier previous recordings. This became the last recording made under the name "The Jimmie Noone's Apex Club Orchestra."

Mildred Bailey (Mildred Rinker), became the first white vocalist to sing with authentic jazz phrasing, and with a feeling for the blues. In 1929, she started the era of the big-band female singers.

Paul Whiteman was the first bandleader to feature a female singer. Whiteman hired Bailey on the strength of a demo record he had heard. While employed by Whiteman, she married the band's xylophonist, Red Norvo. Later, Red Norvo and Mildred Bailey were tagged with the name "Mr. and Mrs. Swing."

The July 27, 1931, recording of Jimmie Noone and his Orchestra, for the Brunswick Label, was made in Chicago, under the name of Jimmie Noone and His Orchestra.

The personnel on this recording was different, the orchestra included, Eddie Pollack (alto), Earl Hines (pno), Quinn Wilson (sbs), Art Jarrett (vcl), and Benny Washington (dms).

The personnel on this recording was different, the orchestra included, Eddie Pollack (alto), Earl Hines (pno), Quinn Wilson (sbs), Art Jarrett (vcl), and Benny Washington (dms).

Four popular songs were recorded *I Need Lovin'* (Creamer-Johnson), under the Brunswick Label, with one reissue, another reissue was made under the Brunswick Label, a 9000 series German (also for the French export market).

The second song recorded was *It's You!* (Razaf-Waller), under the Brunswick Label, and reissued under the Brunswick Label A 9000 series German (also for the French export market).

The third song recorded for Brunswick was *River Stay 'Way From My Door* (Dixon-Woods). The reissue was again by the Brunswick Label. The 9000 series German (also for the French export market). This song became a popular hit in the thirties and therefore sold well.

River Stay 'Way From My Door was written by composers well known through the Tin Pan Alley. Harry Woods (a great artist), wrote *Red Robin, I'm Looking Over A Four Leaf Clover, A Little Kiss Each Morning* (A Little Kiss Each Night), as well as *Heigh-Ho Everybody*, Mort Dixon also collaborated with Harry Woods on this very popular song.

The fourth and last song recorded on this date was *When It's Sleepy Time Down South* (L. Rene-O Reno-Muse). This was a reissue on Brunswick American, Brunswick British, and the Brunswick 9000 series German (also for the French export market).

The song *When It's Sleepy Time Down South* is possibly one of the prettiest songs to be played on a clarinet. Jimmie Noone's clarinet reeks of New Orleans. The atmosphere, the sweet smell of magnolias, and the Mississippi can all be visualized just listening to this beautiful song.

It would be close to two years (1933), when Jimmie Noone would again enter a studio to record his music. This was due to several reasons; the Depression had slowed everything, including music, and the personal problems that Jimmie was having, seemed to add to it.

This was the year that Jimmie's sister, Nita, died. She was a beautiful girl, that possessed a sort of Spanish coloring, and her long black hair seemed to add to her beauty. She had been told to wear a jacket the night that she had gone out for a hairdo, but she had decided it was warm enough without it. At first, she developed a cold, and then quickly it turned into pneumonia.

There was also the personal problem that he was having with his marriage. Jimmie believed a lot of problems had developed due to him being a musician, and working two and three jobs a day to make ends meet. His wife, Loretta (His Sweet Lorraine), was unhappy and both agreed to a divorce. It was not due to become final until the middle of 1934.

Jimmie returned back home to New Orleans, with just enough time for the burial services of his sister, Nita, and then he left for a quick return back to Chicago to play in its cabaret with his orchestra.

Jimmie was now separated from his wife and going through divorce proceedings. He felt very lonely and hurt. The only way he could release his loneliness was by dating, and that was not a problem, women were constantly asking him out. Ask any musician, and they'll agree, that women are attracted to their creative abilities, and will get bold, just to go out with them.

The National Prohibition Enforcement Act of 1919 had stopped the sale of liquor, or its purchase. The enforcement of this act, from the very beginning, had become an impossible task. Alphonse Capone, with the aid of his henchmen's Thompson submachine guns, was able to control liquor better than the government.

Jazz had developed through this Prohibition era, and had survived. The control that gangsters had on musicians did change the fate of their careers. An example of such musicians being controlled as such, were Earl Hines and Jimmie Noone.

Hines and Noone's fame could have been greater, if they had been allowed to travel more out of Chicago, or record with other labels, or even just to have had more broadcast lightly on the radio stations.

On December 5, 1933, the Amendment (Referred to as the 'Noble Experiment'), was repealed after fourteen years of being a dry nation. This twenty-first Amendment freed all Americans to drink alcohol where and when they pleased.

Now that drinking was legal, hotels were able to sell liquor with dinner, and the speakeasies where people could purchase booze illegally had closed its doors, and this created more dancing halls, with bands playing for floor shows.

Musicians were still accustomed to Depression wages with its wage scale for union members quite low, but now jobs were opening up everywhere, and the demand for music increased.

Jimmie Noone in the thirties would still work rent parties, cabarets, weddings, ballroom dances, and whatever else was available. He had often said that, "Rent parties were the best. For about a dollar and a half, he would be hired to play both the saxophone and his clarinet. The musicians were asked to eat free of charge, and usually included chitlins, pig's feet, collard greens, and black-eyed peas."

Rent parties' admission ran about twenty-five cents, as well as the price of a shot of liquor. Sometimes, if Jimmie was having a good week, he'd pay to enter, just to be able to help out his friend's rent debt. He liked these parties because of the food (which he loved), but mainly because he was helping someone from living on the streets.

In early December, before Noone was to begin recording again in the studios, he looked up Quinn Wilson, a bass and violin player, who in 1929 had recorded with the Ellington Band on a daily radio broadcast.

Quinn Wilson later became the arranger and bass player for the famous Earl Hines Orchestra.

In Chicago, on December 15, 1933, Jimmie Noone and his Orchestra recorded for Vocalion. The band members included Eddie Pollack (Bar, alto, vcl), Clarence Browning (pno), Quinn Wilson (sbs), and Benny Washington (dms).

This recording date produced four popular songs of the 1930s that had become hits. The first tune *Dixie Lee* (Alexander Hill), with vocals by Eddie

Pollack, was first recorded for Vocalion. It was reissued on Decca (British), and on Edison Bell Winner (British), and on Jazz Society (French) Label.

The second song recorded was cute and cleverly done *Inka Dinka Doo* (Durante-Ryan) with vocals by Eddie Pollack. The first recording was made under Vocalion, and the reissue was by Decca (British).

The third song recorded was *Delta Bound* (Alexander Hill). Made under the Vocalion Label, and reissued through Jazz Society(French) Label.

On the fourth song, Eddie Pollack plays the baritone and alto saxophone, along with presenting the vocals. *Like Me A Little Bit Less* (*Love Me A Little Bit More*) (Adamson-Lane), this song did not have any reissues.

Teddy Wilson, the piano player, was working with Jimmie Noone at the Lido Club in 1933. Roy Eldridge had worked with Teddy Wilson and Benny Goodman, and made some records on the side. This was right after Eldridge had worked with the McKinney's Cotton Pickers, and while still employed with the Savoy in New York.

Teddy Wilson's accompaniment on the piano while playing behind Billie Holiday is well remembered. When he played with the Goodman Quartet, that group included Lionel Hampton and Gene Krupa.

During the early 30s, Teddy Wilson worked with Jimmie Noone and Louis Armstrong, these gigs provided him the opportunity to play in the Hines style. And the trio with Goodman and Kruba is considered by some, to be the first inter-racial band if someone overlooks the light-skinned Creole's that worked in New Orleans with white musicians.

Zutty Singleton, one of Noone's closest friends, was employed at the Three Deuces as the featured house drummer. The later 30s, he recorded with Sidney Bechet, Lionel Hampton, Roy Eldridge, Mezz Mezzrow, and many others.

After Duke Ellington's recording in 1932 of *It Don't Mean A Thing* (*If it Ain't Got That Swing*), Ellington's band had increased in popularity. The Cotton Club's radio broadcasts helped, along with his tours to Europe. The Duke's band was a polished group, and the big-band sound became a spectacular to watch and hear.

Leon Scott was a trumpet player and a good friend of Noone, and he also played with him in the middle thirties. When he talked about the song *Sweet Lorraine*, he had this to say. "When he played parties in those days, and even when he left Chicago and went to California in the early '40s, people would stop dancing and just stand in front of the bandstand, look at Noone and almost worship him for getting such a beautiful feeling. In my experience with Jimmie, I've seen people expressing their happiness with tears when he played that particular number."[85]

In 1934 Jimmie Noone Performed at the Platinum Lounge with Franz Jackson.

While Jackson was working with Noone at the Platinum Lounge, which was located in the basement of the Vincennes Hotel, he recalled, "Benny Goodman would come down to the joint every night he was in town. He loved Jimmie's style of playing. Benny and Jimmie had the same music teacher. I believe his name was Shepp. Whenever Jimmie would go downtown for his lessons, Shepp would invite Benny Goodman to listen to them play duets."

"The teacher was trying to help Benny learn Jimmie's technique and tonation. Noone had a light, airy and melodic wail, whereas Goodman had a gutty style."

"Although Goodman was the white media's 'King Of Swing', he was never able to perfect that wailing soul tone that was very lyrical and characteristically black."[86]

Franz Jackson continue to tell about Noone, "As a matter of fact, most black musicians never reach Noone's clarinct-playing plateau. The only exceptions that come to mind are Barney Bigard from New Orleans and Buster Bailey of Memphis."

"I could not touch Jimmie Noone with my clarinet and a ten-foot pole. His sound was so beautiful that he made my efforts sound like I was playing a set of plumbing pipes."

"I kept my clarinet in its case the entire period that I played with the Noone Orchestra and I was considered a good clarinet player by my peers. His tone on such songs as his theme song *Sweet Lorraine* was pure, open and big. My tone was a 'legit' clarinet sound but it was tight and closed."[87]

The thirties changed jazz with its Depression and economy which brought poverty and low incomes. But jazz was now taking on "Swing," as there was no longer a need for the trio or the quartet. Now it was time for the big bands to swing.

The thirties changed jazz with its New Orleans flair, its Kansas city riff, and Harlem's Bessie Smith. The creativity of the black musician became apparent, but somehow managed to stay suffocated within all the Black Belt's in every large city.

The suffocation would continue on into the forties, with the outcome of only a handful of black musicians recording and gaining popularity. Jimmie Noone was not one of the exceptional handful, instead he did very little recordings, and as the years continued on, his recordings became lesser.

Chapter Thirteen
The Forties

(Dinky Morris will add his quote here or he can change others I made)

Jimmie Noone walked out of the train station, holding a ticket that verified his train left Chicago at 7:00 AM, as he looked up from his ticket, he heard Zutty Singleton, yelling out, "Jimmie." Zutty held out his hand for a handshake, and Jimmie refused it and hugged him instead.

Zutty questioned him, "Is it true what I've been hearing, that you and Loretta, are now divorced?"

Jimmie replied, "Yeah man, we've been apart for some time now."

Zutty asked, "Man, what happened?"

Jimmie shook his head in wonderment, then replied, "It was the music, and the long hours away from home. That's what it was."

Zutty admitted, "I hear that you'd be leaving and I thought, well you know—I thought that I'd send you off There's a bottle of booze, and an extra-large sandwich. I know how you love to eat."

Jimmie replied, "Man, I'm just taking some time off, while things are slow, guess I'd visit my mother, father and sister's grave. Eat some gumbo, play with the old-timers, stuff like that. But I'm not even going to think about women, not yet anyway."

The train whistle blew as a porter yelled, "All Aboard." They embraced again and promised to hook up when Jimmie returned back to Chicago.

Jimmie seated himself in the "Colored Only Train," and later went into the Cafe Car of the train and ordered his favorite drink, Cafe Brulot. As he sat and looked out, the Cafe's window, he thought about New Orleans.

Memories came to mind as he thought about the young, beautiful Creole girl he had seen once at Picou's Bar. And how he, Freddie Keppard, and old man Picou, had played *Maple Leaf Rag.* What good times he'd had, as he remembered women dancing the Cake Walk, the Black Bottom, the Shimmy, and the Charleston, to their music.

As an older woman passed by him, he looked up at her, and thought that she almost resembled his deceased mother, Lucinda. He thought about her stories of Congo Square, and the African dances and songs performed, and her speaking of the dances on the plantations, to the sounds of a banjo and a fiddle.

He thought about setting up a cutting-contest with the local musicians in New Orleans, and he knew that he had to include Alphonse Picou. He wanted to beat *him* at his own game, that of mastering the song *High Society.*

Stepping off the train in New Orleans, Jimmie took a deep breath of the clean Southern air, switched his luggage to his right hand, and said out loud, "I'm home."

At that moment, the same woman that looked like his mother replied, "Yes Son, we're here."

He knew that New Orleans had its spirits and voodoo, and told the woman, "I've missed everything about this city."

She replied, as she began to walk away, "You'll be fine. God bless you." She then disappeared into the crowd of travelers.

Jimmie hailed down a black and white taxi, and while riding home, he looked out at the city he loved the most. And its mixed races of Cajun, white, French, Creole, Spanish, and Negro. He said to the driver, "The races here are like a large pot of gumbo, all mixed up together, yet blending together just fine." The driver laughed with him.

The smell of the city had remained the same, there was the Mississippi River, with its stench, while over on St. Peter, the odors of Southern Fried Chicken, escaped from various homes, and down on Claiborne, the scent of Creole Gumbo was obvious.

On Claiborne, he also seen a Mam'zelle scrubbing down her steps with red brick dust, which was a common practice. The dust was a protection powder to protect the home from both human and spiritual intruders, and it also became a sign of cleanliness. It was a belief that Creole had, and like his mother used, pertaining to spiritual powers.

Arriving at his home, that he was raised in as a kid, Jimmie visited for a long time with his sister Lottie, until he had stuffed himself with Crawfish,

Seafood Gumbo, Rice, French Bread, alligator pears (avocado with spices), sweet potato pie, and homemade ice-cream.

One of the first things that Jimmie did was call Alphonse Picou at his bar, to arrange for a cutting-contest between them. It was planned for 6:00 PM, as that's when the bar started getting crowded. (A cutting-contest object is to smash the other player, so that they become embarrassed and leave the stage.)

Upon arrival at the bar, Picou and Noone had agreed that whoever stopped playing *High Society* last would be declared the winner. However, the winner was never announced, because while they were playing, a beautiful Creole woman walked into the bar. Jimmie instantly changed from playing *High Society* to *What Is This Thing Called Love?*

For a few minutes, Picou and Noone were playing two completely different tunes, and then after Picou listened to what Noone was playing, it became a duet. While they were playing together, Noone nodded his head to Picou in the direction of the girl. Picou smiled as he acknowledged the beauty of the girl.

As she remained standing, she looked around the bar for her girlfriend she was to meet. Noone checked her out pretty well, he estimated that she was about 5'6", rather thin, young, and that her shape possessed just the right amount of hips and curves. He considered her to be voluptuous.

Her skin was flawless. It possessed a warm glow coloring of something close to honey. She was not a Creole yellow-gal. No, she was more white with a touch of golden honey brown.

Her hair was the lightest of brown, it hung long past her shoulders, and was very straight. Her eyes were green, and it was obvious with her looks that she was of French and Negro blood intermixed. She was a Creole.

She carried a sexual aura about her, something that every man longs and hopes to see in a woman, yet she maintained the look of a young and innocent girl. Her name was Rita Mary Mathiew.

Rita wore a backless evening dress, in a new color that was called, "Flesh Pink," and in a new material called "Rayon." Jimmie secretly had a fetish for women's legs, and he noticed her sheer stockings, and her great legs, that showed with her swanky long split dress.

Picou and Noone had just gotten into the chorus of *What Is This Thing Called Love?* when Rita looked up and realized that the famous Jimmie Noone had been staring at her all this time. She had felt excited. She thought, *He's cute. I wonder if he's single?*

Jimmie thought, *I have got to marry this woman. This is Jove at first sight.*

A young girl at a table stood up and waved to Rita, and as Rita walked toward her girlfriend, she noticed that men had focused their eyes on her. A man from the next table jumped up and pulled out a chair for her to sit next to her friend.

First she thanked him, then took off her silver fox fur coat. She sat down on the chair, crossed her legs, which exposed her black pump shoes, with its small hole opening in her toe.

Noone and Picou stopped playing and talked for a few seconds. Picou walked away to fix drinks for Rita and Jimmie. Jimmie walked toward Rita, as her girlfriend told her, "Jimmie Noone's been staring at you. Did you notice he's wearing the latest, it's one of those chalk-stripe flannel, double-breasted suits. I hear all the men love them, and oh Rita, even his tie matches his handkerchief. Girl, he's hot. Oh watch out, he's coming to our table!" Rita did not reply, "but just sat there and blushed."

Jimmie took a deep breath, to ease his nervousness, and walked over to Rita to ask her for a date. He loved women of all races, but Creole girls were his worst weakness besides food.

They exchanged introductions, then asked her, "Can I join you both for a drink?"

What surprised him is that she said, "Yes."

With a big smile, he sat down. He got up enough courage to tell Rita, "I've never met a woman quite as beautiful as you before?"

After he threw out that line, he followed by asking her out on a date, and she accepted. They agreed she'd wait in the bar until he stopped playing at twelve that evening.

Jimmie and Rita then exchanged information about phone numbers, addresses, place of birth and ages. Jimmie remarked as they spoke of their ages, "I was born in 1895, so that means I am forty years old, and you are twenty-three. That makes me seventeen years older than you. Does that bother you?"

Rita remarked, "Why should age make a difference?"

After a drink, the two musicians got back on the stage. When Jimmie looked out at the audience, he realized how quickly news traveled through the Crescent City. The bar was jammed packed, without any standing room. Picou stood waiting with his clarinet as Jimmie announced loudly, "This song is dedicated to Rita."

Jimmie started playing a few notes, and Picou picked up the tune, he and Jimmie played *Apex Blues* and the sound of two clarinets playing in unison was amazing. Rita sat at her table, tapping her feet to the music.

Couples out on the dance area were having a good time as they danced the Charleston, the Black Bottom and the Shimmy. As the music got hot, then hotter. After the set was over, Rita met some other friends and decided to tag along with them—

Jimmie and Rita decided to go to a cafe and have some coffee.

Jimmie later took Rita home in a taxi, and have the driver wait, as he walked her to her door. Before leaving, he asked her if the date was still on? Then he leaned slightly toward her and kissed her softly on the lips.

Rita went inside her home, and Jimmie got into the taxi. After giving the driver the address of his home, he asked him, "Do you believe in love at first sight?"

The cabby replied, "Man, when you date a woman like that—hell ya."

The next morning, Jimmie's anticipation for his date, began to manifest itself, as he thought about her magnetic charm and sexual appeal, which seemed to be an extraordinary power, she possessed.

Jimmie wanted to get to know Rita better, without dwelling on her looks, however he was only in town for a few more days. He knew he had to work fast. He called the flower shop and asked if their boy could deliver a dozen roses to her. Next, she ran out and purchased a box of chocolate candy, along with tickets to the opera.

That evening as Jimmie dressed for his date, he packed in his suit pocket his Peripatetic Bar. (A slim flask for alcohol) Jimmie had been carrying this since his mother's death, since his heart bad started acting up. He had begun to have something similar to a heart bum, but it was mild, and besides he knew that there was nothing that could be done medically.

Jimmie arrived at Rampart Street, to the home oJRita Mathiew. He knocked on her door and was met by Rita's mother and father. Mr. Mathiew announced, "Please do come in Mr. Noone."

Mrs. Mathiew took his coat and stated, "We've just finished eating some jambalaya. would you care for some, or perhaps join us for some Cafe Brulot?"

Surprised they'd serve his favorite beverage, Jimmie answered, "I still seem to forget that I'm not in Chicago. Only in New Orleans would someone offer me that. Yes, I would like that."

Mrs. Mathiew excused herself and went into the kitchen. Coming out quickly, she told Jimmie, "Forget the Mr. and Mrs. stuff, I name is Ellodi, and my husband's name is John. We have two other daughters, named Wilhemina and Josephine, but they are over at the Vieux Carre with friends."

Ellodi handed Jimmie and her husband, John, their Café Brulot Diabolique. After several sips, Jimmie told her, "This is very good. I remember my mother could fix it exactly like this, you even remember the citrus peel, spices, and of course the brandy."

Rita walked into the room. She was wearing a long green cocktail dress with small spaghetti straps. The garment clung to her small contoured body— like super glue to paper.

Jimmie stood up and took Rita's hand and kissed it, as was the old Creole tradition. He gave her the chocolates. Then greeted her with a hello, then he said, "You are starling."

He looked at her eyes, and quickly he noticed that they matched her dress and the green emerald earrings. He thought, *She looks like a goddess.*

Jimmie looked at his pocket watch and announced, "I think that we had better leave, the opera starts in thirty minutes."

After they had left in a taxi, John told his wife, "Ellodi, that's the man for our Rita. Both of them seem to be smitten. I normally would not like a musician for her, but he's famous, a Creole, and a gentleman."

Ellodi added, "This is the second time she's met with him, and that is a record for her, you know how choosy she is with men."

For the next two days, Jimmie and Rita sent as much time as they possibly could together before he left to go back to Chicago. On his last day in New Orleans, Jimmie proposed to Rita after they rode the seven-cent streetcar to the French Market.

The Merchants at the French Market watched Jimmie kneel down and propose. He asked Rita simply, "I can't imagine living apart from you. Will you marry me?"

Rita replied, "Yes. Oh Yes."

Someone in the market yelled out, "She said yes!" Throughout the entire market, people applauded for her reply. This was a happy day for them both.

Before catching the streetcar back home, Jimmie stopped in a jewelry store and purchased an engagement ring for Rita. When they arrived back to Rita's home, Jimmie met her two sisters, which would soon become, his future sisters-in-law Wilhemina and Josephine were both quite beautiful. They both had long, straight hair and blue eyes. Jimmie thought, "They damn near look Caucasian."

When Ellodi and John Mathiew came into the room, Rita excitedly showed off her ring, while announcing their future marriage. The women started talking about wedding plans, while Jimmie and John took a drink into the parlor, and talked.

The two men's conversation turned into a typical father and future son-in-law type thing. Questions were raised about income, housing in Chicago, religion, and the rearing of children. The date had not been planned, but Jimmie told John, "I want it to be soon, 'cause I do not want to lose her, she's like a cherished jewel."

The following morning, Jimmie and Rita, along with his sister, Lottie, stood at the train depot. As Jimmie bid his farewell's, he promised Rita, "I will return as soon as I finish the recording with Vocalion. That will be either the end of November or the beginning of December 1934."

He kissed Rita then continued, "If the recordings and cabaret dates go as plan, our wedding date that been set for January 1935, should work out."

The Pullman called out for the train to Chicago. Rita grabbed Jimmie and hugged him as hard as she could. He caressed her face, while whispering in her ear, "I love you dearly. We'll be together soon, as man and wife."

With tears in her eyes, she replied, "Hurry back to me, so we'll never be apart ever again."

Boarding the train, Jimmie took one last look at his wife to be, and knew deep within his heart that this was the woman he wanted to spend the rest of his life with. As the train pulled out, they both cried as they waved farewell.

Jimmie Noone arrived back in Chicago on Thursday, November 22, 1934, just in time for his recording date the following day. His side-kick, Eddie Pollack, an alto player, was still there for him. Jimmie was now recording mostly popular hit songs, yet he still managed to maintain his original sound.

The personnel of this recording included, Jimmy Cobb (tpt), Clarence Browning (pno), John Henley (gtr), possibly John Lindsay (sbs), and Benny Washington (dms).

Four hit songs were recorded, *A Porter's Love Song* (To A Chambennaid) (Johnson-Razaf), *I'd Do Anything For You* (Hopkins-Hill-Williams), *Shine All*

The Clouds 11 Roll Away (Mack-Brown-Dabney), and *Lisa* (Gus Kahn-Ira Gershwin-Geo. Gershwin).

Two songs, *A Porter's Love Song* and *I'd Do Anything For You* were recorded on Vocalion, and both were reissued on Brunswick Label. The other two songs, *Shine* and *Lisa,* were also recorded on Vocalion, and reissued on Brunswich (French) Label. The last two songs were labeled as Jimmie Noone and his Club Ambassadors.

The tune *Lisa* that Jimmie Noone recorded in 1934 was created by three masterminds, Gus Kahn, I. Gershwin, and G. Gershwin.

Jazz had now become an established Negro musical structure made and created by the black race, and it was recognized by all as their idiom. It then very quickly became invaded and then developed into being used in white Broadway musicals, plays and operas.

White songwriters and lyricists began composing jazz to music, because the public demanded a repeat to such songs as, *Rhapsody In Blue*.

It was about this time when Paul Whiteman was named, "The King Of Jazz." The qualifications of such fine artists such as, Louis Armstrong, Freddie Keppard, Chick Webb, Duke Ellington, Sidney Bechet, Art Tatum, Willie 'The Lion' Smith, were all overlooked. Any of these black musicians could have been crowned "The King."

"In 1933 Benny Goodman met the jazz entrepreneur John Hammond, who encouraged Goodman to assemble a band for a number of recordings to be made by two English companies; the result showed Goodman to have the necessary organizing ability. In 1934 he organized a swing band."

"In September, he won a spot on the National Broadcasting Society Band. By the time Goodman—whose 'Hot' band had the last hour, 1:00 to 2:00 AM—had been heard on fifty-three NBC radio stations, coast to coast, week after week for twenty-six weeks, success was assured, and the swing era had been ushered in. In short order Benny Goodman became the King Of Swing."[88]

Benny Goodman did give Fletcher Henderson credit for all his arrangements. But, Jimmie Noone had often said that, "To be quite honest, although Goodman had been playing music for many years, Henderson was the brains and the one who really ran and directed the band."

Noone would often see Fletcher Henderson, when he was on the south-side of Chicago, and Henderson would tell rum that he was unable to get a gig.

They'd eat a meal together, and the same discussion would come up that many Negro musicians were facing also.

Henderson would say, "I can't get work being a Negro has stopped me. Now that the swing era has come into play, out there *only* white men are being ruled to perform on the radio and right clubs. The only thing that I can do to survive this Depression and the racial scam is to sell my charts to Benny Goodman."

Willingly, Fletcher Henderson sold charts, but for a very small amount. He usually received anywhere from $25.00 to $35.00 per arrangement. Some jazz books have suggested that the going rate was as high as $50.00, but that is not true.

Selling of musical arrangements without claiming ownership occurred during the Depression, and to receive $35.00 at that time was considered quite a lot. Compare this amount to the average pay around 1939 that Negro musicians earned, which was $4.00 per night or about $1,248.00 a year.

The Goodman Band was considered a success to the white man. And new white Swing Bands, that followed in their footsteps included Jimmy Dorsey, Woody Herman, Tommy Dorsey, Artie Shaw, and Glenn Miller.

The Negro bands that became known in a smaller jazz circle included Fletcher Henderson, Cab Calloway, Don Redman, Jimmy Lunceford, and Chick Webb.

Jimmie Noone's phrasing in the thirties, came within the New Orleans style and it bordered on the brink of Swing. "From Noone came a whole school of players, including Morton's Omer Simeon, Ellington's Barney Bigard, the St. Louis player Buster Bailey, and others; and out of this school came the swing clarinetists of the 1930s and 1940s—Goodman, Artie Shaw, Irving Fazola, Peanuts Hucko, Joe Marsala, and a host of others."[89]

The saxophone in the 1930s took a dominance over the clarinet. It's cause was all about economics. It meant that a three-piece rhythm section could be used in a nightclub. This did create a new type of band, and smaller salaries to musicians as a result.

"Young blacks were identifying the clarinet with whites as a result of the fame of Goodman and Shaw-although there were excellent black clarinetists for models, including Buster Bailey, Barney Bigard, and Edmond Hall. By the mid-1940s the clarinet had very nearly disappeared from jazz, except as it was played by the older players and the dixie landers. The result was to turn the front line, in the main, over to trumpets and saxophones."[90]

Jimmie Noone met with two of his closest friends, Barney Bigard and Zutty Singleton, at one of their favorite restaurants, a place called "Big Butt Mary's." After the three had eaten a large meal, Jimmie told them, "I guess you're wondering why I asked you both for lunch? You see, I wanted to be the first to tell you that I'm planning to get married next month?"

"I know what you two clowns are going to tell me. It's too soon to get serious, but I can't help myself. I feel in love with her at first sight. It was unavoidable. She a real refined Creole woman, intelligent, beautiful, and above all—Sexy."

Zutty looked at Jimmie and just shook his head. Barney stared at him, as if thinking, "You fool." Zutty was the first to speak, "Man. You've gone completely crazy. No woman is all that."

Barney voiced his opinion, "Man. Your head ain't screwed on tight. I think your tight just like that."

Jimmie laughed, then stated, "Listen. I need help. Help me figure how to make arrangements."

Neither Zutty or Barney said anything as they stared at Jimmie. Jimmie knew they'd rebel. No man wanted to see their single male friends become chained down with the manager.

Jimmie asked, "Which one of you idiots will be my best man? I need help trying to understand how I can afford to be married and take care of a wife. This Depression ain't helping matters." Years and Christmas was too demanding to not work. This was the busiest time of the year for a musician.

Noone was scheduled to take his band into the Hotel Vincennes on New Year's Eve, December 31, 1934. The Vincennes Hotel was a six story building, with an elevator located at 601 East 36th Street. It was considered one of Chicago's best hotel, to be owned by a Negro.

For a musician just to be asked to play, there was considered an honor, and much consideration had been given as to who would welcome in the New Year. Noone's band was what Chicago negroes wanted to hear.

New Years in Chicago was a time that negroes dressed up and kick their heels. The Negro Greek sororities and fraternities had sponsored an elegant formal affair. The Negro women wore Paris gowns, and the men wore formal tux attire, along with the musicians.

"If one stands quietly on the Southeast corner of 36th Street and Vincennes Avenue, where the hotel once stood, one might still hear the moaning of Jimmie Noone's clarinet and the rapid, trumpet-like piano of Earl 'Fatha' Hines echoing through the Vincennes lobby from the Platinum Lounge in the basement."[91]

Two days before the groom and the two best men were to leave for New Orleans, they decided to surprise Jimmie and have a stag party for him. The owner of the Hotel Vincennes closed off the Platinum Lounge.

Noone's stage party, ended being nothing but a group of male musicians, that had carried their instruments along, and although they drank and ate heavily, they played jazz all evening. For some musicians, this was one of the few occasions when they could play what they wanted, and to experiment with new tunes and styles.

When the holidays were over, and musicians were experiencing their slow period for the new year, Zutty, Jimmie, and Barney arrived in New Orleans, one day before the wedding. They were back home.

It was Saturday, January 1, 1935. They caught a taxi to Lottie's home and dropped off their luggage. Since the wedding rehearsal at St. Anthony's Catholic Church was not until 6:00 PM, they went to a little restaurant called "Cabaret Orleans."

Zutty looked over the menu and tossed it aside. Jokingly, he said, "I'll order for us this evening."

Barney noticed the wink that Zutty gave him and laughed, "I'm gonna guess it's oysters."

Jimmie replied, "I need a drink. My nerves are shot." Zutty told him, "You're gonna eat some good old Louisiana oysters tonight. Tomorrow's your wedding."

The waitress came over and Zutty ordered, "One extra-large order of oysters in the shell, some hot sauce, a large glass of oyster juice with three shots of scotch, and me and my friend will have one shot of scotch."

When the waitress returned with their order, Zutty took one look at the plate and juice, and busted out laughing, as he also choked saying, "Man, eat up. It's just a snack. You're gonna need all the help you can get on your wedding night. The girl's young, and she's gonna wear you out, man." Jimmie now felt relaxed, and ate up.

Within an hour, the three had arrived at St. Anthony's Church for the rehearsal. Waiting for them were Lottie, Rita, and her parents, John and Ellodi Mathiew. Rita's two sisters were standing off to the side talking to their Priest.

After the rehearsal, the complete wedding party returned back to the home of the Mathiews for a late dinner. Ellodi Mathiew had made arrangements for a formal Creole wedding dinner. Wilhemina and Josephine, helped their mother place the food on the dinner table that included, Red Beans and Rice, Seafood Gumbo, Jambalaya, Oyster Loaf, Stewed Turtle, and Creole Cakes.

The dinner was over. Rita and Jimmie had little time with each other. When the men drove back to Lottie's home, Zutty said to Jimmie, "I have seen pretty girls lots of times, but she is indeed a beautiful woman."

Barney added, "And so are her two single sisters."

When Rita walked down the aisle the next day, all two hundred invited guest watched the procession. The slow tempo of the wedding march, all the guest the opportunity to view her beauty. Rita's hair had been curled into clusters, with small pieces of baby breath flowers that covered her veil. Her green eyes were glossy and wet from tears of joy, and her white dress fit like a glove on her body.

Her father, John Mathiew, felt pride for his daughter, a sadness at losing her, and yet a happiness for her, as he walked down the aisle and gave her away. Her mother, Ellodi, thought about her as a young child, and then now, as she would soon become a woman and a wife, leave her home forever, and a sadness flowed over her.

Jimmie stood with his two best men and felt his heart beat fast, his palms sweaty with nervousness, and yet he knew this marriage was what he wanted.

As Rita approached him, he admired her wedding dress. The lace looked so delicate; the bodice seemed to fit perfectly and the gathering of the dress moved with her body. She reminded him of a perfect doll.

And then those final words from the Priest, "I now pronounce you man and wife. Go in peace. You can now kiss the bride."

It was their first real kiss. As they turned to face their guest, the Priest finalize their wedding vows with, "Ladies and gentlemen, may I present to you, Mr. and Mrs. Jimmie Noone."

The wedding party lasted all day and that night. The bridal couple left early that evening to be alone. After a honeymoon of two days, the couple left on a train back to Chicago with Barney and Zutty.

Rita cried as she left her family, as she had never been away from home before. Rita and Jimmie had made arrangements to stay with Zutty and his wife. The Singletons lived near State Street. Rita was amazed by Chicago. She had never lived in a large city before and being married to the man she loved increased her happiness.

Barney Bigard had gone back to playing with Duke Ellington. Zutty Singleton was still working at the Three Deuces.

Almost a month had gone by and Jimmie's next recording with Vocalion was due to be recorded. He asked Rita to go with him to the studio, so she could see exactly how recordings were made. The recording was made under Jimmie Noone and his orchestra, on February 21, 1935.

The musicians that recorded were, Eddie Pollack (alto), Clarence Browning (pno), Jimmy Cobb (tpt), John Henley (gtr), John Lindsay (sbs), and Benny Washington (dms).

Songs recorded were *Soon (There'll Just Be Two Of Us)* (Hart-Rogers), *Lullaby Of Broadway* (Dubin-Warren), *Lookie, Lookie Here Comes Cookie* (Mack Gordon), and *It's Easy To Remember* (Hart-Rogers).

No vocals were on these four recordings, which were all popular songs. The first recordings were with Vocalion, and the reissues went through Panachord (British).

Jimmie had been doubling up in various clubs, sometimes playing from early evening (6:00 PM), until early morning (8:00 AM).

Jimmie had been working terribly hard as the Depression was still on, and things were getting real tight for Negro musicians. It was January 1936 and Rita and Jimmie's first wedding anniversary when she traveled with him and the band to New York.

Jimmie Noone's recording contract with Vocalion had just expired, and he had been offered to record with Parlophone. When this offer took place, he was not made liable to sign a contract restricting him to record under just their label.

The Parlophone recording personnel included, Guy Kelly (tpt, vcl), Preston Jackson (tbn), Jimmie Noone (clt, ldr), Francis Whitby (ten), Gideon Honore (pno), Israel Crosby (sbs), Tubby Hall (dms).

The first song recorded *He's The Different Type Of Guy,* originally recorded on Parlophone, the reissues came through, Parlophone (British), Oden British (Export Only) (Argentine), Decca (Swiss), and Odeon (Dutch).

The second song recorded was *Way Down Yonder In New Orleans* (Creamer-Layton). Reissues were, Parlophone (British) (Australia) (The reverse on this is by Red Norvo), Odeon (British) (Export Only), Decca, Odeon (Italian).

The third song was *The Blues Jumped A Rabbit*, with vocals by Guy Kelly. There were numerous reissues on this recording, which included, Parlophone (British) (Australia), Odeon (British) (Export Only), Decca, and Odeon (Italian), Parlophone (Swiss), Decca (Swiss).

The final recorded song was, the ever popular hit song *Sweet Georgia Brown* (Bernie-Pinkard-Casey), recorded on, Parlophone (British) (Australia), Odeon (British) (Export Only), Decca, and Odeon (Australia).

After the recording session, Jimmie took Rita to the nearest flower shop and purchased her a corsage of yellow roses. Inside the flower shop, they kissed, as Jimmie handed them to her. They were completely and madly in love.

Nat 'King' Cole had been hired by Ralph Watkins, the owner of Kelly's Stable on 52nd Street, as band pianists, and, while employed at Kelly's, is when Nat and Jimmie Noone became friends.

Several jazz authors have given various accounts of how Nat learned how to sing.

One account is that Cole transformed from a jazz piano player into a pop singer while he was performing in a Los Angeles nightclub, and a drunk customer asked him to sing *Sweet Lorraine.*

Another account is that Cole did not sing as he had a speech problem. And that only after he had received help from a speech therapist was he able to gain the confidence to sing in public.

Another account is one that was told by Jimmie Noone to his wife Rita, and later to Noone Jr., is this, "Me and Nat were close friends while working in Chicago. It was hard to understand him speak due to his stutter. Sometimes he halted, or repeated his words, and it was embarrassing to him."

"I told him the *only* thing that would rid him of stuttering was to sing a ballad. He chose my theme song *Sweet Lorraine* to practice on. As Nat sang, I would accompany him on the keyboard."

"Later, Nat's diction was so perfect, that when he talked on the radio, the Negro community had no knowledge of his race background."

In the Nat 'King' Cole Show reruns on television, Nat Cole told the same story that Noone stated.

On January 15, 1936, Parlophone Label Recorded four songs under the name Jimmie Noone And His New Orleans Band in Chicago. The musicians were Preston Jackson (tbn), Guy Kelly (tpt, vl), Jimmie Noone (clt), Frances Whitby (ts), Gideon Monore (pno), Israel Crosby (sbs), and Tubby Hall (dms).

The songs recorded were, *He's The Different Type Of Guy, Way Down Yonder In New Orleans* (Creamer-Layton), *The Blues Jumped A Rabbit* and *Sweet Georgia Brown* (Bernie-Kinkard-Casey).

It was during this time that Blues vocalists, Bessie Smith, was involved in an automobile accident in Mississippi. Her arm was almost completely tom off, and she was taken to the nearest hospital (white) and was denied admission. Either when she was taken en route to the Negro Hospital, or if she was admitted to the next hospital, is not known in jazz history. It is known is that because she lost so much blood, she died in a short period of time.

And during this time, Natty Dominique was working with bandleader Johnny Dodds. Barney Bigard was with Duke Ellington. Omer Simeon was working in Chicago with Earl Hines. Sidney Bechet was performing in the Noble Sissle Band, along with vocalists Lena Home. Joe 'King' Oliver, or 'Papa Joe' to Louis Armstrong, had been working as a bandleader with his "Savannah Syncopators Band." He was asked to open at the Cotton Club in Harlem, and as he held out for more money, Duke Ellington, was hired instead.

Joe Oliver did record with Clarence Williams, and then, because of a gum disease, his playing deteriorated. In 1937, Oliver left the music business after being connected with promoters that were dishonest and left bankrupt, and sick with pyorrhea.

Sidney Bechet started playing in Greenwich Village in New York, at Nick's Tavern at Seventh Avenue and 10th Street. His quartet were Zutty Singleton, Wellman Braud, and Leonard Ware.

It was during this period that Jimmie remembered he lost contact with his former-wife Loretta, his Sweet Lorraine. And from the Noone family living today, no one seems to know what happened to her. Lorraine still remains a mystery.

Rita Noone (Jimmie's second-wife), was not able to travel to New York for the Decca Recordings, because she was five months pregnant. She was expecting their first child. According to her doctor, he did not advise traveling.

She was due to deliver her child, approximately the first or second week in April 1938.

In New York on December 1, 1937, Noone recorded Jimmie Noone And His Orchestra, and The Apex Club Orchestra on Decca. There was still a big demand for Jimmie's style of music. The musicians used were, Jimmie Noone (cl, ldr), Charlie Shavers (t), Pete Brown (as), Frank Smith (pno), Teddy Bunn (g), Wellman Braud (sb), O'Neil Spencer (dms, vl), and Teddy Simmons (vcl).

The eight popular songs recorded were *Sweet Lorraine* (Cliff Burdwell-Mitchell Parish), *I Know That You Know* (Vincent Youmans-Ann Caldwell), *Four or Five Times* (Marco H. Hellman-Bryon Gay), *Hell In My Heart* (Noone-Williams), *Call Me Darling, Call Me Sweetheart, Call Me Dear* (Scott Dickerson), *I'm Walkin' This Town* (Teddy Bunn), and *Japansy* (John Klenner-Alfred Bryan). All eight recordings, were later reissued by the Swaggie Label.

Jimmie Noone continued to work both in New York and Chicago, while doing a few radio broadcast shows. He was able to find enough work to not have to seek other employment, but he was not as busy as he would have liked to be. Most of his gigs were still in the Black Belt area of Chicago.

In 1937, a live radio broadcast from the Platinum Lounge where Noone continued to work at. It was the basement of the Vincennes Hotel, and Franz Jackson talked about those days. "I remember being with Jimmie Noone at the Platinum, the same time that Fletcher Henderson's Orchestra was at the Grand Terrace."

"One night during our radio broadcast, Chu Berry, the star tenor man with Fletcher's band came down to the Platinum Lounge seeking me out like a cowboy at high noon looking for a gun duel. He jerked his sax from its case and walked upon the bandstand and started blowing. Although we were in the air, Jimmie did not stop him. Noone said, 'Oh, what the hell'!"

"Chu and I had a nonstop tenor sax duel that lasted till the end of the half hour radio broadcast. Chu was a 'Bad' tenor man."[92]

Early 1938 Jimmie was performing at the Lido, Club Morocco, the Stables, and the Platinum Lodge. His band had enlarged to a 12 piece band (big band), and played at Benny Skollar's Swingland. A radio broadcast was performed live at the Cabin Inn, with Noone's band.

Joe 'King' Oliver died on April 10, 1938. Louis Armstrong's "Papa Joe," was gone.

Rita Mary Mathiew Noone went into labor with her first child on April 20, 1938. Husband Jimmie, while elated, jokingly asked his wife to delay the labor for three days, so their child would be born on his birth date of April 23.

The stork arrived on April 21, after Rita had endured a long night of labor. And with a midwife by her side, she delivered to Jimmie Noone, their first child, a son. They had agreed that he would take his father's name and become a Junior. And that his middle name would be taken from her mother's slave name, that of Fleming. Their son's name was James Fleming Noone, Jr.

Their son looked like his father. He was born with black hair, hazel eyes, and weighed six pounds, seven ounces. Jimmie and Rita were such proud parents, that glowed with love and pride for their child. The love they possessed when they had first met had continued on all through their marriage.

As a young boy, they spelled his name, Jimmy and his father's Jimmie. Rita knew that someday they would have the need for the different spelling, and later in life she would find out that she was correct.

As a young boy Jimmy, was never called "Junior." As soon as he learned how to crawl, he was taking pots out of the cabinets and banging his hands on top of them with a spoon to make noise.

His mother and father brought music and musicians into the home, which had started to show with the toy flute the child played with. When Zutty Singleton, Barney Bigard, and other musician friends came over, they would instruct the youngster into the correct method of playing his flute.

Jimmie and Rita were good parents, and their child always came first. They took him to the park and went for lots of walks. One day, Jimmie was trying to show his small son a boomerang, and as it soared in flight, instead of having the capabilities of returning near its thrower, it continued to fly through the air, and never returned.

Although Jimmy was a very young child at the time, it was something that he would remember forever, and when his father told him, "Son. I love you," as they walked away from the park that day.

Rita was a faithful Catholic that attended mass every Sunday. As soon as her son was old enough, she and Jimmie had him baptized. They were determined that their child would be raised in the church. The one thing that they had decided on also was that they would encourage him to become a musician, as he seemed to have a natural talent for music.

Franz Jackson, played with Roy Eldridge at the Arcadia Ballroom in New York City in 1939. He stayed with Eldridge, until he joined up with Earl Hines in 1940.

Jimmie Noone and His Orchestra on June 5, 1940, recorded on the Decca Label. The musicians were Natty Dominique (tpt), Preston Jackson (tbn), Jimmie Noone (clt), Richard M. Jones (pno), Lonnie Johnson (gtr), John Lindsay (sbs), and Tubby Hall (dms).

Songs recorded were *New Orleans Hop Scop Blues* (Geo. W. Thomas) and *Keystone Blues*.

Rita told her husband Jimmie, "Now that Jimmy's had his first haircut, and has gotten rid of all his curls, he looks exactly like his father." Rita reached down and kissed her baby's chubby cheeks, and Jimmie did likewise, and continuing to bend down, he kissed Rita. When he went to pull himself up, he had to hold on to the kitchen chair, while that same sneaky pain he had encountered just last month returned to his chest.

Jimmie had already made up his mind, that when another pain returned, he would tell Rita. He hated the fact that he had not been honest with her throughout their entire marriage.

Jimmie knew that he'd be off the following evening, and perhaps he could take Rita out for dinner, and they could talk. It had been a long time since they had sat down and talked, since their son had been born.

He asked Rita, "Say Sweetheart, how would you like to go out to dinner tomorrow evening, just the two of us?"

Rita ran over to him, as he had taken a seat to ease the pain. She hugged him, and gave him a big kiss, then answered, "I'd love to, but what about the baby?"

Jimmie replied, "We'll get Margaret from next door to come over."

The next evening, Jimmie took Rita to a restaurant called "Lenny's." It was located on State Street, in their neighborhood. As they walked into the restaurant, Jimmie noticed that Rita looked especially nice.

He thought to himself, "It's time to stop hiding my health problems. I love this woman."

She thought to herself, *This is the perfect opportunity to tell Jimmie that I am with child, perhaps two or three months.*

Lenny's Restaurant specialized in serving Italian food. The dining tables were decorated with red and white checkered tablecloths. After being seated by the Padrone of the establishment, Jimmie ordered two glasses offered wine.

After the waiter, had placed their glasses on the table, and left, Rita noticed that Jimmie seemed a bit nervous. So she decided to cut the ice by telling him her news, "Dear. I have something to tell you. I do realize how hard you've been working with your music, and that's why I hate to tell you this."

With her innocent smile beaming, Rita burst out the news with one deep breath, "We are going to have another child. I know that it's very close to the birth of our son—But."

Jimmie reacted completely different from she suspected he would, he jumped up, grabbed her, then hugged her, and yelled out in the restaurant, "I'm going to be a daddy."

The diners in the restaurant clapped and yelled out, "Congratulations."

The thought of two children and a wife made Jimmie remember that old Creole saving that, "A woman was looked upon with wisdom, depending on the large number of children she reared." But he was a musician, just barely making ends met.

Rita sat at the table eating spaghetti and meatballs, as she picked up a napkin to wipe off the pasta sauce from her lips, she told him, "I love you Jimmie."

He replied, "I love you too, baby. There's something that I have got to get off my chest, and let's face it, Rita, I have not been honest with you."

"I've been afraid that I would lose you, if I had told you earlier before we got married. But now, with another baby on the way, I must confess my secret, even if I lose you."

"Since the day that I was born, I have had trouble with my heart. The many doctors and specialists, have always called it an 'Irregular heartbeat', and it's remained the same. As a child, I could not play like the other kids, and when the war started, the Armed Forces did not want me."

Rita had a surprised look on her face, but just sat and listened as Jimmie continued, "If you decide to leave me, or ask the Priest permission for a divorce, I will understand. It's true that I have lied to you, but it was only because I loved you so much."

Jimmie reached for Rita's hand and kissed it, and spoke to her quietly, "Rita. Please forgive me." With tears of compassion, Rita wiped away the teardrops that were starting to trickle down her cheeks.

She replied, "Jimmie Noone, I married you for better or worse, in sickness and in health, and I plan to stick to my vows to God. And as a Catholic, I could never ask our Priest for a legalized divorce. We are both Catholic's, and will live by God's laws."

Jimmie continued to tell Rita about his chest pains, and how they always occurred when he ate heavy or was involved in some type of strenuous activity. And as he spoke he could fell the tears trying to escape, "And what's even worst, is I'd been sneaking off while at practice, to grab extra steak sandwiches. I now weigh over 240 pounds, which increases pressure on my heart. I've been a complete jerk, not telling you any of this."

Rita spoke to him rather calmly, "Starting tomorrow, you'll reduce your intake of food, we'll eat more vegetables, and desserts after dinner are out. And we'll take a stroll every evening." Jimmie felt reassured. Finally, he had told the truth.

Several months later, Rita was starting to show her pregnancy, and she put on her nightgown. She sat at her dresser table and began to comb out her long, beautiful hair. That night, she noticed that it was growing—as it flowed down her back in curls. And she thought of all the women she knew, that had to resort to using a hot curling iron, to get their hair to behave.

Jimmie walked into their home after playing at a nightclub, as Rita was brushing out her hair. He took one look at Rita and greeted her while thinking, "Those green eyes can look so mysterious sometimes. My God, she's even more beautiful when she's pregnant, I wish I could afford to keep her that way."

Tommy Ladnier, had recorded, *Play That Thing* in 1923, with Jimmie Noone, had now earned the respected title, "The Sensational Cometists."

It was in 1938, when Tommy Ladnier had returned from playing for five years in Europe, and with Mezz Mezzrow, had recorded a series of records. After being in Europe for so long, when he returned back to the States, his fame was short-lived, when he died the following year at the young age of thirty-nine.

In the jazz book, *Hear Me Talkin' To Ya*, Buster Bailey mentions Ladnier, "Then there was Tommy Ladnier. Did you ever hear any of his records?

There's a guy who has a natural swing. Listen to the way he plays on those records. The way he takes a melody and swings it. That's what I mean by swing."[93]

Jimmie Noone was still continuing to play at cabarets, nightclubs, honky-tonks, and small cafes on the south side of Chicago. There was The Lido, The Club Morocco, The Stables, and the Platinum Lounge.

By late 1937, and early 1938, Noone had enlarged his orchestra to include such musicians as Albert Wynn on trombone, and Bill Winston on drums. These musicians completed his twelve-piece band that he had been working toward for the last two years.

The size of Noone's band fit into what was happening with big bands at that time, however, the public was leaning toward the swing style, and Jimmie's music remained strictly in the New Orleans Jazz style.

Jimmie Noone returned back home to New Orleans in 1938, while touring the South. It would become the first time in over twenty years that he would be paid to play in his city. When he had come home to visit numerous times for family matters, his playing capacity was just to be with other fellow musicians, with no pay involved.

The reception that he received in New Orleans surprised him. He really had no idea that his name was so well known in his home town. Because he was still recording with the Decca Label, his stay was a short one, due to the numerous engagements that he had waiting for him in Chicago.

That same year, he performed at Benny Skollar's Swingland, which was actually the old place called Dave's Cafe, with the owner changing its name, to give it more class.

"Dave's Cafe was a Caesar's Palace in miniature: It provided excellent entertainment along with the gambling. The Cafe was at 343 East Garfield, and was a class cabaret, where you could light your evening fire and lose your tomorrow."[94]

Jimmie Noone once again worked at a cabaret that was run by the mob. "In fact, Sam 'Golf Bag' Hunt was the mob's overseer of gambling for the entire South side. Golf Bag got his nickname during his day as a torpedo for Al Capone: he would track down his prey with his shotgun concealed in a golf bag."

"Joe Luis, the heavyweight boxing champion, brought the club in 1940; his partner was Charlie Glenn, the sportsman and Cadillac salesman. They changed the name once again: This time from Swingland to Rhumboggie."[95]

Jimmie later became employed by the Cabin Inn, where he performed several radio broadcasts, however none were ever recorded. Musicians that were playing off and on with him, when time permitted were, Baby Dodds, Louis Armstrong, Ted Poston, and numerous others.

During an interview that the author of this book had with William 'Bill' Russell, he said, "I heard Noone play at the Platinum Lounge, over on 601 East 36th Street. He did four shows nightly that featured the Jimmie Noone Orchestra. He played New Orleans music, a style familiar to Omer Simeon and Albert Nicholas."

"The last great year of Chicago jazz was 1939. That February the fans could hear Wingy Manone at the Three Deuces on State Street, where Jimmy Mac Partland and Art Tatum were doing singles upstairs."

"Gene Krupa was at the College Inn at the Hotel Sherman, Stuff Smith was at the La Salle Hotel, Bob Crosby's Bobcats were at the Blackhawk Restaurant and Fletcher Henderson was at the Grand Terrace."

"But Swing was coming in. Chicago had long been fond of this style of musicianship—inventive, but less driving than jazz—with its improvisations written down on a page of music, only the riffs being invented on the spot."[96]

Gunther Schuller described Swing as, "Swing in its most general sense means a regular steady pulse, 'as of a pendulum', as one Webster definition put it. On a more specific level, it signifies the accurate timing of a note in its proper place."[97]

Jimmie Noone had called Zutty Singleton in New York. Jimmie talked about work and the weather, "Man, last night I worked at Club Lido. At six in the morning, it was ten degrees above normal with twelve inches of snow. That damn hawk felt like a giant razor blade slashing my frozen face."

Zutty replied, "Listen Face, I ain't exactly living in any warm climate myself I just called to tell you real fast that I'll see you and Rita next week. Kiss baby Jimmy for me. Bye." The phone went dead.

When Zutty arrived in Chicago the following week, Jimmie met his train that had arrived from New York. After they usually hug and calling each other the word, "Face," which was how Zutty referred to everyone, they caught a cab.

Jimmie told the cab driver, "Club Lido, at 344 East 55th Place." As the cab came into the South Parkway area, the line outside the Club Lido showed good attendance for that night. The cabby stopped in front of the club, then announced, "Sir. That'll be $1.25."

At the entrance door of the Lido, Jimmie and Zutty, were met by the manager, James Keys. He asked them, "Fellows, did you see the new marquee over the entrance door?" Before they could speak, Keys grabbed them both by the arm and held them there as they looked up. In big block lettering, the sign read, "Jimmie Noone." And below his name, *in* somewhat smaller letters, it read, "And his Brunswick Recording Orchestra." And the final line read, "In An All Star Colored Revue."

Zutty remarked to Jimmie, "Damn it, Face. You're getting to be a big star. Well, I'll be damned!" Zutty turned to James Keys and said, "It's nice, man. It looks good."

As Noone, Keys, and Singleton walked into the club, Keys told Zutty, "Me and Jimmie would love it if you'd sit in on the first set, then I'd like you both to try out the new menu. It's Chinese and American cuisine. Oh course Jimmie, Rita said that you can only eat Chinese. I promised her. Sorry." Jimmie just shook his head, knowing that she was in control of his bad eating habits.

Jimmie looked at his pocket watch quickly, and told Zutty, "I've got to get backstage and make sure the band's members are here. Come on with me."

They entered the musicians' dressing room. Jimmie looked at himself in the mirror while combing his hair straight back. His suit looked unwrinkled, white shirt clean, tie on straight, his stomach, however, had that spare tire effect. Assuring himself that he looked fine, and realizing that all the band members were there, he was ready to go on stage.

The Lido featured three shows nightly, which highlighted such talented people as Jeneva Washington (Star of 'Rhapsody in Black'); Hank Gilliam (Tenor); Bobby Caston (Personality Plus); Lola Porter (Soubrette) Muriel and Paul (Dancers Demons); Clarence Weems (Master of Ceremonies); and The Club Lido Quadro (Delectable Dancing Damscls).

The first show at the Club Lido was a sellout. A snow blizzard had taken over the city, but people were still out partying. Jimmie opened the first set with his theme song *Sweet Lorraine* and the crowd went wild with applause and enthusiasm.

Noticing a chest pain, Jimmie sat down for his next song and played on a stool, which seemed to help a lot. The crowd wanted to hear *Sweet Lorraine* again. This time, his clarinet rested on his enormous big belly, as the tone became fluid, when he played long passages in the low chalumeau register.

Jimmie made the announcement that a very good friend of his was out in the audience, someone that he had grown up with, and who had a Creole nickname that meant "Cute." He continued, "This musician has played with the greatest: John Robicheaux, Louis Armstrong, Fate Marable, Earl! Hines, Jelly Roll Morton, Barney Bigard, Sidney Bechet, Lionel Hampton, and numerous others. Ladies and gentlemen, please give a round of applause to Zutty Singleton."

As Zutty walked up on stage, the women went wild. He was a fine-looking man. He relieved the drummer, sat down, and Jimmie said to him, "Let's play our favorite."

Zutty nodded as the introduction for *Apex Blues* started. The crowd loved those twelve-bar blues that they played, and many in the audience had said later that it was too bad that they weren't recorded that night.

Jimmie's playing created phrases from both registers for his solos, instead of just playing from one or the other, as most clarinet players do today. The best qualities that came forth that night on Apex Blues was Jimmie's fill-in of phrases. Using his New Orleans idiom style, he could fill in notes that most clarinet players would skip over, so that they could take a breath.

In Chicago around 1937, the popular clubs and the popular musicians that were in demand were: At the Grand Terrace Ballroom-Count Basie And His Orchestra; The '29' Club-Johnny Dodds' Band; The Swingland-Carrol Dickerson and His Orchestra; The Platinum Lounge-Jimmie Noone's Band; The Three Deuces-Roy Eldridge And His Band.

At The Savoy Ballroom-The Orchestra of Andy Kirk with Roy Eldridge; The Congress Hotel-Bob Crosby And His Orchestra; The Club Plantation-Jeter Pillar's Orchestra.

Chicago was the leading city for music during this time, however, in Boston at The Roseland State Ballroom-Artie Shaw's Band, with Billie Holiday and Max Kaminsky, were in popular demand. In Washington at The Music Box-Jelly Roll Morton; in Seattle at The Palomar Theater-Duke Ellington And His Orchestra.

Chapter Fourteen
The Terminus

Young Jimmy Noone Jr. was about to turn six in two days, when he asked his mother about his father being taken away by an ambulance. She explained to her son, that his daddy was dead. Then she added, "He left you his diamond ring, a gold watch, and his clarinet. Only a good daddy would do that. He wanted you to grow up and play clarinet, just like he did." Neither mother nor son would ever forget that fatal day in April of 1944. Jimmie Noone was dead.

C. Picou

On December 11, 1940, The Jimmie Noone Trio recorded on Bluebird Label, in Chicago. Musicians used for this recording were Jimmie Noone (clt), Gideon Honore (pno), John Simmons (sbs), and Ed Thompson (vcl).

The four songs recorded were *Moody Melody* (Jimmie Noone), *Then You're Drunk* (Ed Thompson), *I'm Going Home* (Joe McCoy), and *They Got My Number Now* (Joe McCoy). This was the band's last recording for the year of 1940, on the Bluebird Label.

Joe Williams, a vocalist, had made his first professional debut in 1938 with Jimmie Noone. He also was working with Noone on radio work and nightclubs, at the Cabin Inn and the Platinum Lounge, where they did live broadcast nightly.

The Great Depression was still in existence, causing long soup lines in every city, unemployment, and crime was everywhere in the United States. And World War II was continuing, with Hitler calling most of the shots. In 1940, the German Army had invaded Netherlands, Belgium, Luxembourg, along with the invasion of Paris.

Leon Scott was quoted about when he worked with Noone in a magazine article entitled *Storyville*, dated June 1, 1972, that was written by Johnny

Simmen. Scott said, "I worked with Jimmie continuously, moving to the Midnight club on 31st and Indiana. We stayed there for a while."

"Jimmie was a nice guy, very easy to get along with and very accommodating. Anything anybody wanted, he played it. In other words, he satisfied the public. He moved from the Midnight club to the Cabin Inn."

"We played at the Cabin Inn with the big band and played gigs mostly with the small group. We actually needed a regular job with the small band as Jimmie had so much work in the better districts. On the Gold Coast we called it."

"The big band only played at the Cabin Inn. I enjoyed playing with Jimmie, he wouldn't have anyone else but me at that particular time. Jimmie would get through playing, and say he thought he'd like to go to Chinatown. We'd go, he'd eat one thing after another—everything on the menu, he had a tremendous appetite. Tiny Parham too, it was nothing to see him sit down and eat two chickens."

"The Cabin Inn where, incidentally, I played with Chippie Hill also, was a club where they didn't have anything but female impersonators—the whole line, they had twelve in a line, plus the whole show, was all female impersonators. We had a ball there."

"I'll never forget when they were getting ready to take a picture of the band before the Cabin Inn closed. Jimmie had discovered Joe Williams could sing and was trying to get him out at the club."

"He was doing very well. When they were taking the picture Jimmie said, 'No. Not Joe, this is not for singers.' But when it came out, it had Joe's head peeping round, trying to get into the picture."[98]

In the jazz world, Count Basie's Band had highlighted the tenor saxes of Lester Young and Hersha] Evans. Lester Young was considered harmonically ahead of his time, as his tone sounded more like an alto sax, rather than a tenor. Hershal Evans, who blew a much more mellower horn (His recording of *Blue And Sentimental*), still remains a classic.

Duke Ellington, a fine composer, pianist, and bandleader, in 1939, had Billy Strayhorn with his band. Their collaborations as arrangers and alternate pianists helped produce, *Take The A Train* and *Chelsea Bridge*. That same year, after Ellington brought out his share of his contract from Irving Mills, he was able to operate toward his own ambitions.

Chick Webb's band had become very popular with Ella Fitzgerald's vocalizing. She had married Webb and remained with his band, even when other bandleaders tried to get her to join them. When Webb died in 1939, Ella, took over the job of bandleader, and the group stayed together for three more years.

Mary Lou Williams, a piano player, composer and arranger, had been labeled as, "The first great female instrumentalists." Her arrangements were written for bands, such as Louis Armstrong, Earl 'Fatha' Hines, Benny Goodman and Duke Ellington.

Fletcher Henderson had joined up with Benny Goodman upon becoming employed, and was hired as Goodman's pianists.

At a Cafe called "Jack's," Jimmie Noone called out, "Jack, I'll have the usual." Jack turned to his cook and yelled out, "One BBQ with everything and one chicken sandwich and a slice of apple pie."

The cook behind the grill knew it was Jimmie ordering, and stuck his head out of the kitchen, and welcomed him with a wave.

Jack showed Jimmie to a nearby table and told him, "Man. Rita was in here talking about your orders. She said that I should not serve you what you normally order. She knows that you sneak in here, and how often the cook tells her everything."

Jimmie replied, "I've been having a little trouble with my heart man, not my stomach. She's just concerned about my health and weight. Just ignore her."

Jack answered, "Considered it done."

While walking away he told Jimmie, "She's really a beauty. I can see why you married her man." Jimmie smiled at the remark, and also at the food that was being served him.

While eating, Jimmie felt guilty. He wasn't kidding anyone, not even Rita. He wanted to stop eating so much, but he was hooked, and that's what worried him the most. He knew that he had to get a grip on his eating habits, however he had no idea how to start the process.

Jimmie walk d down State Street after eating at Jack's. His thoughts were on his family, and the fact that after working all these years, he had not contributed much in the way of proving them any worldly possessions. And he had spent so much time working on the South side of Chicago that he wondered if he'd ever play more in the white clubs.

As a Negro musician, Jimmie became forced to realize that the hours he was working were starting to take a toll on his health. When he was younger, he could work easily the 90 to 120 days straight one-nighters. A club might sign him up for a contract that lasted three months or four months.

While a white band would check into one of the nicer hotels and play an engagement of perhaps sixteen to as much as thirty-eight weeks of the year.

Walking up the steps to his home on State Street, Jimmie placed his key in the door, and opened it. He saw his young son walking toward him as he said, "Da Da—Hi Da Da."

He reached down and picked him up, while calling out, "Rita, where are you?" With Jimmy in his arms, he quickly walked into the bedroom, where he found his wife laying on the floor.

"Oh My God!" Jimmie said, as he placed his son down, and reaching for Rita's wrist, felt her pulse, which seemed rather slow. He picked up the telephone, called the operator, and requested, "Send for an ambulance immediately, my wife's passed out."

At Saint Mary's Catholic Hospital, Jimmie paced up and down the halls, as he waited for the doctor to finish his examination and tests. Zutty arrived at emergency, walked to Jimmie and said, "What happened, Face? I got your call."

Jimmie held his head down and told Zutty, "Apparently she fainted on the floor, I don't know what happened, but it could be related to the fact that she's about three months pregnant."

Zutty continued to talk to Jimmie to keep his mind occupied. "Where's the baby?"

Jimmie looked up and seemed to relax somewhat as he said, "Oh, he's with our neighbor, Mrs. Jones. When I got to the house, he was behaving quite well, and had in his hand that fife I gave him. You know Zutty, I think it's time we got him another instrument. Do you think he'd like to play the clarinet?"

Zutty fell out laughing. "I do think he is. He's definitely your son Jimmie Noone."

The emergency doctor entered the waiting room and asked, "Mr. Noone?" Jimmie jumped up and replied, "Yes sir."

The doctor introduced himself, then stated, "Your wife will be fine. Perhaps she's just been doing too much for someone a little over three months pregnant."

Shaking the doctor's hand while thanking him, the Physician remarked, "You may now go and see her. However, I would like for her to stay overnight, so we can monitor her condition, before we release her."

Jimmie sounded very grateful when he answered, "Thank you so much. Yes, I'll go see her right away."

Jimmie turned to Zutty, as if to indicate that he wanted him to go see Rita, but Zutty told him, "You two should be alone. I'll wait here for you. Now go on."

Jimmie rushed away quickly from Zutty, and when he reached Rita's hospital room, he swung the door open, and as it squeaked to open wider, he saw his wife lying in bed. Rushing to her bedside, he kissed her, then spoke quickly, "Rita, I'm sorry this happened. I had no idea the amount of work you've been doing since Jimmy's been born."

Rita sounded weak when she asked, "Where's our baby? I've been worried and no one would tell me anything."

Jimmie reassured her, "Our son is with our neighbor, Mrs. Jones. Now don't forget she raised thirteen children herself, so she knows what she is doing."

"The doctor said that you'll be spending the night here, so I'll have Mrs. Jones keep our son for the time. When you get home, I'll be helping you more with the household, and if that's not enough, we'll bring in other assistance."

"I'm just glad that you're fine, 'cause I don't know what I would have done if something bad happened to you. Now get some rest tonight, and I'll pick you up when the doctor releases you tomorrow." They kissed and Jimmie left the hospital with Zutty.

Jimmie Noone was pacing up and down the halls of St. Mary's Catholic Hospital, in Chicago, anxiously awaiting word from the maternity ward, where his wife Rita, was in labor with their second child.

Jimmie knew his mind was confused, all he could remember was that it was July and the year was 1941. He also knew that he had canceled three gigs since his wife had gone into labor twenty-four hours ago. His main concern at the moment was his wife, but he also knew he was losing money not working at the Cabin Inn.

Finally, when the sunset showed through the windows of the hospital, the doctor came out with his announcement, "Jimmie, your wife has just delivered a beautiful baby girl, mother and baby are just fine. Congratulations!" They shook hands before the doctor left.

I Walking into Rita's all white hospital room, which smelled of antiseptic cleansers, he witnessed the most natural pose he had ever seen. Rita looked motherly, yet gorgeous, he thought as he kissed her, while smiling at the beautiful baby girl that she held in her arms. And then Jimmie spoke quickly to his wife, "She looks like an angel. What shall we call her?"

Rita smiled. "Her name will be Sylvia."

The proud parents looked down at their pink blanket bundle as Sylvia began sucking her fingers. Jimmie said, "She looks like you, except for the hair color."

Sylvia's hair was a pitch-black coloring, she had round oval eyes, the color of the sky. She was as white as a sheet in skin-coloring, it was obvious she was a Creole-of-color.

Jimmie decided to take a few weeks off from work, so he could help Rita make the adjustment of having two kids to take care of. The free time that being off of work provided him to compose new scores for his band, and one tune he wrote that he recorded was called, "Goodbye, Don't Cry."

When Jimmie started back to work several weeks later, his new gig was at the plush establishment called "The Yes Yes Club." The musicians that he had working with him were considered the best, they were, Frank Smith (pno), Johnn Frazier (sbs), and Wally Bishop (runs).

Frank Smith, a piano player, now Jiving in Chicago, as of 1991, who now suffers from severe pain from being an invalid, and having back trouble, but could still remember the days of the Yes Yes Club.

In May 1991, when Franz Jackson went over to Frank Smith's home, this is what they recorded for the author, as quotes for this book.

F. Jackson asked Franklin Smith, "How did you happen to play with Jimmie Noone in the first place?"

F.S. replied, "I started at the Platinum Lounge yeah-well, that's when I started. I don't know how they picked me, 'cause I'll tell you Jimmie Noone was very particular and he had looked around. But I think the guy that got me in the group was Bill Winston."

F.S. "Franz, let me give you an idea of how I felt. George Dixon, how proud he was to carry his instrument-his case. When he was a youngster coming up and how proud he was to be a musician. And I used to be the same way, but now, I don't want to be connected with it anymore. It was just different back in those days, the guys were honorable, all the fellows I met were princes, almost all of them."

F.S. Smith continues, "People have pushed the truth about Jimmie Noone, yeah, they've pushed this whole thing out of shape. When we were down in the Platinum Lounge and up until several years after Jimmie had left that club, Benny Goodman was always there."

F.J. Franz Jackson replied, "Benny Goodman—well the first thing that got me against Goodman, or down on Goodman—well number one, he used to— and I always gave Jimmie hell about this—the only thing I could find wrong is he would let them guys come in and record him on those wire recorders."

I had a wire recorder and I knew what it was all about, and I knew that what they recorded would come out on records later. Well, I was right. They recorded us at the Yes Yes Club.

Franz continued talking, "What Franklin Smith is referring to is—Benny Goodman, found it easier to record Jimmie's music, rather than write it down, it was convenient, as this music was intricate. Also, since he had played with Jimmie since the Platinum Lounge days (1937), he had witnessed a 'Musical Pillage'."

Goodman did not use Jimmie's recordings, he just straight out played his music, without any payment of any kind. Another example of musical pillage, was when in '37, the Jimmie Noone And His Orchestra Band, which consisted of Franklin Smith, recorded for Decca in New York.

Those eight songs that were recorded later became reissues for the Swaggie Label. However, the seven musicians that produced these records, never received any additional income or royalties from the sale of these recordings. The same thing happened with the recordings that were made on January 15, 1936, and June 5, 1940, at the Yes Yes Club in 1941. All those recordings became reissues for the Swaggie Label. It can be heard on an album entitled Jimmie Noone 1936–1941, Swaggie #S1226.

Also, part of that same record contains recordings that became Johnny Dodds last recording, which also featured Jimmie, and that recording became his second last recording date, besides his private sessions and radio broadcast. The recording features two songs, *New Orleans Hop Scop Blues* and *Keystone Blues*.

On July 17, 1941, The Jimmie Noone Quartet recorded at Yes Yes Club. The musicians that recorded were Jimmie Noone (clt), Frank Smith (pno), John Frazier (sbs), and Wally Bishop on drums.

The songs recorded were: *A Porter's Love Song To A Chambermaid* (Razaf-Johnson), *Blues For Roy, Goodbye, Don't Cry* (Jimmie Noone), *Lady Be Good* (Gershwin), *Memories Of You, Honeysuckle Rose* (Waller-Razaf), and *Body And Soul*.

The above seven titles and Jimmie's theme song, 'Sweet Lorraine' were privately recorded by John Steiner at the Yes Yes Club, in Chicago. These were not professional recordings. Of the seven tunes, six became issued later by Swaggie #S1210, and *Body And Soul* was released from this recording session on Swaggie Label #S1226, which also featured Franklin Smith.

John Steiner became involved in recording Noone, after he had called Steiner, and said he was making a recording for Victor Records. And because he wanted copies of his group recording for Victor's A & R man, Steiner agreed.

1The Yes Yes Club was located just south of the loop, at the upper end of State Street. This area was crowded with Honky Tonk's, and on the same block were Burlesque Theater's, other bars, and a Nickelodeon Arcade next door. Because State Street was a crowded area, and noisy from the establishments surrounding the club, Jimmie recommended the recording take place early, after his first set.

The Yes Yes Club was considered plush for State Street, and this club was actually something more of a saloon, where the musicians played behind the bar. It was a unique bar.

A Cardioid Microphone (A long metal arm supporting a heart-shaped microphone), was used for the recording of the second set. The acoustic from the ensemble, combined with the force and intensity of Jimmie's clarinet, was cause to move the recording equipment back further away from the band, this caused the cash register at the bar to be heard in the background.

The night of their third set, the band started off with their theme song *Sweet Lorraine* and then recorded *Goodbye Don't Cry*. These recorded songs were then listened to by Jimmie with headphones, and he said, "Yes. This is good for the instrumental part, but we need a singer. I asked someone to sit in with us, but he hasn't showed up yet."

Because the singer had not arrived yet, John Steiner and Jimmie Noone decided to wait around for a while. Jimmie told the rest of the band members that further recordings would be done, and that the material could later be used for issuing or selling. No written contract had passed hands, and Jimmie could only request that everything be placed on hold, as he still was committed to the Victor Label.

The recordings that they made at that time with sixteen inch discs, which became a problem placing them onto a ten inch or 78 RPMs, as they were just too long. The Victor Label later said that they had lost or either misplaced the recording of *Goodbye, Don't Cry*. However, a Mr. Sherburn, many years later, was able to find a way to reproduce these songs, on an album called The Jazz Makers.

This album featured the Jimmie Noone Quartet at the Yes Yes Club, on side B, and side A is entitled, *A Jam Session Broadcast*, it featured Louis Armstrong, Jack Teagarden, 'Bud' Freeman, 'Fats' Waller, Al Casey and Wilmore 'Slick' Jones.

In all due fairness to the Swaggie Label, and to Mr. John Steiner, a few things should be mentioned. Jimmie Noone had asked Steiner to record him, because he trusted him and his judgement. Also, on August 1, 1942 (almost a year later), the American Federation of Musicians declared a ban on recordings. So no contract ever took place, and because of Noone's early death.

The recordings that were taped at the Yes Yes Club, became valuable to jazz history, especially since a singer never arrived to possibly mistreat the instrumentalists in the quartet. Also, if these recordings had never been reproduced by Swaggie, our young generation would have missed out on a part of pioneering jazz musicians in the thirties.

Lucky for Swaggie that they realized Jimmie Noone's music had not been recorded as much as it possibly could have, and until their reissues were produced, his work had become very limited. They were able to release approximately thirty percent of Noone's recorded work, and a few songs that had never been previously issued.

Because of Noone's reissues also, many other clarinetists of today are able to listen to his traditional New Orleans Jazz style, and he therefore becomes an influence and an inspiration to other musicians.

After Jimmie Noone's daughter, Sylvia, had been born, and his son had turned three years old, is when Noone really began to suffer severe pains associated with his heart. He started acting a little bit quieter, as he worried about his health. He had taken to drink whiskey, to stimulate his heart due to his chest pains. No one at this time knew about his condition, many thought he was simply drinking more.

Jimmie had to double up on his jobs, due to the popularity he had in Chicago on the south-side. The people of color kept his music alive, and the money that he was making was very little. The Depression had just ended, but the economy had not adjusted to the change.

Jimmie still continued to play golf, and this was his only exercise. After working two jobs daily, Noone played golf with Zutty Singleton and Ed Pollack. They would play eighteen holes at Jackson Park, around 4:00 AM (negroes still were not permitted to play at golf during the day).

Jimmie would run home after playing until the early morning hours, change clothes and have breakfast, then he'd meet his friends on the course. By 7:00 AM, their day was finished, and it was time to go home and get some rest.

Musicians in all the big cities were speaking of a possible jazz revival that a few recording studios were contemplating. Delta Records contributed to the revival when they recorded the Kid Rena's Jazz Band, which consisted of Louis 'Big Eye' Nelson, Albert Glenny, Alphonse Picou, Jim Robinson, and Willie Santiage. Their style of music had been sweeping throughout the United States and Europe. This music had taken on the name of "Free Expression."

Another cycle in music occurred in 1940, which later became known as "The New Orleans Jazz Revival." This switch in New Orleans jazz happened, with the decline of Swing in the early forties.

"Because most of the New Orleans musicians did not record until they migrated to Chicago in the early 1920s, much of what is known about an 'authentic' New Orleans style was gleaned from recordings made by New Orleans musicians during the revival of Dixieland and New Orleans jazz in the 1940s."[99]

"The revival of interest in the origins of jazz grew swiftly during 1940. Record companies, keenly aware of sales tendencies—even in minority markets—not only stepped up the issue of jazz recordings by contemporary bands but also began dusting off old master-pressings so that they could organize regular reissues from the so-called Golden Era of the 1920s."[100]

"The New Orleans men who had remained home or returned home tended to play in an order style. When Louis and Bechet locked horns in stirring choruses on Coal Cart and Perdido Street Blues in New Orleans jazz (Decca) it was a thrilling display of two-way improvisation."[101]

When Noone took his quartet and big band down South for the New Orleans Jazz Revival, he had to make advanced traveling plans. Jimmie became one of the first native New Orleanians, to be asked back to his hometown for the revival.

The demand for original hot New Orleans music was being sought after by the younger generation, that had never heard early jazz music performed.

Ed Pollack, who still has a good memory about the trip to New Orleans had this to say in his interview, "Jimmie drove a Pierce-Arrow car—a big convertible with tires on the outside of the car. The fellows that went down to New Orleans included myself, Jimmie, Frank Smith, Wally Bishop and Franz Jackson. Man, we drew the crowds and people in like flies, when we went down South."

Franz Jackson remembered the man that had booked the tour down South. "That Tour-Guy-He just didn't have it-It was a bad tour. This man didn't even know how to split up the money between musicians and receive his percentage basis. I had to figure everything out for him. I don't remember if we gave a dance or not down in New Orleans, but we were entertained nicely by the Auto Craft club."

In the Jimmie Noone Bio-Discography written by Harm Sagawe, which is at Tulane University Library, Baby Dodds reported that around the end of 1941, he played in Jimmie Noone's band together with Mada Roy on the piano, and Bill Anderson, was on bass.

About this time, Lester Young departed from the Basie Band, and Sidney Bechet was performing regularly at Nick's in Greenwich Village, in John Hammond's Spirituals To Swing shows, and with Eddie Condon's Group at Town Hall.

"Bechet was in demand during the mid-1940s because of the Dixieland Revival, which involved him in groups with Bunk Johnson and other 'Revived' players who were not of his caliber."[102]

In 1949, Bechet moved to Paris, where he lived for the rest of his life.

In New Orleans, Oscar 'Papa' Celestin, who had worked with Jimmie Noone before going to Chicago, had been involved in an automobile accident, and had broken his leg. His band disbanded temporarily. From when Celestin had formed his first band in 1917, and until 1941, he continued to play New Orleans style music, with the exception of a few years during the Depression.

In 1941, Oscar Celestin died. His funeral was considered one of the largest in New Orleans, except in 1961, when the author's great-great uncle, Alphonse Picou, passed away. At Picou's jazz funeral, there were ten thousand people that celebrated his burial.

Many jazz musicians have had jazz funerals in the following of traditional New Orleans Creole customs. Creole's believed that when a child is born into the world, we should cry, and rejoice when someone dies, a t then know that they are leaving behind all their problems, trials, troubles, and tribulations.

After the recording date of July 1941, Jimmie Noone did not go into a recording studio again until the year of 1943. This came about from the sixteen month-long strike of the American Federation of Musicians.

Noone did keep busy performing at socials, air broadcasts, nightclubs, and other various jobs. His popularity stayed based in the "Windy City."

Throughout the years of 1942, and part of 1943, Noone's activities as a musician were nothing out of the ordinary. He was able to use this slow period to his advantage by spending more time with his wife Rita, his son Jimmy, and his young daughter, Sylvia.

The American Federation Of Musician's strike that had occurred in August 1942 stated that there were to be no instrumental records made. This caused a hardship for all musicians and delayed progress with jazz.

This ban was not lifted until the fall of 1943, when Decca signed with the Union. This created many new independent labels to start up and fall into the same terms of unionism.

It was more than a year after 1943 that Victor and Columbia stepped up a join the masses. "As a result of the ban, no mass audience heard Earl Hine's Band, in which people like Gillespie, Parker, and Harris were playing the new music, encouraged by tenor saxophonists—arranger Budd Johnson and singer—trumpeter Billy Eckstine."[103]

Joe Williams talked about the musician's strike, and when he replaced Rubel Blakely, Ramp's former male singer. "That was some band. In the brass section Hamp had Joe Morris, Joe Newman, Lamar Wright and Joe Wilder on the first trumpet. Arnett Cobbs was blowing lots of tenor sax, Eric Miller was on guitar, George Jenkins played drums, and Milt Buckner rounded out the rhythm section on piano."

"The Musician Union's recording ban of 1943 prevented me from recording with that fine group of musicians. That was a crucial time in jazz history. I believe the inability to record delayed my career at least ten years."[104]

Franz Jackson, tenor saxophonists and clarinet player, throughout this time period was keeping active with jobs. At the well-known Three Deuces, he had joined Roy Eldridge's Band in 1939. "I rejoined Roy Eldridge at the Arcadia Ballroom in New York City in 1939. Prince Robinson was with the band on clarinet. He had an excellent style that was reminiscent of Jimmie Noone. I like hearing him better than I did hearing myself. He had a jump style that really kicked off. I stayed with Roy until I joined Earl Hines in 1940."[105]

Jimmie Noone was doing a lot of road traveling with his small quartet and his large ten-piece band. World War II had caused a gas rationing, which added to terrible traveling conditions for the Negro. The only means of travel was by way of the train, and other restrictions if negroes traveled below the Mason-Dixon Line.

Until the NAACP prevailed upon the Office of Defense and Transportation, to ease its ban on charter bus travel for Negro bands, many musicians stopped playing.

Only five buses became available for Negro traveling bands, and with the gasoline shortages, the fans were not able to travel and see their favorite musicians.

"Two other wartime curbs, a twenty percent amusement tax and the midnight 'Brownout' curfew, severely hurt business. The bands might have turned more to recordings to supplement their reduced performing income, but in 1942, the American Federation of Musicians called a recording ban that dragged on for two years."[106]

On Jimmy Noone Jr.'s birthday, April 21, 1943, when be turned five years old, his parents gave him a birthday party. Included were all the musicians kids that his father had known and worked with.

Rita and Jimmie gave their son his first clarinet that year. Because he had played the fife, then the flute, the clarinet was something that seemed fairly easy for him to play. It was obvious that he was adapted to music.

Finally, the strike against every United States record company had ended in November 1943. After a long year and a half, musicians were able to go back into the studio and record. The recording studios could hardly wait to make records again, and everyone was rushing to get their record out to the public as soon as possible.

In 1943 Noone had started suffering with severe heart pains, they were so painful that even a shot of whiskey, or laying down to rest, did not relieve the shortness of breath, or the burning in the chest, that he was experiencing.

This was also the year that the Noone family had packed up and moved from Chicago to Los Angeles, California. The move to California was one of economics, as Jimmie had secured a contract to play for six months (That turned out to last for a year), at a club called The Streets Of Paris Cafe, which was located on Hollywood Boulevard, in Hollywood, California.

Leaving Chicago, Jimmie Noone, had asked Ed Pollack to go with him, but he refused because of the family members he had in Chicago. Pollack had been with Jimmie the longest, even since the Platinum Lounge days, and parting was difficult. When Jimmie left, he gave Pollack his golf clubs. Pollack decided at that time to quit music, mostly because of the pay, and also because he wanted to go into the hairdressing business. Jimmie took ten members of his band to Los Angeles, which included Franz Jackson and Walt Nickelson.

As soon as Rita and the kids arrived in California, after several days, they had to pack up and return to Chicago, as there was a housing shortage in Los Angeles.

This return trip put a financial burden on Jimmie, along with additional stress. When Rita returned back to Chicago, Jimmie went to see a doctor about his heart. The doctor told him, "There is nothing that we can do. You have what is called a 'Chronic Mocardium' heart ailment, which cannot be repaired."

The doctor gave Jimmie a prescription, that he said, "The pills will reduce the pain, and make you more comfortable. If you could reduce your weight from 240 to 200 pounds, and start an exercise schedule, it could possibly prolong your life by a few years. If not Jimmie, I'm afraid your life will be cut very short."

I After leaving the doctor's office, Jimmie stood outside thinking about what he had been told, and for the first time in his life, he was terrified. With so much to think about, he forgot that Zutty would be arriving soon to pick him up, and he started walking down the street. A car pulled up and stopped near him, and it was Zutty. He yelled to Jimmie, "Hey man. Get in. It's too damn hot to be walking."

As they drove away, Jimmie rested his arms onto his rather chubby stomach that had lost its waistline, as he told Zutty everything the doctor had said, as tears quickly dribbled down his face.

Zutty drove around Los Angeles, as Jimmie talked about his condition and what they ought to do. Finally, they both agreed not to tell Rita, as she was so sensitive, and Jimmie believed that she had enough to worry about with the kids, and then having to move back to Chicago. Plus, he confessed to Zutty, he had no idea how to tell his wife that he could die at any time, or perhaps in a few years.

Jimmie told Zutty, "Face. If anything happens to me, make sure that Rita and the kids are fine, and especially little Jimmy. It's obvious that my son will become a musician, and that somehow worries me."

Zutty added, "Music is in his blood, just like the rest of us Creole's. He already knows his scales. Hasn't he already had lessons from every musician that you've ever played with?"

Jimmie smiled, "That's just it. I'm afraid he'll suffer the same life I've had to live."

Zutty reassured Jimmie, "If the worst that could happen to the boy is that he takes to music after you, the world will be better for his music. Now stop worrying." They then went to band practice, knowing that nothing had really been settled, nor could it be.

When Jimmie Noone arrived in Los Angeles, it was the summer of 1943. The growing interest in New Orleans music and Dixieland Jazz had become quite popular in the "Sunshine State."

Kid Ory had returned to his home in Los Angeles, where he was making a decent living, raising chickens. Barney Bigard had left Ellington in 1942, after growing tired of touring on buses and trains. Bigard was now freelancing in Hollywood recording studios and at Billy Berg's Club.

Jimmie had put himself on a nutritional diet, and was exercising as much as he possibly could, mostly with Jong walks in the park. His schedule was very demanding, and he was not getting much rest. Also, whenever he had the spare time, he would either call on the telephone, or go out to look for housing for his family, as he hated being separated from them.

It had been two years since Jimmie Noone had made a recording, and his public was demanding to hear him play again.

On November 16, 1943, The Capitol Jazzmen recorded on Capitol Label in Los Angeles. Musicians included, Billy May (tpt), Jack Teagarden (tbn, vcl), Jimmie Noone (clt), Dave Matthews (ten), Joe Sullivan (pno), Dave Barbour (gtr), Art Shaphiro (sbs), Zutty Singleton (elms).

The songs recorded on November 1943 were *Clambakd In B-Flat* (Joe Sullivan), *Casanova's Lament* (Dick Larkin), with vocals by Jack Teagarden, *Solitude* (Eddington-DeLange-Mills), *I'm Sorry I Made You Cry* (N.J. Clesi), with vocals by Jack Teagarden.

The reissues were through Telefunken Capitol, which are German issues, the band is labeled as Die Capitol Jazzmen. The recording *Clambake In B-Flat* reveals the superb playing of Jimmie's old friend Zutty, and Jimmie's remarkable solo.

There are two choruses in fast tempo in which Jimmie shows his capabilities of a clarinet player. He plays with intense, powerful emotion, it's truly amazing how he can play both the upper and lower register, with such ease.

One cannot detect that Noone's health was failing, as he sounds exuberant! His lyrical sense and tone could be compared only to Sidney Bechet.

The recording became a reissue by Swaggie Records in 1984 and was titled, The Capitol Jazzmen 1943–1947. Dave Dexter, who produced the original recording, knew in advance from Noone that he was quite ill. Dexter had made arrangements with Noone to have a replacement musician available for him, if he was to have to leave sick.

Dave Dexter, was the Writer and Producer at Capitol Records, and the replacement he had in waiting for Jimmie, was a clarinetist by the name of Heinie Beau.

After the recording session had lasted *only* three hours of Jimmie's blowing, and Dexter began talking of working another three additional hours, Beau was substituted for Jimmie. Jimmie was not physically capable of working another three hours.

This recording session was to be Jimmie's last recorded music, except for the radio station recordings that were to follow. Although not many jazz articles have been written about Jimmie's replacement, Heinie Beau, he was indeed capable.

Beau, recorded two songs, as Noone's replacement, *Mighty Lak'A Rose* and *Stars Fell On Alabama* featuring Jack Teagarden's Chicagoans.

This recording also featured many great jazz musicians, and just to name a few names on the album: Benny Carter, Coleman Hawkins, Buster Baile, Bill Coleman, Max Roach, Nat 'King' Cole, Red Callender, Benny Goodman, Barneyt! Bigard, Red Norvo, and Nappy LaMare. The album is unique, as it features larger than life musicians.

In the early '40s, the union scale was about $40.00. Jimmie Noone said that he earned $41.00, which would have been for six hours. So it's obvious that these musicians loved their jazz, as the recordings were very tedious work in the studios. Musicians today have an easier time in the studios with air-conditioning, nice plush recording rooms, etc., but that was not the case in the '40s.

The linear notes on this Swaggie S.1406 album that Dave Dexter, Jr., wrote regarding how reissues were made are rather interesting. "Listeners may be interested in knowing that all these time-tested masters were originally transcribed on 12 and 16-inch acetate discs, then transferred to 78 R.P.M. masters after I designated which takes to press."

"There was no recording on tape, no splices, no editing, no removal of clams and clinkers by skillful engineers. What you hear now is precisely what was played forty years back. And thank God, there were no inhuman, mechanical synthesizers in the studio to muck up the music."

Many of Jimmie's best musician friends that had relocated to Los Angeles in the 1940s had learned how sick Jimmie had gotten. Mutt Carey, Zutty Singleton, Buster Wilson, and Ed Garland had decided to help Jimmie find a home for his family.

They looked everyday, either for an apartment, a home, a duplex, a studio, and even a room. Nothing could be found in any neighborhood, due to the prejudice in the city. Also, Los Angeles did not have established Negro areas, such as in the 1990s.

Finally, Ted Le Berthon, of The Los Angeles Daily News, wrote an article pleading for someone to rent a home to Jimmie Noone. He wrote that article on September 14, 1943, and he was fired for it.

The following year 1944, which was several months later, Jimmie's family had located a home. He was able to send for them, and they were once again reunited as a family. They resided at 2711 Cimmarron Street, in Los Angeles.

At that time Jimmy Junior was just about to turn six years old, and his sister, Sylvia, a beautiful girl, was just a young child, and not quite three years old. Finally, the pressure of home hunting had ended. However, it had taken its toll on Jimmie's health.

With things back to normal for Jimmie, he had started back to eating healthier instead of going out to eat. His diet was more sensible and he exercised by walking with his children in the park.

Jimmie was exercising, eating properly, and yet his health was deteriorating. The pills that the doctor had given to him to take for pain, no longer worked.

In the book *Jazz Masters*, author Martin Williams wrote, "In February 1944, Orson Welles had a half-hour weekly broadcast of Standard Oil on a regional CBS Network, through California and neighboring states."

"Welles loved New Orleans jazz, and, with the original idea of featuring one number on one show, asked Marili Morden if she could assemble a band. She called up Matt Carey (Who had managed to stay part-time in music although he spent twenty-two years as a Pullman Porter), Jimmie Noone (Appearing locally with a more or less swing style group), pianist Buster Wilson, guitarist Bud Scott, bassist Ed Garland, and Zutty Singleton. They were all delighted to be asked and jumped at the chance."[107]

Kid Ory, trombonists, had come out of retirement, and he "had his big chance in 1944, when Orson Welles was running a broadcast series for Standard Oil, and invited him to form a band."

Ory's first group had Mutt Carey on trumpet, Jimmie Noone on clarinet, Buster Wilson on piano, Bud Scott on guitar, Ed Garland on bass and Zutty Singleton on drums. "All these men had been famous during the 1920s and early 1930s, and had left New Orleans in the general exodus to seek their fortune in Chicago and elsewhere."[108]

The show was such a grand success, and mail started coming into the radio show for more New Orleans music, that Orson Welles asked the band to continue with the radio station as a weekly feature. From that famous radio show that produced such good music, four recordings were made, on four separate labels.

The first radio broadcast that was recorded was on March 15, 1944, a radio broadcast under The Kid Ory's Creole Jazz Band was recorded by Carousel Label. The musicians were Mutt Carey (cnt), Kid Ory (tbn), Jimmie Noone (cit), Buster Wilson (pno), Bud Scott (gtr), Ed Garland (sbs), and Zutty Singleton (dms). The song recorded was 'High Society' (Williams Steele).

Reissues were under the Jazz Record Society (French), and Jazz Collector (British). Jazz Record Society AA 105, has Jazz Record Society 0034 in wax, and is issued under Jimmy Noone And His Orchestra.

Although Jimmie was still continually having chest pains and had to sit down for the recording of *High Society*, he still was able to play this song in his typical New Orleans counterpoint, all the way through the complete song. The only musician that could have performed this one tune as well at the time would have been Alphonse Picou.

On Wednesday, March 22, 1944, a recording of The Kid Ory's Creole Jazz Band. The musicians used were the same from the March 15th recording. The song recorded was *Sugar Foot Stomp.*

The next recording date was March 29, 1944, Kid Ory's Band radio broadcast, produced under Jazz Record Society (French) AA 105. The reissue has Jazz Record Society 0033 and is issued under Jimmie Noone And His Orchestra. The song recorded was *Muskrat Rumble* (Kid Ory).

The musicians used were Mutt Carey (cnt), Kid Ory (tbn), Jimmie Noone (clt), Buster Wilson (pno), Bud Scott (gtr), Ed Garland (sbs), and Zutty Singleton (drns).

The following Wednesday evening, The Orsen Welles Radio Broadcast produced another recording on April 5, 1944. The song recorded was *That's A Plenty*, which had no reissues. The song recorded dates back to about 1911, when Clarence Williams was a young piano player living in New Orleans, and was also a song that Sophie Tucker sang at the Orpheum Theater in the Crescent City.

The musicians used were Mutt Carey (cnt), Kid Ory (tbn), Jimmie Noone (clt), Buster Wilson (pno), Bud Scott (gtr), Ed Garland (sbs), and Zutty Singleton (dms).

The following Wednesday, which was April 12, 1944, became Jimmie Noone's last recording date. The song recorded was an old Armand Piron tune titled *Panama Rag*. Since Ragtime was an earlier form of jazz that remained popular until the 1920s, this was an ideal song for Kid Ory's Creole Jazz Band to perform.

Panama Rag was recorded on the Jazz Society (French) Label, then reissued on Jazz Collector Label (British).

The following day of the recording, Jimmie invited Zutty Singleton and his wife, Marge Singleton, over to his home for dinner. After eating, he told them, "I've been very sick. I'm not sure how much longer I have to live, but there are things that we need to talk about."

Jimmie talked about his children, and how he wanted them raised. He told them that he had gone to see the Priest at their church, and had made his confession to God. He talked about Zutty taking care of his musical instruments, and saving his B-flat Albert System clarinet for his son, Jimmy.

The following week, on the morning of Wednesday, April 19, 1944, while Jimmie Noone was shaving at 7:00 AM, in his bathroom, Rita heard him fall to the floor, from the kitchen where she was making coffee. When she entered the bathroom, she found her husband dead from a heart attack.

Rita Noone ran and called the Paramedics, while her two children watched, not understanding why their father had collapsed onto the floor. Rita was stunned and numb when she called Zutty to come right over to the house.

The Paramedics arrived within a few minutes, and administered CPR, but it was to no avail. Ihe pumped his heart, but nothing seemed to work.

When Zutty arrived, he knew from Rita's phone call what had happened, and he was shocked and despondent. The Paramedics rushed Jimmie Noone's body to the hospital, in hopes of reviving him, yet they knew there was no hope.

Young Jimmy, who was about to tum six years old in two days, asked his mother about his father, while holding tightly onto his sister Sylvia's hand.

Rita took her son for a walk while Zutty watched Sylvia, and she explained to her son, that his daddy was dead. Then she said, "He left you his diamond ring and his gold watch and his clarinet, and only a good daddy would do that. He wanted you to grow up and play clarinet just like he did."

Memorial services were held at The Chapel Of Angelus at 1:00 PM, on April 22, 1944. Three days after Jimmie Noone had passed and left this world, became his funeral day.

His best friends were all in attendance which included, Kid Ory, Mutt Carey, Zutty and Marge Singleton, Bud Scott, Orsen Welles, Joe Sullivan, Mat Matlock, and Nappy Lemare.

The Pallbarer's at Jimmie Noone's funeral were George W. Vann, Charles Barlsdale, Bud Scott, Zutty Singleton, Eric Henry, and Dooley Wilson.

Jimmie Noone was buried at Hollywood's Evergreen Cemetery. What is so dreadful is that he was at the peak of his popularity and success. Noone never lived to see true fame. He had always lived as a poor man, although he was a pioneer of jazz.

The poor life that Jimmie Noone lived as a musician shows, even to this day, at his gravesite, that still remains without a headstone.

He came from Basin Street and Storyvill and New Orleans' famous red-light district in 1917. He migrated to Chicago with his clarinet, and played with such greats as: Joe King Oliver, Freddie Keppard, Tommy Ladnier, Louis Armstrong, and Jelly Roll Morton, and brought his new sound and style, the traditional New Orleans style of jazz.

Yet as a famous and great jazz pioneer, Jimmie Noone still waits for a headstone, and the recognition that he never received when his Apex Blues rang through the South side of Chicago.

Jimmie Noone's death certificate showed his immediate cause of death to be: chronic myocarditis, due to a coronary artery sclerosis.

Noone died at the age of forty-eight years old. His wife Rita, had become a young widow at the age of thirty-six years old.

Jimmie Noone was able to prove that the teachings he had received from Lorenzo Tio Jr., and Sidney Bechet, favored a European classical tradition, which later branched out into the New Orleans style of music.

Rita, Jimmie's wife, was not able to tell her husband, that she was expecting their third child, who was born in 1944, and named John David Noone. He was named after his grandfather Johnny Noone, who had married a free-slave girl named Lucinda.

After Jimmie's death, Rita, with the help of other musicians, family, and friends, was able to raise her children by herself.

The world of music will never forget the pioneer of jazz, Jimmie Noone. His *Sweet Lorraine* and *Apex Blues* will always be listened to. Generations of clarinetists, have become influenced by Noone's clarinet, such as Omer Simeon, Barney Bigard, Benny Goodman, Pee Wee Russell, and even today—Musicians are listening to his sweet playing clarinet.

Jimmie Noone Discography

Compiled records from Harm Sagawe from Tulane University Library, and Stanley Dance, Jazz Writer and Author

ABBREVIATIONS

INSTRUMENTS:

Alto	alto saxophone (AS)
Bar	baritone saxophone (BS)
Bbs	brass bass (BB)
bjo	banjo (BJ)
cnt	cornet (Cnt)
clt	clarinet (C)
dms	drums (D)
gtr	guitar (g)
pno	piano (P)
sbs	string bass (SB)
tbn	trombone (TB)
ten	tenor saxophone (TS)
tpt	trumpet (TP)
tu	tuba
vol	vocal (V)
vln	violin (VL)

LABELS:
Microgroove and unusual labels (like Decatur, or Jazz) are not abbreviated.

AFCDJ—Association Française des Collectionneurs de Disque du Jazz (French)

AM—American Music (American)

BB—Bluebird (American)

Bilt—Biltmore (American)

Br—Brunswick. The following prefix letters, or absence of them, denote the nationality:

LABELS:

A 9000 series	German (also for the French export market)	
	A 500000 series	French
	03000 series	British
	1000 series	French
	1200 series	British
	4000 series	Canadian
	6000 series	American
	7000 series	American (race)
	800000 series	American (Collectors Series) (black and gold label)
	80000 series	Canadian (Blue label)
	500000 series	French
Brs—British Record Society (American)		
Cap—Capitol (American)		
Car—Carousel (American)		
Col—Columbia (American)		

The nationality of other Columbia issues is denoted by the following prefix letters:

DF—French

DZ—Swiss

LF—French

Cx—Claxtonela (American)

Dec—Decca (American) The nationality of all other Decca issues is denoted by the following prefix letters, or the absence of them:

DM—British (expert only)

F (four digits)—British

30000 series—Swiss M—British (export only)

EBW—Edison Dell Winner (British)

GEN—Genett (American)

Gal—Gazelle (Swedish)

HJCA—Hot Jazz Club of America (American)

Hag—Harmograph (American)

HRS—Hot Record Society (American)

JC—Jazz Collector (British)

JI—Jazz Information (American)

JRS—Jazz Record Society (French)

JS—Jazz Society (French)

Mel—Melotone (American)

Od—Odeon. The following prefix letters, or absence of them, denote the nationality:

A.2300 series—Italian

or—British (export only)

Labels:

Ok—Okeh (American)

280000 series—Argentine

Pana—Panachord (British)

Par—Parlophone. The following prefix letters, or absence of them, denote the nationality:

A 6000 series—Australian A

7000 series—Australian R—British

PZ—Swiss

Para—Paramount (American)

Pur—Puritan (American)

Re—Regal (British)

Sil—Silvertone (American)

Spt—Supertone (American)

Sto—Storyville (Danish)

Tel Cap—Telefunken Capitol (German)

Tpl—Temple (American)

UHCA—United Hot Clubs of America (American)

VJR—Vinilyts Jazz Reissues (American)

Voe—Vocation (American) The nationality of all other Vocation issues is denoted by the following prefix letters:

S.—British

V.—British

Jimmie Noone Recording Dates

OLLIE POWERS' HARMONY SYNCOPATORS

Chicago, September 1923

Alex Calimese (first cnt), Tommy Ladnier (second cnt), Eddie Vincent (tbn), Jimmie Noone (cit), Horace Diemer (alto), Glover Compton (pno), John Basley (bjo), William 'Bass' Moore (bb, tu), Ollie Powers (dms, leader).

1502-1 Play That Thing	Cx 40263, Pur 11263
1502-3 Play That Thing	Para 20263, HG 851, Gzl 1039 Cx 40263, Pur 11263, Am?
1 502-4 Play That Thing	Storyyille Kb 101
1505-5 Play That Thing	Para 12059, UHCA 79
1505-6 Play That Thing	ll6, Jazz 5003 AFG? Storyyille KB-101 Pm 12059, HG 874 Pm 12059, HG 874

Note:

A. Para 20263, Cx 40263 and Harmograph 851 as "Ollie Powers Orchestra": 874 as Clarence Young's Harmony Syncopators; Gazell 1 039 as OlliePowers and His Orchestra, with Tommy Ladnier.

B. Take-4 is said also to be issued on Para 20263 and Para 120598.

C. Wesley M. Neff states that the above "Personnel was given by Horace Diemer and checked against recollections of Glover Compton and Bill Dover."

D. Stanley Dance notes: Alec Calamese-as 1st cornet and banjo and bass by Dago.

E.

<u>**OLLIE POWERS**</u>   <u>**CHICAGO**</u>   <u>**OCTOBER 1923**</u>

Alex Calamese, Tommy Ladnier (cnts), Eddie Vincent (tbn), Jimmie Noone (cit) Horace Diemer (alto), Glover Compton (pno), John Basley (bjo), William 'Bass' Moore (bbs), Ollie Powers (dms, vcl).

1538-1 Jazzabo Jenkins (Shelton Brooks)	Para 12059
1538-2 Jazzabo Jenkins	Para 12059, Hmg 874, Pur 11263

Note: Harmograph as Clarence Young's Harmony Syncopators.

<u>**KING OLIVER JAZZ BAND**</u>   <u>**CHICAGO**</u>   <u>**OCTOBER 15, 1923**</u>

King Oliver, Louis Armstrong (cnts), Eddie Atkins (tbn), Jimmie Noone (cit), Lil Hardin (pno), Johnny St. Cyr (bjo), Baby Dodds (dms)

81300-3 Chattanooga Stomp   Col 13003-D Col DF 3079 (Oliver and Picou)

Col LF 225, Col DZ 3079,
RJCA HC 63, Bilt 1057, VJR

11

81301-1-2-3   Junk Man Blues Rejected (Joe Oliver)

October 16, 1923
81302-5
London (Cafe)

Blues   Col 14003-D, HJCAHC 17, BILT 1054,

KING OLIVER'S JAZZ BAND CHICAGO 15,1923

Joe Oliver, Louis Armstrong (cnts), Eddie Atkins (tb), Jimmie Noone (cit), Lil Hardin (pno), Johnny St. Cyr (bjo), Baby Dodds (dms) VJM 11.

813003	Chattanooga Stump Col 13003-D DF/DZ-30798, LF-225
81301-1-2-3	Junk Man Blues BM 1057, HJCA HC-63,
81302-1-2-3	London (Cafe) Blues Rejected

CHICAGO, OCTOBER 16, 1923

81302-5	London (Cafe) Blues	Col 14003-D, Ph B-23573-H, Bm 1054, HJCAHC-17, VJR-26
81303-2	Camp Meeting Blues	(Joe Oliver) as above
81304-2	New Orleans Stump	Col 13003-D, DF/DZ-3079, LF-225, Bm 1057, HJCA HC-(Oliver & Picou) 63 VJR 11

NOTE:

A. Buster Bailey stated he was the clarinetist player. However, a comparison with the Powers and Cook recordings up to 1926 proves that the same clarinetists Jimmie Noone is responsible.

COOK'S DREAMLAND ORCHESTRA, JANUARY 21, 1924 DOC COOK, RICHMOND IND.

Charles 'Doc' Cook (dir), Freddie Keppard, Elwood Graham (c), Fred Garland (tb), Jimmie Noone, Clifford King (cl, as), Joe Poston (as), Jerome Pasqual! (ts), Jimmy Bell (vn, p), Stan Wilson (bj), Bill Newton (bb), Fred Hall (d), Tony Spaulding (pn).

11727-B	Scissor Grinder Joe (Gillespie-Stocco)	GNT 5374, Sil 4044	(Kahn-Simons)
11728	Lonely Little Wallflower	GNT 5373, Sil 4045	(Clark-Leslie Warren)
11729-A-B	So This is Venice	GNT 5360	
11730	MoanfulMan	GNT 5373, Sil 4045	Man
11731	The Memphis Maybe (Gillespie-Cook-Moll)	GNT 5374, Sil 4044	Belongs to Someone
11732-A-B Else	The One I Love (Jones-Kahn)	GNT 5360	

NOTE:

A-Moanful Man is better known under the title—*My Daddy Rocks Me*.

B-Edison Bell Winner 4056 (So This Is Venice) is by Harry Reser's Orchestra (Paramount Master), not Cook's Dreamland Orchestra, as was once believed.

LILLIE DELK CHRISTIAN CHICAGO, MARCH 5, 1926

Lillie Delk Christian(contralto), ace by Johnny St. Cyr (bjo).

9573-A	Sweet Man	Ok 8317
9574-A	Sweet Georgia Brown	Ok 8317

JIMMIE NOONE (ADDED), CHICAGO JUNE 15, 1926

Lillie Delk Christian (vcl), Jimmie Noone (clt), Johnny St. Cyr.

9717-A	Lonesome and Sorry (Davis-Conrad)	Ok 8356-A
9718-A	Baby O' Mine (Jones)	Ok 8356-B
9718-B	Baby O' Mine (Jones)	Ok 8356

NOTE:

A: Mx 9718-A was probably exclusively issued on the later small red Okeh label.

<u>COOKIE'S GINGERSNAPS</u> <u>CHICAGO JUNE 22, 1926</u>

Freddie Keppard (c), Fred Garland (tb), Jimmie Noone (cl-v), Joe Poston (as-ts-v), Kenneth Anderson (p), Johnny St. Cyr (bj) (unknown percussion, possibly Cook).

9768-A	Messin' Around (vocal: Noone-Poston) (Cooke-St. Cyr)	Ok 8390-A
9769-A	High Fever (Sanders)	Ok 8369-A
9770-A	Here Comes The IIot Tamale Man	Ok 8369-A
9771-B	Love Found You For Me (vocal: Noone)	Ok 40675
<u>DOC COOK</u>		

<u>COOK AND HIS DREAMLAND ORCHESTRA CHICAGO, JULY 10, 1926</u>

Doc Cook (dir), Freddie Keppard, Elwood Graham (cl), Fred Garland (tb), Jimmie Noone (cl), Joe Poston, Clifford King (cl, as), Jerome Pasquall (cl, ts), Kenneth Anderson (p), Robert Shelly, Johnny St. Cyr (bj), Rudolph 'Sudie' Reynaud (bb), Bert Greene or Andrew Hilaire (d, vi), breaks probably by Poston and Noone.

142414-1	Here Comes The Hot Tamale Man!	Col 727-D
142415-2	Brown Sugar (Barris)	Col 813-D Re G-8804
142416-1	High Fever (Sanders)	Col 813-D Col 813-D
4338		
142417-1	Spanish Mama	Col 727-D

Note:

A: Regal as Raymond Dance Band.

B: George Mitchell (cl) replaces Keppard; Jerome Carrington (p) replaces Anderson.

COOK AND ms DREAMLAND ORCHESTRA. CHICAGO MAY 6, 1927

142981-3	Sidewalk Blues	Col 862-D
142982-1-2-3	The Sermon	Rejected

LILLIE DELK CHRISTIAN. MAY 6, 1927

Acc. by Richard M. Jones' Jazz Wizards; Artie Starks (cl), Richard M. Jones (p), Johnny St. Cyr (bj), Jimmie Noone (cl).

80841-A	It All Depends On You	OK 8475
80842-AB	Ain't She Sweet?	OK 8475

Note:

A: Acc. by Jimmie Noone (cl) and Johnny St. Cyr (g).

'DOC' COOK AND HIS 14 DOCTORS OF SYNCOPATION CHICAGO, JUNE 11, 1927

George Mitchell, Elwood Graham (c) Bill Dawson, Fayette Williams (tb), Jimmie Noone (cl), Joe Poston (as) Billy Butler (as, vn), Clarence Owens (ts), Jerome Carrington (p), Johnny St. Cyr (bj), Bill Newton (bb), Andrew Hilaire (d, v).

144317-2	Alligator Crawl	Col 1298-D
144318-2	Willie The Weeper	Col 1070-D

LILLIE DELK CHRISTIAN. CHICAGO, DECEMBER 12, 1927

Lillie Delk Christian (vcl), Jimmie Noone (cl), Johnny St. Cyr (g).

82046-A	My Blue Heaven (Whiting-Donaldson)	**OK** 8536
82047-A	Who's Wonderful! Who's Marvelous? Miss Annabelle Lee (Clare-Pollack)	**OK** 8536

Note:

A: Acc. by Louis Armstrong and His Hot Four: Louis Armstrong (c, v), Jimmie Noone (cl), Earl Hines (p), Maney Cara (bj).

CHICAGO, MARCH 30, 1928

145859-2	Hum And Strum (Do-Do-Do, That's What I Do)	Col 1430-D
145860-1-2-3	I'm A Broken-Hearted Blackbird	Rejected
145861-2	I Got Worry	Col 1430-D
145862-1-2-3	The Treat By The Gang	Rejected

JIMMIE NOONE'S APEX CLUB ORCHESTRA CHICAGO, MAY 16, 1928

Jimmie Noone (cl, vi, dir), Joe Poston (cl, as, vi), Earl Hines (p), Bud Scott (bj, g), Johnny Wells (d).

C-1937-C; E-7355	I Know That You Know	Voe 1184, Br 80024, Jso AA-587
C1938-C; E-7356	C1938-C; E-7356 Sweet Sue-Just You	Voe 1184, Br 8002
C1939-B; E-7357	Four or Five Times	Voe 1185, V-1026, Mt M-12543, Br 80025, A-500320
C1939-C; E-7357	Four or Five Times	Voe 1185, Spt S-2228

C1940-B; E-7358	Every Evening (I Miss You)	Voe 1185 Mt M-12543, Br 80025
Cl 940-C; E-7358	Every Evening (I Miss You)	Voe 1185

Note:

A. The original cream-and black label Vocation 1185 uses take Con on both sides; the latter gold label uses takes Band C; Brunswick 80025, though marked-C, is in fact pressed from a dubbing ofC-1940-B.

B. Poston switches to clarinet for 31bars in unisone with Noone over Hines on *Sweet Sue*.

C. Brunswicks of the 80000 series also appeared on Canadian Brunswick (blue label) with the same order numbers.

D. Brunswick 300320 (French) as Jimmie Noone and his Club Ambassadors, title as Four or Five Times, composers as (Heyman-Mills).

JIMMIE NOONE'S APEX CLUB ORCHESTRA CHICAGO, JUNE 14, 1928

Jimmie Noone (ell, vcl), Joe Poston (al, cl, vi), Earl Hines (p), Bud Scott (bjo, gtr), Johnny Wells (d).

C-2015	Ready For The River (Kahn-Moret)	Voe I188, JSo AA-527
C-2016;E-7403	Forevermore (Gotthelf-Burnett)	Voe 1188, Jso AA-527

LILLIE DELK CHRISTIAN VOCAL WITH LOUIS ARMSTRONG & ms HOT FOUR, CHICAGO, JUNE 26, 1928

Louis Armstong (tp, vi), Jimmie Noone (cl), Earl Hines (p), Maney Cara (g).

400954-B	You're A Real Sweetheart (Caesar-Friend)	OK 8607, Tpl 527
400955-B	Too Busy!	OK 8596
400956-A	Was It A Dream?	OK 8596
400957-A	Last Night I Dreamed You Kissed Me	OK 8607, Tpl 527

Note:

A: Tpl 527 as Louis Armstrong and His Hot Four, with the second title simply as Last Night.

JIMMY NOONE'S APEX CLUB ORCHESTRA CHICAGO, JULY 2, 1928

Jimmie Noone (cl), Joe Poston (al), Earl Hines (p), Bud Scott (bjo, gtr), Lawson Buford (bbs), Johnny Wells (d).

C-2111	Apex Blues	Voe Rejected
C-2112	Oh! Sister Ain't That Hot	Voe Test
C-2113	Blues (My Naughty Sweetie Gives To Me)	Voe Rejected

Note:

A: There may be tests extant of all the above. Title and band title as given on the test pressing of C-2112. The matrix number is typed on the white label, there are no digits, in the wax, however.

STOVEPIPE JOHNSON-VOICE WITH PIANO, Gm AR & CLARINET CHICAGO, JULY 2, 1928

Stovepipe Johnson (vcl), Jimmie Noone (cl), Earl Hines (p), Bud Scott (gtr).

C-2114   I Ain't Got Nobody (Williams-Graham)

Note:

A: The reverse is Don't Let Your Mouth Start Nothing, Your Head Can't Stand.

<u>JIMMIE NOONE'S APEX CLUB ORCHESTRA</u> CHICAGO, JULY 6, 1928

Jimmie Noone (cl), Poe Poston (alt), Earl Hines (p), Bud Scott (bjo, gtr), Lawson Buford (bbs), Johnny Wells (d).

C-2121	Sweet Lorraine	Voe Rejected
C-2122	King Joe	Voe Rejected
C-2123	Monday Date	Voe Rejected

Note:

A: Tests may be extant of these as well.

<u>JJMMJE NOONE'S APEX CLUB ORCHESTRA</u> CHICAGO, JULY 23, 1928

(Same musicians as of 7-6-28 recording).

C-2111	Apex Blues	Voe Rejected
C-2112	Oh Sister! Ain't That Hot?	Voe Rejected
C-2113	Blues My Naughty Sweetie Gives To Me	Voe Rejected

CHICAGO, JULY 24, 1928

(Same musicians as of 7-23-28 recording).

C-2121	Sweet Lorraine	Voe Rejected
C-2122	King Joe	Voe Rejected
C-2123	A Monday Date	Voe Rejected

JIMMIE NOONE'S APEX CLUB ORCHESTRA CHICAGO, AUGUST 23, 1928

Jimmie Noone (cl), Joe Poston (alt), Earl Hines (p), Bud Scott (bjo, gtr), Lawson Buford (bbs), Johnny Wells (d).

C-2258-A	Apex Blues (Noone-Hines-Poston)	Voe 1207
C-2258B	Apex Blues (Noone-Hines-Poston)	Voe 1207 Br 80023, Jso AA-581
C-2259-C	A Monday Date (My Monday Date) (Hines)	Voe 1229 BR 80026, Voe v.1026, UNCA41
C-2260-C	Blues (My Naughty Sweetie Gives To Me) (Swanstone-McCarron-Morgan)	Voe 1215, BR 80026

Notes:

A: At least some copies of Voe 1207 with C-2258-A in wax have reversed labels.

B: Voe V.1026 is Jimmy Noone and His Apex Club Orchestra. Br 80023 and Voe Vl026 as on Monday Date, UNCA 41 as a Monday Date.

JIMMIE NOONE'S APEX CLUB ORCHESTRA CHICAGO, AUGUST 25, 1928

Jimmie Noone (cl), Joe Poston (alt), Earl Hines (p), Bud Scott (bjo, gtr), Lawson Buford (bbs), Johnny Wells (d).

C-2266-A-B-C	Oh Sister! Ain't That Hot? (Donaldson-White)	Voe 1215
C-2267-B	Oh Sister! Ain't That Hot?	Voe 1215, AFCDJ A-030
C-2267	King Joe	Decatur 515,
C-2268-A	Sweet Lorraine (Burwell-Parrish)	Voe 1207, Br A-500320
C-2268-B	Sweet Lorraine (Cliff Burwell)	Br 80023

Notes:

A: Br 80023 as Jimmie Noone and his Club Ambassadors, composer as Noone.

B: King Joe is Bud Scott's own composition, and certainly his dedication to the great King Joe Oliver with whom he had recorded in the Windy City for several years.

CHICAGO, DECEMBER 11, 1928

402206-A	I Can't Give You Anything But Love (Fields-Mc Hugh)	OK 8650
402207-B	Baby (Fields-Mc Hugh)	OK 8660, Par R 2234

Note:

A: Par R 2234 (Race Series No. 16) as Lillie Delk Christian with Orchestra.

CHICAGO, DECEMBER 11, 1928

402208-A	Sweethearts On Parade	OK 8650
402209-B	I Must Have That Man	OK 8660, Par R 2234

LILLIAN DELK CHRISTIAN VOCALS WITH LOUIS ARMSTRONG AND HIS HOT FOUR CHICAGO, DECEMBER 12, 1928

Louis Armstrong (tp), Jimmie Noone (cl), Earl Hines (p), Maney Cara (g).

402206-A	Sweethearts On Parade	OK 8650
402209-B	I Must Have That Man	OK 8660, Par R 2234

Note:

A: Par **R** 2234 (Race Series No. 15) as Lillie Delk Christian With Orchestra.

JIMMIE NOONE'S APEX CLUB ORCHESTRA CHICAGO, DECEMBER 27, 1928

George Mitchell (ct), probably Kid Ory (tb), Jimmie Noone (cl, vi), Joe Poston (at, cl, vi), Alex Hill (p), Jurue Cobb (bjo), Bill Newton (bbs), Johnny Wells (d).

C-2710-A	It's Tight Like That (vl-JN, JP, JC) (Dorsey-Whittaker)	Voe 1238 Jso AA-522, NommM-10
C-2710-B	It's Tight Like That (Dorsey-Whittaker)	MU 31024 Voe v 1001 Dec MG-36265
C-2711-A	Let's Sow A Wild Oak	Voe 1238 JSo AA-522
C-2711-B	Let's Sow A Wild Oak (Gay)	Voe 1238 JSo AA-522
C-2712	She's Funny That Way (Whiting-Moret)	Voe 1240

Notes:

A: On 2712-Joe Poston plays clarinet behind Jimmie Noone's vocal.

B: The complete title is: She's Funny That Way (I Got A Woman, Crazy About Me).

C: On 2710-A Noone sings: "The Little Black Rooster Told The Little Brown Hen," on 2710-B, "The Little Brown Rooster Told The Little Black Hen."

D: Voe V.1007-As Jimmie Noone and His Apex Club Orchestra.

JIMMIE NOONE'S APEX CLUB ORCHESTRA CHICAGO, FEBRUARY 26, 1929

Jimmie Noone (cl), Joe Poston (al), Alex Hill (p), Junie Cobb (bj), Bill Newton (bbs), Johnny Wells (d).

| C-3005 | St. Louis Blues (Handy) | Voe Test (Swaggie JCS-33787) |

C-3006	Chicago Rhythm (Grossman-Kanter)	Voe 1267 AFCDJ A. 024

JIMMIE NOONE'S APEX CLUB ORCHESTRA CHICAGO, MARCH 2, 1929

Jimmie Noone (cl), Joe Poston (alt), Alex Hill (p), Junie Cobb (bjo), Bill Newton (bbs), Johnny Wells (d).

C-3031	I Got A Misery (Yoell-Scharlin-Jacobs)	AFCDJ A. 030

Note:

A: I Got A Misery has some similarity to Melancholy.

JIMMIE NOONE'S APEX CLUB ORCHESTRA CHICAGO, APRIL 27, 1929

Jimmie Noone (cl, vi), Joe Poston (alt, vl), Alex Hill (p, possibly vi), Bill Newton (bbs), Johnny Wells (d).

C-3378	Wake Up! Chill'Um, Wake Up!	Voe 1272 Spt S-2254
C-3379	Love Me Or Leave Me (Kahn-Donaldson)	Voe 1272 Spt S-2254

Note:

A: The third vocalists may be either Alex Hill or Johnny Wells-The latter is said to have been a singer before he joined Jimmie Noone's band.

B: C-3378 and 9-Zinky Cohn replaces Hill, Newton omitted.

JIMMIE NOONE AND HIS APEX CLUB ORCHESTRA CHICAGO, JUNE 21, 1929

Jimmie Noone (cl), Joe Poston (alt), Zinky Cohn (p) probably Junie Cobb (bjo), Bill Newton (bbs), Johnny Wells (d).

C-3683   Anything You Want   Voe 15823

Note:

A: The above title is actually St. Louis Blues, a fact which may account for the company's rejecting the recording of the current title (cf February 26, 1929). There is no composer credit for Anything You Want on the label.

JJMMIE NOONE'S APEX CLUB ORCHESTRA CHICAGO, JUNE 24, 1929

Jimmie Noone (cl), Kid Ory (tr), George Mitchell (cnt), 'Little Mitch' George Mitchell (cnt).

C-3710	Someone's Falling In Love	Voe Rejected
C-3711	Serenading The Moon	Voe Rejected

JIMMIE NOONE AND ms APEX CLUB ORCHESTRA CHICAGO, JULY 11, 1929

C-3844	Birmingham Bertha (Clarke-Akst)	Voe 1296
C-3845	Am I Blue? (Clarke-Akst)	Voe 1296
C-3848-A	*My Daddy Rocks Me* (With One Steady Roll)	BR 7096 BR4966 BRA 500196 MU-31024 BRS 1008 Spt S-2232 Voe v. 1001 A-500196 DECCA BM 31024 DEC MG-36265
C-3849-A	Apex Blues	BR 7096, Br 4966 BRA500196 Voe 2777 BRS 1008

Note:

A: Label of Voe 1296, reads May Alex. Voe 2779 as Jimmie Noone And Orchestra.

B: Brunswick's 7096, 4986, as The Club Ambassadors. Br A 500196 as Jimmie Noone and his Club Ambassadors. BR 4966 is a Canadian, 500196 a French issue.

C: BR 7096 is the original issue, Voe 2779 was reissued as late as 1934, and is thus the first reissue.

Jimmie Noone And His Apex Club Orchestra cmCAG0, JULY 18, 1929

Jimmie Noone (cl), Prestonn Jackson (tb), possibly Joe Poston (alt), Zinky Cohn (p), Wilbur Gorham (bjo), *Bill* Newton (bbs), unknown (d) May Alix (vi).

C-3898	Ain't Mis Behavin' (Razaf-Waller-Brooks)	Voe 15819
C-3899	That Rhythm Man (Razaf-Waller-Brooks)	Voe 15823
C-3900	Off Time (Razaf-Waller-Brooks)	Voe 15819

Note:

A: The drummer is probably not Johnny Wells. Voe 15819 and 15823 reads Mae Alix.

JJMMIE NO0NE'S APEX CLUB ORCHESTRA cmCAG0, SEPTEMBER 24, 1929

Jimmie Noone (cl), Joe Poston (cl, alt), Zinky Cohn (p), Wilbur Gorham (gtr), Bill Newton (bbs), Johnny Wells (d), Elmo Tanner (vi).

C-4397	S'Posin' (Razaf-Denniker)	Voe 1415
C-4398	True Blue Lou (Coslow-Robin-Whiting)	Voe 1415

JIMMIE NOONE'S APEX CLUB ORCHESTRA CffiCAGO, SEPTEMBER 26, 1929

Jimmie Noone (cl), Joe Poston (alt), Zin.Icy Cohn (p), Wilbur Gorham (gtr), Bill Newton (bbs), Johnny Wells (d), Elmo Tanner (vi).

10	Through: (How Can You Say We're Through?) (McCarthy-Monaco)	Voe 1416
C-4618	Satisfied (Caesar-Friend)	Voe 1416

JIMMIE NOONE'S APEX CLUB ORCHESTRA CHICAGO, OCTOBER 15, 1929

Jimmie Noone (cit), Joe Poston (alt), Zinky Cohn (p), Wilbur Gorham (gtr), Bill Newton (bbs), Johnny Wells (d), Helen Savage (vi).

C-4647	I'm Doing What I'm Doing For Love (Yollen-Ager)	Voe 1436
C-4648	He's A Good Man To Have Around (Yolien-Ager)	Voe 1436

THE SAVANNAH SYNCOPATORS CHICAGO, OCTOBER 21, 1929

Jimmie Noone (cit), Joe Poston (alt), Zinky Cohn (p), Wilbur Gorham (gtr), Bill Newton (bbs), Johnny Wells (d), Helen Savage (vi).

C-4687	My Melancholy Baby (Norton-Burnett)	Br 7124, Br 1086
C-4688	After You've Gone (Creamer-Layton)	Br 7124, Br 1086

JIMMIE'S BLUE MELODY BOYS CHICAGO, OCTOBER 25, 1929

Jimmie Noone (cit), Joe Poston (alt), Zinky Cohn (p), Wilbur Gorham (gtr), Bill Newton (bbs), Johnny Wells (d), Elmo Tanner (vl).

C-4692-3	Love Me	Voe Rejected
C-4694	Love	Voe Rejected
C-4695	Song Of The Sands	Voe Rejected
C-4725-B	Love (Goulding-Janis)	Voe 1439
C-4726-B	Love Me	Voe 1439

JIMMIE NOONE'S APEX CLUB ORCHESTRA CHICAGO, FEBRUARY 3, 1930

Jimmie Noone (cl), Joe Poston (alt), Zinky Cohn (p), Wilbur Gorham (bjo), Bill Newton (bbs), Johnny Wells (d).

C-5358	El Rado Scuffle (Rose)	Voe 1490
C-5359	Deep Trouble (Rose)	Voe 1490

Note:

A: Wilbur Gorham on banjo and guitar, replaces Cobb.

JIMMIE NOONE'S APEX CLUB ORCHESTRA CHICAGO, FEBRUARY 6, 1930

Jimmie Noone (cl), Joe Poston (alt), Zinky Cohn (p), Wilbur Gorham (g), Bill Newton (bbs), Johnny Wells (d), Elmo Tanner (vi).

C-5370	Cryin' For The Carolines (Young-Warren)	Voe 1466
C-5371	Have *A* Little Faith In Me (Young-Warren)	Voe 1466

CHICAGO, FEBRUARY 18, 1930

C-5521	Should I?	Voe 1471
C-5522	I'm Following You	Voe 1471

JIMMIE NOONE'S APEX CLUB ORCHESTRA CHICAGO, MAY 16, 1930

Jimmie Noone (cl), Eddie Pollack (alt), Zinky Cohn (p), Wilbur Gorham (g, bjo), Bill Newton (bbs), Johnny Wells (d), Georgia White (vi).

C-5754	When You're Smiling (The Whole World Smiles With You) (Fisher-Goodwin-Shay)	Voe 1497
C-5755	I Lost My Gal From Memphis (Tobias-De Rose)	Voe 1497

Note:

A: Eddie Pollack-cl-as-bar-v-replaces Poston. Georgia White on vocals added.

CHICAGO, MAY 28, 1930.

C-5766	On Revival Day (Raza£)	Voe 1506, Spt S-2233
C-5767	I'm Drifting Back To Dreamland	Voe 1506, Spt S-2233

JIMMIE NOONE'S APEX CLUB ORCHESTRA CHICAGO, JULY 1, 1930

Jimmie Noone (cl), Eddie Pollack (alt, cl), Zin.Icy Cohn (p), Wilbur Gorham (bjo), Bill Newton (bbs), Johnny Wells (d), Elmo Tanner (vi).

C-5900	Virginia Lee	Voe 1518
C-5901-2	So Sweet (Gillespie-Kanter-Shawn)	Voe 1518
C-5903-A	San (McPhail-Michels)	Voe Test (Swaggie JCS-33786) (LP)
C-5903-B	San	Voe Test (Ace Of Hearts AH 84)

JIMMIE NOONE'S APEX CLUB ORCHESTRA CHICAGO, JULY 29, 1930

Jimmie Noone (cl, vl), Eddie Pollack (alt, vi), Zinky Cohn (p), Wilbur Gorham (g), Bill Newton (bbs), Johnny Wells (d).

C-5950-A	You Rascal You (Theard)	Voe 1584
C-5951-A	Bring It On Home To Your Grandma (Theard)	Voe 1584

CHICAGO, AUGUST 23, 1930

C-6107	Little White Lies	Voc 1531
C-6108	Moonlight On The Colorado	Voe 1531

JIMMIE NOONE'S APEX CLUB ORCHESTRA CHICAGO, OCTOBER 30, 1930

Jimmie Noone (cl), Eddie Pollack (alt), Zinky Cohn (p), Wilbur Gorham (bjo), Bill Newton (bbs), Johnny Wells (d), May Alix (vi).

C-6465	Something To Remember You By (Dietz-Schwartz)	Voe 1554
C-6466	Three Little Words (Kalmar-Ruby)	Voe 1554

Note:

A: The above label reads Mae Alix.

JIMMIE NOONE'S APEX CLUB ORCHESTRA CHICAGO, JANUARY 12, 1931

Jimmie Noone, Eddie Pollack (els), Zinky Cohn (p), Wilbur Gorham (g), Bill Newton (bbs), Johnny Wells (d), Mildred Bailey (vi).

C-7300	He's NotWorth Your (Dixon-Rose-Warren)	Voe 1580
C-7301	Trav'lin' All Alone (Johnson)	Voe 1580

JIMMIE NOONE AND HIS ORCHESTRA CHICAGO, JULY 27, 1931

Jimmie Noone (cl), Eddie Pollack (alt), Earl Hines (p), Quinn Wilson (sbs), Benny Washington (d), A Jarrett (vi).

C-7913-A	I Need Lovin' (Creamer-Johnson)	Br 6174, 1234, A 9134
C-7914-A	It's You! (Razaf-Waller)	Br 6192, A 9135
C-7915-A	River, Stay 'Way From My Door (Dixon-Woods)	Br 6192, A 9135
C-7916-A	When It's Sleepy Time Time Down South (L. Rene-O. Rene-Muse)	Br 6174, 1234, A9134

JIMMY NOONE AND ms ORCHESTRA CHICAGO, DECEMBER 15, 1933

Jimmie Noone (cl), Eddie Pollack (bar, alt, vi) Clarence Browning (p), Quinn Wilson (sbs), Benny Washington (d).

C-686-1	Dixie Lee (Alexander Hill)	Voe 2620, EB W 99, Decca F 3904, JSo AA324
C-687-1	Inka Dinka Doo (Durante-Ryan)	Voe 2619, Decca F 3904
C-688-1	Delta Bound (Alexander Hill)	Voe 2620, Jso AA 524
C-689-1	Like Me A Little Bit Bit Less (Love Me A Little Bit More) (Adamson-Lane)	Voe 2619

JIMMIE NOONE AND HIS ORCHESTRA CHICAGO, NOVEMBER 23, 1934

Jimmie Cobb (tpt), Jimmie Noone (cl), Eddie Pollack (alt), Clarence Browning (p), John Beasley (g), possibly John Lindsay (sbs), Benny Washington (d).

C-858-A	A Porter's Love Song (To A Chambermaid) (Johnson-Razaf)	Voe 2888, Br 500513
C-859-A	I'd Do Anything For You (Hopkins-Hill-Williams)	Voe 2862, Br 500513
C-860-A	Shine (All The Clouds II) (Mack-Brown-Dabney)	Voe 2888, Br A 500514
C-861-A	Lisa (Gus Kahn-Ira Gershwin-Geo Gershwin)	Voe 2862, Br A 500514

Note:

A: Br 50013 and A 50014 as Jimmie Noone and his Club Ambassadors.

B: Jimmy Cobb (t) added. John Lindsay (sb) replaced Wilson.

JIMMY NOONE AND HIS ORCHESTRA CHICAGO, FEBRUARY 21, 1935

Jimmie Noone (cl), Jimmy Cobb (tpt), Eddie Pollack (alt), Clarence Browning (p), John Henley (g), John Lindsay (sbs), Benny Washington (d).

C-903-B	Soon There'll Just Be Two Of Us (Hart-Rodgers)	Voe 2907, Pan 25720
C-904-A	Lullaby Of Broadway	Voe 2908, Pan 25749
C-905-A	Lockie, Lockie, Lookie Here Comes Cookie (Mack Gordon)	Voe 2908, Pan 25763
C-906-A	It's Easy To Remember (Hart-Rodgers)	Voe 2907, Pan 25720

JIMMIE NOONE AND ms NEW ORLEANS BAND CHICAGO, JANUARY 15, 1936

Jimmie Noone (cl), Guy Kelly (t, vl), Preston Jackson (tb), Frances Whitby (ts), Gideon Honore (p), Israel Crosby (sb) Tubby Hall (d).

90575-A	He's The Different Type Of Guy	parR-2303, PZ-1115, Dec 18439 60379, M-30859, Od 286228, OR-2303 Dec 33061
90576-A	Way Down Yonder In New Orleans (Creamer, Layton)	parR-2281, A-7296, Dec 18440 60380, Od 286229, A-2329
90577-A	The Blues Jumped A Rabbit	parR-2303, A-6739 PZ-1115, Dec 18439 60379, N-30859, Od 286228, OR-2303
90578-A	Sweet Georgia Brown (Bernie, Pinkard, Casey)	parR-2281, A-7296, Dec 18440 60380, Od 286229, A-2329

A: Decca 30859 is a Swiss, Odeon Swing A.2329 an Italian, and Odeon Or 2281, 2303 are Dutch issues. Parlophones A 6739, A 7296 are Australian issues. The reverse of Par A 6793 is by Red Norvo.

JIMMIE NOONE AND HIS ORCHESTRA NEW YORK, DECEMBER 1, 1937

Jimmie Noone (cl), Charlie Shavers (t), Pete Brown (as), Frank Smith (p), Teddy Bunn (g), Wellman Bruad (sb), O'Neil Spencer (d, vl), Teddy Simmons (vi).

62830-A	Sweet Lorraine (Mitchell Parish)	Dec 7553, Voe S-216 Swa 1226, B58046
62831-A	I Know That You Know (Vincent Youmans-Ann Caldwell)	
Swa 1226		B58046
62832-A	Bump It (The Bumps) (Jimmy Noone-J. Mayo Williams)	Dec 1584, 3863, 60457, 60524,-- Voe S-216
62833-A	Four or Five Times (Marco H. Hellman-Bryon Gay)	Dec 1584, 3519, 60336, M-30398, Voe S-209, Br 03303
62834-A	Hell In My Heart (Noone-Williams)	Dec 7553
62835-B	Call Me Darling, Call Me Sweetheart, Call Me Dear	Dec 1730, Od 286359
62836-A	I'm Walking This Town (Teddy Bunn)	Dec 1730 Od 286359
62837-A	Japansy (John Klenner-Afred Bryan)	Dec 1621

Note:

A: Some copies of Brunswick 03303 use a dubbed master from 62832-A.

JIMMY NOONE AND ms ORCHESTRA CHICAGO, JUNE 5, 1940

Jimmy Noone (cl), Natty Dominique, Preston Jackson (tbs), Richard M. Jones (p), Lonnie Johnson (gt), John Lindsay (sbs), Tubby Hall (d).

93030-A	New Orleans Hop Scop Blues	Dec 18095, 25104, 60335, M-30315, Br 03169, A-82725 Swa 1226, Swa 75, De8283, 18039
93031-A	Keystone Blues	Dec 18095, 25104, 60335, M-30315, Br 03169, A-82725, Swa1226, Swa 75, De8283, 10087

Note:

A: Br 82725 (German) as Jimmie Noone U.S. Orchester.

JIMMIE NOONE TRIO
CHICAGO, DECEMBER 11, 1940

Jimmy Noone (cl), Gideon Honore (p), John Simmons (sbs), Henry Fort (despite the labels)-sb/Ed Thompson (v).

053725-1 Qu 014	Moody Melody	BB B-8609, R7127
033726-1	Then You're Drunk (Ed Thompson)	BB B-8649, R7127 IA 18
033727-1	I'm Going Home (Joe McCoy)	BB B-8649, R7127 IA 18
053728-1	They Got My Number Now (Joe McCoy)	BB B-8609, R7127 Qu 014

JIMMIE NOONE QUARTER
YES YES CLUB, CHICAGO, JULY 17, 1941

Jimmie Noone (cl), Frank Smith (p), John Frazier (sb), Wallace Bishop (d).

Sweet Lorraine	Swaggie S-1210, Forsgate WOP-69-0
A Porter's Love Song, To A Chamberm (Razaf-Johnson)	Swaggie S-1210aid Forsgate WOP-69-0
Goodbye, Don't (Jimmie Noone)	CrySwaggie S-1210, Forsgate WOP-69-0
Blues For Roy	Swaggie S-1210, Forsgate WOP-69-0
Lady Be Good (Gershwin)	Swaggie S-1210, Forsgate WOP-69-0
Memories Of You (Blake-Razaf)	Swaggie S-1210, Forsgate WOP-69-0
Honeysuckle Rose (Waller-Razaf)	Swaggie S-1210, Forsgate WOP-69-0
Body And Soul (Sour-Heyman-Eyton-Green)	Swaggie S-1226 <LP Forsgate WOP-69-0

Note:

A: The above seven titles and the theme of Sweet Lorraine were privately recorded by John Steiner at the Yes Yes Club, Chicago. These are not professional recordings.

<u>THE CAPITOL JAZZMEN</u> HOLLYWOOD, NOVEMBER 16, 1943

Jimmie Noone (cl), Billy May (tp), Jack Teagarden (tbn, vi), Dave Matthews (ten), Joe Sullivan (p), Dave Barbour (gt), Art Shaphiro (sbs), Zutty Singleton (d).

104-A	Clambake In B-Flat (Joe Sullivan)	Capitol 10009, Telefunken Capitol C 80089, Capitol 20738
105-A	Casanova's Lament (Dick Larkin)	Capitol 10010, Telefunken Capitol A 10010 C, Capitol 20738
106-A	Solitude (Ellington-De Lange- Mills)	Capitol 10010, Telefunken Capitol A10010 C, Capitol 20738
107-A	I'm Sorry I Made You Cry (N.J. Clesi)	Capitol 10000, Telefunken Capitol C 80089, Capitol 20738

Note:

A: Telefunken Capitol are German issue, band title as: DIE CAPITOL JAZZMEN.

KID ORY'S CREOLE JAZZ BAND HOLLYWOOD, MARCH 15, 1944

Kid Ory (tbn), Mutt Carey (cnt), Jimmie Noone (cl), Buster Wilson (p), Bud Scott (g), Ed Garland (sbs), Zutty Singleton (d).

| High Society (Williams Steele) | Carousel 2501, Jazz Record Society AA 105, Jazz Collector NI |

Note:

A: Jrs AA 105 has JRS 0034 in wax, issued as by Jimmy Noone And His Orchestra.

KID ORY'S CREOLE JAZZ BAND HOLLYWOOD, MARCH 22, 1944

Mutt Carey (cnt), Kid Ory (tbn), Jimmie Noone (cl), Buster Wilson (p), Bud Scott (gtr), Ed Garland (sbs), Zutty Singleton (d).

| Muskrat Ramble (Kid Ory) | Jazz Record Society AA 105 |
| Sugar Foot Stomp | Orsen Welles, Radio Broadcast |

Note:

A: The above has JRS 0003 in wax, issued as by Jimmy Noone And His Orchestra.

KID ORY'S CREOLE JAZZ BAND HOLLYWOOD, APRIL 12, 1944

Mutt Carey (cnt), Kid Ory (tbn), Jimmie Noone (cl), Buster Wilson (p), Bud Scott (gtr), Ed Garland (sbs), Zutty Singleton (d).

| Panama Rag (Armand Piron) | Jazz Society AA 558, Jazz Collector N 1 |

Note:

A: JS AA 558 has SOF 1529 in wax. The reverse has Mutt's Blues, and despite the label, the clarinet is not J. Noone.

B: All the above titles under *Kid* Ory's name are broadcasts by Orsen Welles.

Epilogue 1991

It was Jimmy's last performance at the U.S. Grant Hotel, the room was filled to capacity. The New Orleans Good Times Society and Marching Band was present along with its singer Rosie Tatum. An example of the songs played that night were as follows: IT'S TIGHT LIKE THAT, LET'S SOW A WILD OAT, FOUR OR FIVE TIMES, RHYTHM MAN, SLEEPY TIME DOWN SOUTH, YOU RASCAL YOU, APEX BLUES, and SWEET LORRAINE. It was at the end of March 1991.

The similarity between Jimmie Noone Sr. and Jimmy Noone, Jr's clarinet playing is indeed Close. The resemblance can be compared on the song Sweet Lorraine. Jimmy Jr. learned the trill quite well at six years old from his father, and it still burst through out this song.

I can remember when Jimmy was a teenager playing music with my brother Teddy, that when he played Sweet Lorraine, then he played it from knowing the notes and from rehearsals over the years. Now—decades later, he played with the "New Orleans Style," as if it were embedded within him.

Jimmy proved to me and the audience that night, that he was a "master clarinet player." He captured the attention of the audience with his New Orleans style playing of the high register, and then being able to sweep into the low register, and play back and forth in both registers, precisely like his father did almost on every song.

The composing and writing that Jimmy wrote for his band, was done with expertise. Jimmy had taken music that had been written in the 1920's and translated that music into something that the public could understand in 1991. While at the same time preserve the originality and basic composition of the songs.

This Saturday evening was the last public performance that Jimmy Noone played at, but it was also his best. Along with the bands best playing and Rosie's best singing. This was the night that Rosie did not need a clarinet backing her up in the background, she was on her own, and proved her singing capabilities.

After the two sets were over, Jimmy told me "that he was going home as he felt tired." I asked him, "if he wanted me to come along, as he had not driven into town alone, since he started having eye problems." He told me, "I'll be fine." But being a woman with intuition, I knew what he really meant was, "I'm sick and I have to get home immediately."

When Jimmy arrived home, he did call me and told me that he had arrived safe, and for me not to worry. We talked about our upcoming trip we had planned to New Orleans. I told him that the travel agent left a message to come over and pick up our tickets, this we had planned to get married the same week of the jazz festival. We then planned to see each other on Wednesday.

On Wednesday night I told Jimmy when I arrived, "I'll have to go home tomorrow morning early, as my daughter Leslie is coming back home with her husband now that he is back from Saudi Arabia."

This was the last evening that me and Jimmy had together. We both appeared to feel very well, with no health problems whatsoever. We talked about needing a vacation, while visiting New Orleans, and all the Creole food that we would eat.

It was a happy and enjoyable evening, I told Jimmy how "sexy I thought he looked when he played the saxophone," so he got out his sax, put on one of our favorite records, BODY AND SOUL, by Dexter Gordon, and he played along with him. Then he played his cassette tape of CECILE and sang along with the music. When I mentioned how beautiful the song was, he said, "It's as beautiful as you are."

We went to sleep that night, while I lay on his chest, listening to his heart beating. He kissed me goodnight, and the next morning I went home, while he went to work.

This was the last time that I had seen Jimmy waving goodbye to me. As I left that morning, I thought how well he seemed to be, and he was not having any stomach disorders at all.

It was April 27, 1991, when I drove into the city of La Jolla, California, The day was typical for San Diego, so I had the sunroof open on my Nissan Pulsar, and I was driving from Southeast San Diego to see Jimmy Noone, Jr.

We had been dating since 1988, for a total of three years, and just rece4ntly decided he had to stop the long compute expense and time being in heavy traffic for hours. Then we both agreed that moving to La Jolla for him to work would save money, time, and gas. We used Wednesdays as our date night, so he did not schedule any gigs or even a rehearsal on our day. Sometimes we had a weekend night to do things together.

Jimmy had rented a duplex, yet he called it a house. It was located at 729 Draper Street, La Jolla. The bedroom was also used as a living room, and there was a small kitchen and bath. Walking around the entire area only took not even five minutes.

I had his key and entered his place. There was a note taped to the refrigerator door. It read, "Cecile, we got a whole night alone, take this money and go to the liquor store and get a nice bottle of champagne or cognac. If you want to take a hot bath, I got you some bubble bath stuff in the bathroom."

After getting some champagne and chilling it, I placed a jazz album on his stereo, ran some hot water into the tub and submerged myself into bubbles. Almost in a sleep mode, I heard Jimmy's key in the door, and then he yelled loudly, "Precious (one of my nicknames,) where are you?" I replied, "In the tub, I'm getting out." Grabbing a towel, and before I could get all the way out of the tub, he walked inn, grabbed me, and started hugging me. (Jimmy was a hugger.) Then we kissed for what seemed like forever, he then looked at me smiling and said, "You are the most beautiful woman I've ever had the pleasure of asking to go to bed with me. Did you know that" I took a good look at jimmy as he walked further into the room. He was cute in a funny kind of way, because he was almost short, had wild black-graying curly hair, that always looked scattered, yet his smile outweighed what little else you could say of him. It was also obvious that he had not been out in the sun for a longtime, as his skin color was completely white. He also looked white. He was unique. He was different, that is what I liked about him.

Later, after love making, I rested my head on Jimmy's hairy chest, (yes, he was very hairy,) then he asked me, "What jazz album did you play?" (This was our game trying to outguess the identify of jazz artist's.) I replied, "That the great DEXTER GORDON, and his quartet. The name of the album is Manhattan Symphonie." He replied, "You're correct."

Jimmy then said, "Now let us talk about your book, and my music. How are you coming along with your book, "Apex Blues"? Are we both dealing with our creatively and artistically properly? You realize that people like us, need to control that aspect of our lives."

I replied, "The book is near completion; however, we need to talk about the ending and what we'll add." Jimmy smiled, then said, "The ending is the best part for both of us, especially since I now have my band."

I added, "You are the best . I can talk to you about it because you understand. Damn, I love you."

Jimmy got up and started putting on clothes, while talking, "Let's get dressed, and walk down the street and get some Chinese food, then we'll talk more." I stated, "Only if you promise not to eat so much this time. You have got to start eating right because I worry about you."

The next morning, Thursday, I left Jimmy's home, while he went to work. We did not get much sleep that night because Jimmy was terribly sick with stomach pains. I knew it was not the Chinese food since I felt o.k., but that it might be the amount of food he ate. He had ordered his favorite: Egg Foo Young, Wonton's, and Shrimp Chow Mein.

Later that day, I left a message on Jimmy's tape recorder that said, "Jimmy I got a letter from Franz Jackson, and he is going to give me some quotes for my book, Apex Blues, regarding your father's music playing during the late thirty's.

"That night, when 9:00 P.M. arrived and Jimmy had not called me, I began to worry, especially since he was feeling sick when he went to work, but I could not talk him into calling in sick that morning."

About 10:00 P.M., Jimmy called me, and he told me very calmly, "A co-worker had taken him to Scripps Hospital in La Jolla, because he had gotten real sick at work, and that he had been admitted into the hospital immediately that same day."

I shuddered with the thought of Jimmy being in the hospital, and I also knew the dreadful fright he must be experiencing from the immediate awareness of danger. He hated doctor's and hospital's ever since his father had been taken to one and died.

And then he told me, "Now listen precious, the Doctor say that I have pancreatitis." I became so hysterical that I was yelling, "Jimmy, what in the hell does that mean?"

Very calmly, he told me, "Now, Cecile, calm down. Do you really think that I will let these doctor's make a mistake? Hell no. Would you please drive out to La Jolla tomorrow morning to my place, and get me some toothpaste, underwear, shaving stuff, and bring yourself over to the hospital when you are done. I need to see you really bad. Damn. I need you."

Becoming calm. I guess from his calm voice, I said, "Jimmy, I'm sorry to yell, but goddamn, I think that I'll come out right now and see you, since I know I will worry all night if I don't." He quickly replied, "Stay calm. Get some rest on that bad back and come out tomorrow morning."

I hung up the phone, looked at the clock, and knew it was too late to call Lorraine Noone, (Jimmy's daughter,) as it was almost 11:00 P.M., and this was just to be a simple operation without any complications. Before I went to sleep that night, I prayed for over an hour for Jimmy, then finally I went to sleep.

The next day, before I left home to go to the hospital, I tried to call Lorraine at her apartment, but she did not pick up, and I knew it was too early for her to be at work. She owned the D LA RANS BEAUTY SALON, over on Skyline Drive in Southeast San Diego.

It was about 8:00 A.M., when I drove towards La Jolla. My plan was to go to his apartment, get his toiletries, then visit him before he had surgery. Then I would go to Sant Mary's Catholic Church for Good Friday services which didn't start until noon. But first I just had to see Jimmy and make sure he was doing well.

Walking into his home, the scent of no air, plus a manly sort of musk smell was present. I noticed the quaint scent and sort of wondered why he left all the windows closed, since there is hardly any theft or crime in La Jolla.

Entering the bedroom was like stumbling along an obstacle course, through piles of Postal Worker's work uniforms.

After gathering his requested toiletries, I left never knowing that this would probably be the last time I would walk into his own personal little world and view his private life, with all his musical possessions.

I can still remember placing the key in the dead bolt, but as I was closing the front door, I walked back in to make sure the stereo was shut off, and that is when I noticed dexter Gordon's record. I just had to play "Body and Soul." I felt that in some way I needed to hear it one more time. I needed that sound.

Finally, I was going to leave his place, when I caught a glimpse of viewing Jimmy's nearly completed composed song labeled, "Alphonse's Blues." It was laying on top of his drafting table, right where we had been writing the words to a twelve-bar blues song. (Jimmy thought that after I had written Apex Blues and Alphonse Picou's biography, that I could write both into a screenplay and he would write all the music for it.)

Arriving at Scripps Memorial Hospital in La Jolla, I parked the car, then took the elevator to his hospital room, where I found him in room 717B, laying in a hospital bed. He was moaning loudly in terrible pain. His eyes were closed when I first seen him, then his eyes opened as he became wrenched in violent pain. Yet with the pain, he sensed my presence, and spoke slowly with a soft voice.

"Cecile, baby, I just knew that you would come." H stared at me, while trying to smile, as I bent down to kiss him on the cheek.

I had never seen Jimmy look like he did. He looked like he had a rough night and was feeling like shit. But I never mentioned that, instead, I suggested he use his toiletries, and brush his teeth, and comb his hair.

I took out his hairbrush from the bag and started brushing his hair. I then did what he said he hated the most, I brushed his thinning soft yet curly hair straight back this always bugged him, yet made him smile especially when I would say, "Damn, you look just exactly like your daddy with your hair combed straight back."

But this time when he went to smile, a pain in his stomach made him frown. I became instantly worried. As soon as his pain subsided, he told me, "Let us talk about the ending of your book, 'Apex Blues'."

I told Jimmy, "Jimmy, I think that we should wait until you are feeling better, if that's o.k.?" His voice got louder with excitement as he talked, "HELL NO. it ain't O.K., look Cecile you know time is running out for me, don't you? Remember what that voice in New Orleans said? After my surgery, you will automatically know how to end the book. All I could do is just nod my head, as reality was starting to give me a kick. I knew, I always knew, that I had not had a typical dream, ever since 1989, and time was running out.

I looked up at the blood transfusion bottle dripping into his vein's while another I.V. bottle leaked the morphine straight into his body system. I looked at Jimmy and again our thoughts became one, as he spoke. "They had to give me blood, and I know what your thoughts are about that, especially with aids and things going around. Now be my Cheri and give me a kiss."

After our kiss, the phone rang at Jimmy's bedside. It was his doctor, he told him, "You have been examined, and we've taken x-rays, only to discover that you have a ruptured spleen. A nurse will be preparing you for surgery immediately."

I could hear the phone call as Jimmy was holding it by me. I looked at him then begin praying, "Please help Jimmy dear God, this is getting really touchy." I then bent down towards the bed, and gave him a kiss on his lips, as his arms went over me. Knowing how he loved to be hugged, I held onto him, as I began to feel the urgent rush of fear swelling within me.

A nurse enters the room smiling. She grabbed hold of the high blood instrument equipment while saying, "Time for a blood-pressure check."

I moved away and used the opportunity to use his hospital bed phone, to call his daughter, Lorraine. But the hospital bed phone operator would not give me an outside line, after trying for several minutes. Since the hospital nurse was adjusting his I.V. device, I told Jimmy, "I will be back in a few seconds. I am just going to use the phone in the hall."

Placing twenty cents into the pay phone, I dialed Lorraine's phone number. Then a phone operator came on the line, "That will be thirty cents more please." I had forgotten I was calling out of the area. Getting a connection, I told Lorraine, "This is Cecile. Your father's been admitted into Scripps Memorial Hospital in La Jolla. Jimmy is in acute pain, and his doctor plans on operating on him immediately. He is awake and aware of the surgery, so there's no need for you to close your shop and come all the way out here. I will call you when the operation is over."

Lorraine told me, "I will call Lisa my stepsister, because she works at the hospital in the business office. She can visit you both on her lunch hour, and she can call me if you cannot."

Entering Jimmy's hospital room, he appeared to feel fine, when he mentioned, "Before I go into surgery, remember what I said about the ending of your book, I do not think you should change it from what we both know to be the ending. It will be a good surprise for any jazz reader. The plot ending can also be connected to my father's past and bring it around to my music if we use the great Joe Williams. Now remember he knows me through my father, so he will be the male singer to sing, "Cecile." He will be the one to popularize it, with a wide spectrum of music listeners. No one could sing that beautiful song like him."

Jimmy continued while in pain, "While my composed song hits the Billboard Magazine, what will be called my second band? It should be composed of all Black musicians, no other race. We will be the band that returns to play, "Sweet Lorraine," High Society," "It's Tight Like That," and all the other songs my father made famous. Plus, all the music that we have obtained from Tulane Archives will be played. That music is over sixty years old."

The "Jimmy Noone New Orleans Marching and Good Times Society Band would he composed of San Diego's best Black musicians. We'd have, Chuck Mc Pherson (dms,) Aubrey Faye (tp,vo,) Rosie Tatum (vo,) Daniel Jackson (s,) Oliver Luck (tb,) Winfred Steward (vo,db,) Preston Coleman (db,) and others."

I asked Jimmy, "What if my book was timed to be printed by a publisher, when you presented your new band? It could be your dream come true. Your band would become so popular, that your Motherland would seek you out. Yes, the New Orleans Heritage Jazz Festival would call you up for a return visit."

Jimmy reached for my hand, while severe pains overtook him. He began moaning and twisting in pain, then rolled in the bed. Still holding my hand, he was able to tell me, "Precious take my ring and my watch, and if anything happens to me, give them to your son Chris. And in your book emphasize that me and you-a Noone and a Picou once again had a part in jazz history, along with your brother Teddy Picou. Now, it will be up to another new generation to finish where we left off. Another Picou and Noone."

The nurse came into the room, seen Jimmy in agony and told him, "I am going to administer more morphine into your I.V., as one hour has already passed."

I was no nurse, but hell, I had never even been a volunteer candy striper, but I had been on permanent disability long enough with various pain pills that I knew about morphine every hour would only be given in severe cases. This was becoming really mind-blogging.

I noticed that the nurse had pushed her little intercom button, while relaying the message, "I need some assistance in room 717B immediately."

Jimmy was still moaning in pain, while two additional nurses came in to help. One nurse was trying to adjust the drip for the I.V. that contained the morphine, while the other two nurses were having Jimmy lay flat down in his bed and remain calm.

I told Jimmy, "I think I will go outside for a few minutes, to get some fresh air and to call Lorraine."

He spoke softer than usual and said, "Please Precious stay with me, I need you here. Cecile, oh how I love your name, it is as beautiful as you are."

When he went to move in the bed, I told him, "Remain still sweetheart, then it will not hurt so much."

Quickly he grabbed my hand, while the look on his face said a lot, there was the I love you stare, then a look of absolute terrible excruciating pain.

I noticed the sweat on Jimmy's brow, and how sweaty his hands were as he tried to hold my hand. Then I looked at the digital machines hooked up to him, his blood pressure reading had reached, "Oh No." Then I looked at his pulse rate, and it had surged to one-hundred ninety or higher, and then I yelled, "Jimmy please don't do this! Please don't leave me."

He whispered the words, "I love y..", he didn't finish you. "When I looked at him, his complexion had turned as white as a sheet. Then a nurse screamed very loud, "Code Blue, Code Blue."

All this time I just stood there watching him die. About fifteen nurses and one doctor, on the hospital staff came running into the room. I put my hands over my mouth, but yelled very loud, "Jimmy, oh my God, Jimmy."

I watched emergency procedures being started on Jimmy. There was the pumping of the heart, the orders for a shot from the doctor, along with other measures. I witnessed Jimmy fighting for his life, as he struggled against death.

Some nurses finally noticed that I was still in the room. They politely asked me to leave. I quickly looked at him before walking out of the room, I knew that Jimmy was now leaving me. I wanted to scream at the top of my lungs, "No! No!" yet I kept moving towards the waiting room, while deciding it was a must that I had to call Lorraine immediately.

Looking in my purse for more change, I discovered that I was absent of coins. Therefore, I had to call the operator and call Lorraine collect. I told his daughter, "Lorraine, Jimmy just had a heart attack, and they're trying to revive him, you had better come right out here immediately." She responded, "I still have a customer in the chair with a perm, I will come out as soon as I can finish up. Also, I talked to Lisa, and she will meet you soon. I will see you in a little while."

Waiting in the reception area, the life that me and Jimmy had shared, flashed in my mind. Then I looked up and it was Lisa, (Lorraine's stepsister.) We hugged, then I told her, "I've been waiting for you to arrive. I began to tell her that Jimmy was slipping very fast, and that I had been sent out of the room."

About ten minutes later, a head nurse came out of the room, found me, and stated, "Cecile, the doctor would like to talk to you in his office. Please follow me."

Me and Lisa walked down a hall to the doctor's office, a little past the nurse's workstation. We were asked by the head nurse, "Please have a seat." The doctor walked into the room and sat. I knew something was up since this was Jimmy's attending doctor, and the nurse assigned to Jimmy.

The doctor then told us, "There was nothing that we could do to save him. The patient went into a cardiac arrest, and after twenty-five minutes of emergency procedures, there was no further hope."

I just sat in the chair dumbfounded, unable to move. I suddenly felt like I was having a bad nightmare, or that perhaps I had gone to sleep, and wasn't even aware of it.

I asked myself, "How could Jimmy be dead? How could he possibly of had a cardiac arrest? He did not even have a heart problem that I knew of."

As the doctor continued to talk my mind started playing trick with me, and the doctor continued…"We did all that we could, I am terribly sorry. The hospital staff would like to have a coroner's examination, to determine the correct cause of death."

I remember wondering if I was going crazy. A voice was speaking, "Is there anything that we can do for you?" And then, "Are you alright?"…Then suddenly I came out of some type of trance and replied, "I will be just fine. Yes, I will be just fine!"

I knew that I was crying, and I could sense the presence of Lisa crying also. As I got up to leave, I pinched myself on the arm, just to make sure that this was for real. Because, in less than thirty minutes I was talking to Jimmy and he was alive.

The man that I had loved, and was going to marry soon in New Orleans, had just died, and I felt like maybe I should join him. And then a flash in my brain said, "He told you that this would happen, and you knew it also. The real shocker is that it occurred on Good Friday, the last day anyone would expect death to happen."

The doctor was calling my name, "Ms. Picou, would you like to go into the room and see Mr. Noone?" With red eyes, I looked up and replied, "Yes if I can." The nurse walked me into room 717b, and I just stood there looking when she stated, "We cannot take those tubes out until the corner examines him." Then with a gentle pat on my shoulders, she left me alone with Jimmy.

I could feel uncontrollable hysteria about to overtake me, as I put my hands on his face, which was not even cold yet. I kissed him on the lips. Crying I rested my head on his shoulders…Which I knew was for the last time. I wept laying on him, just like a little baby would do.

Jimmy was gone to be with God, and I was left to be all alone. I knew that I had been with him off and on for most of our lives, but the last three years had been ours and ours alone. What he had accomplished in his lifetime, I had witnessed it all, and now even his death. Laying on his shoulders, all I could think of to tell him, as I held his dead boys was, "You did it your way, yes you sure did."

I waited at the hospital for Lorraine to arrive for over ninety minutes, and then I decided to leave. I felt like I was about to explode with hysteria. Lorraine was to be met by Lisa, who would tell her that Jimmy had died, because I knew mentally that I could not handle that task.

Driving home from La Jolla into the city of National City, I knew that I was in some state of shock, as I cried all the way home. When I put the car in park and got out, I remember picking up a bag of clothes, that the hospital staff had given me, that belonged to Jimmy.

As I turned the key into my home door, the realization came over me that indeed Jimmy had died. The creative venture that we had undertaken in 1988 was now over. The ending of my book would be Jimmy's success, but also his death. Another Picou, or some other sibling could keep jazz alive. Or maybe another generation from the Noone family might be the chosen ones.

My book was almost completed, except for the ending, which now had to be Jimmy's death…Not quite the ending we had planned…But me and Jimmy really knew it would be this way…Jimmy knew and I knew…We had always known ever since we had traveled to New Orleans and I heard a voice speaking to me while I was sleeping.

"Jimmy Noone, Jr. created joy just by being in a room. By adding one of his reed instruments, the recipients of his playing, which filled the room with a sense of awe at his ability to turn a phrase of music into an earful of beauty, invariably drove the people into cheering and applauding following his solos. He was my friend and I treasure his memory."

Jude Hibler – Owner, The Jazz Link magazine (1988-1992)

Chronological Order of Events
for Jimmy Noone Jr.

1958 Jimmy Noone Jr. discharged from Navy. He started working for U.S. Postal Service and worked at night as a jazzman playing the saxophone.

1961 Jimmy's younger brother, John Noone joined the Navy.

1963 Jimmy Noone Jr's daughter born and named Diane Lorrain Noone. Jimmy married his first wife Ruth Johnson and later married Ellen Alabama, no kids from either of these marriages.

That same year Jimmy played at Jazzville, a San Diego nightclub and purchased an organ to change his style of music. He was playing an Albert System Clarinet.

1964 He also began playing music at the Sportsman club in southeast San Diego. The Sportsman Club was purchased by a group of Black San Diego Charges football players, because they did not feel welcomed in white bars. Guest that performed there were: Cannonball Adderley and Little Richard.

That year he opened at the Sportsman Club with his organ, and played saxophone and was band leader. During that time, his hair looked like Albert Einstein, and he played rhythm and blues with a little blues and jazz. He worked there for three years playing four days in a row.

1967 Jimmy's brother married in New York to Bea, and she presented John with a son they named John Raymond. He was born May 24, 1968.

1967 to 1984 Jimmy was an instructor for the San Diego City Schools, working part time and evenings.

1968 his sister, Sylvia Noone, (nicknamed Cookie) married Walter Clark, and they lived in Cincinnati, Ohio.

1968 to 1973 Teddy Picou and Jimmy Jr. composed and wrote five songs and recorded at Studio West, a recording studio located at 50th and Ruffner Street. All arrangements were by Jimmy and lyrics by Teddy.

1968 Jimmy returned from Georgia after a divorce to San Diego and worked at the Sportsman Club and San Diego State University without a degree, but with his expertise he taught jazz history and improvisation.

1980 Jimmy's mother died.1

1980 the song recorded by Jimmy (Logan Avenue Blues) becomes the selection included on the Homegrown Album. Jimmy is rehired at the Post Office in La Jolla full time.

1982 Jimmy played at a Black nightclub called, "The Black Frog," playing alto sax and piano. Jimmy answers an ad in the San Diego Reader newspaper as the Cottonmouth D'Arcy band that needed a clarinet to play in the style of Sidney Bechet or Johnny Dodds, and he gets the job.

1983 Jimmy has a birthday, becoming forty-four years old.

1983 A new band is formed with members being Teddy Picou and Chris Del Villar, a banjo player, they are called, "The Sophisticated Swing Band. They recorded a live jam session that featured the "Cottonmouths D'Arcy's with five songs.#1A.

1983 Jimmy begins the attempt to play New Orleans music in the idiom of his father, and he preferer's using an old buffet clarinet, which is the Boehm System with half the key missing.

1984 Jimmy stops teaching students at San Diego City Schools District as instructor and becomes proficient in Alto, and soprano Sax, clarinet, composer, vocalists, banjo, piano, upright bass, and guitar. Jimmy played an albert-system clarinet with lots of trills, octane, leaps, and other devices his father used.

1984 Jimmy recorded "Do What Ory Says," featuring Hall Smith's Creole Sunshine Orchestra on April 21st, at Pasadena City College Harbeson Hall, Pasadena, California. A total of thirteen songs and the album was produced by Stomp Off Records #S.O.S. 1078.

1985 Jimmy notified by John R.T. Davies, leader of the Rhythmic Five and Six, that on June 20, he was selected to record for Stomp Off Records in Burnham Bucks England, for a recreation of Kid Ory's Band of 1944, with Stomp Off Records #S.O.S. 1121.

1987 Jimmy became a member of the JIMMY AND JEANNIE CHEATHAM SWEET BABY BLUES BAND. He toured Europe where they played in Japan at a jazz concert. In September of that year the Cheatham's played a two-day attendance of 18,000 fans at the San Francisco Blues Festival. The Cheatham's had just released their newest album "Homeward Bound," with guest saxophonist Cleanhead Vison.#3
Jimmy now lives in his deceased mother's home in Southeast San Diego, after legal arrangements are made with his siblings. Jimmy transferred to the Post Office in La Jolla, California that was located on 11th and Wall Street.

1988 in the summer Jimmy performs with the Sweet Baby Blues Band at the tenth annual Playboy Jazz Festival in Long Beach. In the recording studio that Jimmy has set up he composes and writes to a song called "Cecile." Along with that composition he proposes marriage to Cecile. They talk marriage and decide on a date in 1991. The song had sort of a medium Bossa Nova beat combined with a New Orleans style. Jimmy wanted this song to be his theme song for his new bank, sort of what Sweet Lorraine was to his father.#4

1988 Jimmy records seven songs in his recording studio onto a tape to market and solicit for him to make an album. He calls it a "self-contained orchestra," as it features him playing the clarinet, flute, soprano, alto, tenor, and baritone saxophones, electric bass, drums, banjo, and keyboards.#5

1988 in July Jimmy meets with Dr. Oliver W. Luck, a trombonist who played with Duke Ellington, Louis Bellson, Cab Calloway, and himself. He met with Jim Merod who attended Princeton, Stanford, and taught at Cornell University. He also writes for the Jazz Works column and the San Diego Voice and Viewpoint Newspaper and the Jazz Link Newspaper.#6

1988 in the summer the author (Cecile,) has decided to write the biography of Jimmie Noone Sr. (Jimmy's father). The arrangement that was made with Jimmy that he would form a New Orleans Band. We agreed to complete this task with three years, (1991.)

1988 Jimmy played saxophone at the Bella Via, and Jim Merod recorded five sets of music.

1988 in August Jimmy was requested by Fro Brigham (a local musician) to assist in a salute to jazzman Leon Petties (who he went to school with). The money raised was to help Leon with his medical bills from arthritis and emphysema. At the Oasis Club on 3184 Market Street, San Diego. This fund raiser opened our eyes to a musician's life that had no insurance. Leon Pettis passed away several months later. #8

1988 in September, Jeannie and Jimmy Cheatham and their Sweet Baby Blues Band performed at the Monterey Jazz Concert, this band was progressing into a blues group.

1988 in December, Jimmy met with Stanley and Helen Dance and I interviewed him as a writer to compose an article on him.

1988 Jimmy at Christmas time was swamped with gigs for the holidays while playing music with the Cheatham's.

1988 December 31, for new year's eve, the Cheatham's were booked to play on a Princess Cruise that circled around Long Beach Bay. Their gig was scheduled at 8:00P.M. and at 10:00P.M, the crowd was amazing.

1989 on January 1st, Jude Hibler called from the Jazz Link magazine and said that the article that I wrote on Stanley Dance was now in print, along with the interview from a phone call I did on musician Spike Robinson, who was due to play at the Loft in San Diego. These two articles made Jimmy proud of my writing accomplishments.

1989 Jimmy lost twenty pounds, moved into Cecile's home, finds a renter for his home, has a haircut after six months, and lost his wild hair look.

1989 We spent time with David Crowne and his wife at their home. He worked at the University of California, San Diego, and he became interested in me drafting a book on Jimmy's father. He was also in charge of the literature department at the university, and never asked me about my writing abilities.

1989 When Jimmy moved into my home, my den became a music room. Jimmy had numerous instruments. He owned an upright piano, four saxophones, two clarinets, a banjo, a guitar, a portable piano, and hundreds of cassette tapes.

1989 In February the Cheatham's played at the San Diego Jazz Festivals Jazz Outreach Program. It was a free jazz concert during Black history month in Southeast San Diego and was at the Educational Cultural Complex. They had two performances on 2-18-89, at 8: 00P.M and 10:00P.M., it was a jazz and blues-soul show. The band has just performed at the Blue Note in New York City, and at the Monterey Jazz Festival.

1989 in April, the article I had written on Stanley Dance came out in print, Jimmy was excited about it. Jimmy makes plans to travel to New Orleans trip.

1989 in May, a celebration of the Jazz Link's one year anniversary was held at the Horton Grand Hotel at 31 Island Street, it was called, "Links to Jazz Celebration." Many musicians attended.

1989 the Cheatham's new recorded album was released entitled Jimmy and Jeannie Cheatham and The Sweet Baby Blues Band recorded, "Back To The Neighborhood." #9

1989 A performance for the Cheatham Band at the Seattle Jazz Festival/Gig Harbor Festival, in Seattle, Washington.

1989 on May 7th, Jimmy played at the Jazz Mine to play with other musicians. The Mine was an exceedingly small record shop, where not more than twenty people could cram into. It was requested for Jimmy to play first When The Saints Come Marching In.

1989 on April, me and Jimmy met his daughter Lorraine Noone, at the San Diego International Airport, to fly to New Orleans. This was the trip that me and Jimmy had planned for over the past year. His brother John was to arrive earlier, and he was to get a rental car and pick us up at the New Orleans airport.

1989 Jimmy had earlier called Pete Fountain and had arranged to join him on stage in New Orleans. But, when he went backstage, he was not allowed to join the band, and there was no explanation for that incident.

1989 John and Jimmy visited their grandmother's old neighborhood where they had lived for several years. The section of Carrollton Street and St. Charles Avenue, then we indulged in our favorite Creole snack, Café Au Lait, and beignets, (a little square doughnut.)

1989 in June the Jazz Link Newspaper featured a five-page story of Jimmy that had been written by Stanley Dance and it was reprinted with permission of the editor, Jazz Journal International, London. It was entitled Jimmy Noone- a well-kept San Diego Secret. Stanley had authored the complete story of Jimmy's life in the article. It was volume 11, issued # 15.

1989 in September, Jimmy received mail from Tulane University/Hogan Jazz Archive/ Howard-Tilton Memorial Library. They sent requested files on Jimmie Noone, Sr., and Alphonsc Picou. The curator at Tulane was Mr. Bruce B. Raeburn and with Alma D. Williams, Associate Curator of Graphics, they provided information requested.

1989 The author sent a promotional package which was a tape that was recorded with John R.T. Davies in Europe, and sent to the New Orleans Jazz

Society, headquarters for the New Orleans Jazz festival to Doretha (Dodie) Simmons. She called and said she would let Bill Russell borrow the tape.

1989 Dodie and Bill reviewed the tape and invited the Cheatham Band to play at the New Orleans Jazz Festival. When Jimmy found this out, he became extremely excited.

1990 in March, Jimmy was notified that he had been selected for a gig scheduled for March 10th, as a salute to Charlie Parker, presented by the San Diego Jazz Society. The billing in the newspaper read: "A salute to the Masters, featuring Down Beat Poll winner, Nick Brignola,(jazz baritone saxophonist) and Frank Strazzeri, (jazz pianist) and special added attraction, Jimmy Noone." At the San Diego Convention Center. After the performance, Jimmy remarked, "that he was proud of his performance, and that Nick and Frank were excellent performers."

1990 on March 11th I showed him my airplane ticket to return to New Orleans. He knew that I was to meet with Bill Russell, plus we found out that our good friends David and Georgia Crowe would be meeting us days later in New Orleans. I was to leave three days before him. Later, Jimmy told me he was losing his vision in his left eye-his only good eye, as his right eye was plastic and only served a cosmetic appearance.

1990 This was the year for the Cheatham's to perform in one of the most popular jazz festivals. The New Orleans Jazz and Heritage Festival was to run for two weekends. Taking place on the grass infield of America's oldest and possibly most picturesque horse racing track. It was scheduled for Friday, Saturday, and Sunday, April 27,28, and 29th, and on Friday, Saturday, and Sunday, May 4, 5, and sixth.

1990 on April 23rd the day before I was to go to New Orleans, I received a letter from George Buck, and he gave me a list of six names of people to connect with that had connections with jazz in his city and their phone numbers.

1990 Jimmy asked me to marry him on the specific date of May 1,1991 in New Orleans, we finally decided to sign a marriage agreement to protect both his daughter's inheritance and my children's.

1990 David Crowne and Jimmy started planning on the research information they wanted from Tulane regarding Jimmie Noone, Sr.

1990 Jimmy had high-blood problems that he checked daily, which probably came from stress on his job, plus he had gained more weight. It became obvious that he should have become a full-time musician, and not working at the Post Office. He was naturally musically talented.

1990 on April 24th, Jimmy drove me to the airport in his red Camaro. I was worried if we might make it, as his car had caught on fire three times, since I had first started dating him. After arriving in New Orleans and checking into the hotel, I called Jimmy's brother John, and together we scheduled our research on his and Jimmy's father.

1990 After starting our research and driving to what used to be Storyville-across Iberville on our left, was a sign in the middle of the divider, which read: "New Orleans famous district, where famous musician Jimmie Noone played."

1990 We drove to what used to be Picou's bar, which was located on 2441 London, then to what used to be the home that Alphonse Picou lived in, located at 1624 St. Peter Street, then seen the home Jimmie Noone, Sr. lived in.

1990 with John driving we visited the Palm Court Jazz Café and Records Center, looking for George Buck. A girl working there asked me when Jimmy would be in town, and we replied on Thursday evening. She suggested we return on Friday night, so he could meet Danny Barker. She also suggested that Jimmy bring his clarinet with him, so he might possibly sit in with Danny.2

1990 Me and Job went to meet Bill Russell (or the Guru, he is called,) a somewhat fragile man appeared at the door. I introduced myself, and when he allowed us to enter his apartment, it had the appearance of a jazz library-plus a used music store. Against every wall and floor space available were boxes and boxes, marked from A to Z. The first box I seen was marked "Armstrong, Louis." That followed down to Lester Young.

1990 Along a far wall in a room that might have been a living room in Bill Russel's home, laid a banjo in an instrument case marked on the outside, "Johnny St. Cyr." As soon as he began talking about Alphonse Picou, his face lit up and he smiled. What turned out to be a twenty-minute interview turned out to be over three hours. This man knew everything about jazz musicians, and he showed me documented proof on everything he said.

1990 Bill Russell gave me all the information I needed for my book, and he invited Jimmy to sit in on a set at Preservation Hall. Because Jimmy was not with me, and I knew how much this honor would mean to him, I accepted on his behalf. We left Mr. Russell's apartment exhausted and tired, now it was time for dinner, and to pick up my son Chris at the airport.

1990 Finally after waiting for Chris and three flights later, his arrival was late due to a storm in Texas. It was also time for David and Georgia to arrive at the airport, but they were delayed until the next day, along with Jimmy's arrival.

1990 The next day we went to Preservation Hall, located at 7266 St. Peter Street, which is perhaps where a tourist might hear some original New Orleans Jazz. Bill Russel invited us to visit. Bill showed us some photocopies of Alphonse Picou and unwrapped from an old newspaper a clarinet that originally belonged to Alphonse. It looked old and worn, with rubber bands, and glue around the instrument. We told him that Jimmy would be in town the next day. He gave us a recorded tape of Alphonse's album that was recorded with Papa Celestin.

1990 The next day Georgia and David Crowne arrived just before we were leaving to go to Tulane University. At Tulane we met Alma Williams, who was the Assoc. Curator of Hogan Jazz Archives, who I had been corresponding with. She gave me more information on Picou and Noone Sr. While David was searching the archives for old historical written music, for which Jimmy's new band could play. It was music from over sixty years, like 1920, that was written by Armand Piron and Jelly Roll Morton.

1990 That evening the curator at Tulane invited us all back later for a social hour. We met Danny Barker, Al Rose, Peggy La Bord, and other television personalities, and writers. Danny Barker's grandfather was Isidoire Barbarin, who played with the great Onward Brass Band, and he played alto. While Paul Barbarin (drummer,) and Jimmy Noone, Sr., married two sisters. Danny was anxious to play with Jimmy at the Palm Court, the following night.

1990 At the airport Jimmy did not arrive on his scheduled flight, so we went back to the hotel, and in my room, Jimmy had left me a note, the read: "Sorry I missed you, I am across the street at Denny's eating with David and Georgia." When they returned, I told Jimmy everything we had been doing since our arrival, and that he had two sit-in gigs to do, and his smile was radiant.

1990 Returning back to Palm Court Café, Jimmy had his saxophone and clarinet with him. While on a break Danny asked me, "Say, does Junior here really know to play that clarinet? Because I have met Junior's in here that did not know what they were playing." I reassured him, that he was exceptionally good. When Jimmy was ready to go on stage, I whispered in his ear, "You will do excellent. He laughed when I told him that, and it made him smile as he walked up on stage. Jimmy played three songs in their next set, then came off stage. The best song he did that night, was Sweet Lorraine, as it reminded me of what his father's music might have sounded like when he lived in New Orleans.

1990 Jimmy's next big gig was playing at Preservation Hall. He finally met Bill Russell, who showed him Alphonse Picou clarinet, that we had already seen, plus Bill had it all set up with the musicians, that Jimmy would sit in and play. Preservation Hall had black walls and bleacher seats, so me and Georgia sat on the floor, it was that crowded, and what an experience it was for everyone.

1990 Before leaving Preservation Hall, we thanked Bill Russell and Jimmy agreed to stop by his home for our last visit on April 29th after the jazz festival, when Jimmy's performance was over. I felt honored to present the history of New Orleans in my book, and tell how jazz all started in New Orleans, and what better way it was to write about Jimmie Noone, Sr., now I had all the information I needed to author a book.

1990 Sunday, April 29th, and the New Orleans Jazz and Heritage Festival had a large attendance. Jimmy was scheduled to meet the band members at the Landmark Hotel, located at 920 North Rampart Street. The band was scheduled to play at 4:40P.M. to 5:40 p.m., so we left to drop Jimmy off with the Cheatham's. Red Collander was due to play with them .#10

1990 The music features of the festival are numerous such as, jazz, rhythm, blues, gospel, plus the food included Cajun, Creole, Caribbean, Italian, African or soul. Along with crawfish pie, file gumbo, Oyster-Rockefcller, bisque, etouffee au gratin, and many other mouth-watering dishes.

1990 Our group which included, Georgia, David, Chris, and me walked an hour early to where the Cheatham's would perform, and the area was already crowded. We met up with Jimmy and the band behind the stage and he told me, "I will be glad when this is over, I never thought that we would ever play in New Orleans. Damn, I wish my mother and father were alive to see this." I told him "They are watching from heaven, now go play your best, those people in the audience want you guys' back again next year."

1990 Jimmy went to set up his instruments, he had taken his clarinet, his alto and soprano sax. After the band had performed two songs the audience was screaming and standing up from their seats. Dodie walked up to us and said, "They really are good. Why is this great band only playing for one day, this is roots music, this is the type of music, people want to hear. Next year, things will be different for this band." The ending song brought the crowd screaming and cheering, and they came back on stage two times.

1990 Everything in New Orleans was now done. It was time to pack our luggage and return home the next day. Finally, after celebrating everything that we had accomplished in such a brief time by 4:00A.M. we finally got in bed. That morning I woke up and looked at the clock and it was 6:42 A.M. it seems that I was only sleeping for a little over two hours. I looked at Jimmy and he was snoring with a harsh noise. I was not sure if that was a dream that I had just had, or a vision, or was I in a state resembling sleep or in a trance? But I had heard a voice speaking to me.

1990 The voice that I heard was loud enough that even Jimmy's snoring did not cover it up. It was not my voice, not that low, rather higher pitch voice of a woman. Whatever form of sleep that I was in, I became aware of what Jimmy had to do.

1990 The voice that spoke to me in my sleep said, "If Jimmy does not change his eating habits, drinking, and smoking within one year, he will die." That voice scared the hell out of me. It did. How often do people hear warnings like that in their sleep. It was being told to me.

1990 I was so scared from that dream, that I made Jimmy wake up, and I told him what I had heard in my sleep. All he did was tell me, "That's probably your Creole voodoo, in practice, now go back to seep, tomorrow we go home."

But I could not go back to sleep, I was completely awake. Jimmy's health, I knew was not good. Being over fifty, he had high-blood pressure, then his feet were always swollen and pain-ridden with gout, then there were his ulcers, with lots of upset stomach aches, and I could go on and on. Plus, he was dead set against having a physical, the only positive thing I knew he would do, is to play his music.

1990 Jimmy had already told me numerous times, "death will take me early in life, in the same matter that my father died." I thought about the fact that I was living with a man that wanted to marry me in a year, and yet he knew that he was going to die at an early age. On the night of my dream, I had no idea that I would never forget this dream and that it would be exactly one year to that date, that Jimmy would die. I was already freaking out, and this was just a dream.

1990 It was now Monday morning and time to return to San Diego. The group decided to meet in the coffee shop before everyone's departure. Jimmy would leave with the Cheatham's, then Chris, then Georgia and David. Jimmy asked me "What happened last night, did you have a nightmare?" Then I told him about my dream, and he said, "When we get back home, we both will go on diets, and clean out our systems." He then promised to pick me up at the airport, then later that night, he told me, "Precious, I'll go on a diet, don't worry, for you I'd do anything, that's how much I love you."

1990 Before everyone left that morning over breakfast, we all decided to return to New Orleans next year (1991) when Jimmy had his new band for the jazz festival. Everyone agreed this had been the best vacation and researching of jazz. And I had finally received the research that I needed.

1990 After John returned the rental car back, he met me at the airport, and we still had about an hour before our flights left. We went to the bar for our final drink together, and I had already told John about my dream and he was concerned about his brother. John's final words to me were: "Is there a way you can get Jimmy to go on a diet? Or could you call his doctor and ask him to give him a physical? I do not want you or Lorraine, calling me about my brother this year or next, I want us to be together again, next time this year."

1990 It was time for us to depart our separate ways, and John mentioned how he missed his wife and boys. I gave John a kiss on the cheek, and told him "Please do not worry, and me and Jimmy will see you either the end of April or the first of May 1991. That morning became the last day that John would ever see his brother alive.

1990 While traveling back home, I said a silent prayer to God, and thanked him for guiding me to the musicians and information I needed to tell a story on Jimmie Noone Sr., which has never been written before.

1990 Jimmy picked me up at the airport, and after arriving home, we had a long talk. I told him, "I demand that you go to the doctor for a physical." He kissed me and said, "Cecile, you are tough, and you have gotten the point across, tomorrow, I will call the doctor. I promise I will." Jimmy kept his promise to me the next day, he did call the doctor, but not for an appointment, but to have a prescription refilled for his high-blood medicine. When I found out what he had did, I nearly hit the roof!

1990 That night we had a real verbal argument, and I must have called him every cuss word that a sailor knows. And then he had the nerve to ask me to ride with him to Los Angeles the next day for his recording with the Cheatham band. That same night he told me, "In order to get the time off from the post office, I went to the doctor, and got a written slip that I was having medical problems." I allowed my doctor to take my blood pressure and he told me, "You are on the verge of a nervous breakdown, and it is all stress related. You do not need the week suggested, you need about four weeks."

1990 In reality Jimmy was off on stress leave, but he did not look at it that way. I did agree to ride up to Los Angeles with him if he promised to eat properly while we were away from home.

1990 The Cheatham's recording was to take place at the Sage and Sound Recording in Hollywood, so we stayed at a hotel in the area, and I started working on chapter one of my book. But on day two, Jimmy told me I would have to go with him as we needed to check out of the hotel, and the recording session was only scheduled for a half day.

1990 The first time that I had seen a recording being made was when my brother Teddy, recorded his album "Experience." This recording was made with a different type of enthusiasm, as the musicians had just returned from New Orleans, and everyone was still remembering the audience two encores.#3

1990 Jimmy and David were making the necessary preparations for a new band, they were a perfect team. David was the brains behind the band, while Jimmy was the band leader, and composer. Before they had received the written music from Tulane, they were rehearsing New Orleans jazz, with a group of musicians that met weekly at David's home, (they were not making public appearances, but playing for fun.)

1990 Me and Jimmy had invited Red and Mary Lou Callender over to our house for dinner. Our other friends Dayna Carroll and Helen Drysdale found out that Red was coming over. Helen the photographer, asked if they could come over and meet Red, plus take some photos.

1990 I had cooked red beans and rice, corn bread, and baked chicken. All our company that day loved my cooking and Red said, "Oh, you really know what to do with beans," as he served himself some more. Our guest Helen took pictures with her camera, which she now displays at various exhibitions she does for various colleges. The day ended, as the Cheatham's were due to play their first set at 8:30P.M.

1990 The Cheatham's performance at Elarios Bistro and Sky Lounge in La Jolla, was a restaurant with a separate bar and lounge. It was somewhat small-where the correct atmosphere fits into the sound of jazz. It sits atop the Summer House Inn, on the eleventh floor, which brings into view a fantastic scenic landscape. After dark, the complete range of vision is seen with lights all around the club windows.

1990 The Cheatham's filled the club for both shows, with standing-room only audiences. They packed the house exactly like Elarios when they appeared at New York's Blue Note, and other East Coast jazz Clubs.

1990 The following day, after their first night's performance, Dirk Sutro, wrote a review in the Los Angeles Times entitled "Sweet Baby Blues Knows What It Means To Swing."

1990 Jimmy had been working full time at the Post Office while playing every evening nightly for five days straight. Because the Post Office was in La Jolla, all he had time to do was change out of his uniform, grab some food at a fast-food restaurant, and he was ready for his second job.

1990 During this five-day period, he had gained about seven or eight pounds, I finally told him, "You are gaining too much weight, you are not eating any fruit or vegetables, and damn Jimmy, you are smoking about two packs a day. I want to be your woman, not your mother. I should not have to tell you how to take care of yourself." He responded with, "Cheri, you are right, I will do better. Let us get away next weekend, and spend some time together, and talk things over. Would you like to go down to Ensenada? Its warm down there this time of year, and the weather would help your back a lot."

1990 We traveled down to Ensenada, checked into a motel, and started the afternoon with a walk along the beach. The sunset was a beautiful red-orange color, and I could sense that Jimmy was starting to unwind and relax and get rid of the stress he carried around. While walking down the beach, I stopped to take off my tennis shoes that were starting to get wet and sandy. I told Jimmy, "Take off your funky shoes and socks, and give your feet some air." When he did, I made him stop walking so I could check to see—if what I had seen was correct.

1990 And I was right. Jimmy's feet had swollen up about two time the size that they were, and he had little stocky feet. Needless to say, I got mad at him, and then started acting like a natural black—b.i.t.c.h. I told him I was fed up with his shit. I did not know how to get him to the doctor. But because he was neglecting his health, I did not see how I could marry him the following year. (I thought this threat would knock some sense into him.) I also realized nothing was working, absolutely nothing.

1990 After Ensenada, Jimmy had a band rehearsal to attend, John had called and we agreed that I call Jimmy's doctor and try to set up some type of appointment.

1990 David Crowne received the written music from Tulane Archives. Some of this music dated back to the period of 1917 to 1920, which made this music over seventy years old, and some of it had not been played since. The challenge that they faced was finding the correct musicians that could read, plus they had to be enthusiastic about playing old New Orleans music. First, they decided to use the band that had been practicing with them over at David's house. Jimmy's job was too tedious, but something that he loved to do. He had to write all the parts for all the musician's, which was to include anywhere from eight to a ten-piece band.

1990 Jimmy went out and purchased a small drafting table to write his music on. Then on a cassette tape, David recorded all the tunes that had remained popular, and had been recorded on earlier records. The rest of the music would have to be played by the musicians, before knowing what it would sound like.

1990 Jimmy's next step was finding a singer, but he did not want just any singer, she had to be someone that was adaptable to New Orleans music. While Jimmy was looking for a singer and not finding anyone, while talking to his daughter (Lorraine) he mentioned that he was looking for a singer. She suggested that her and Rosie come over and try out. She mentioned that Rosie had done a little singing with a band that played top ten songs.

1990 Upon arrival, the two girls started singing while Jimmy played the piano. He came right out and told Lorraine "that she was tone-deaf (insensitive to differences in musical pitch,) and for her to let Rosie sing." When Jimmy played Otis Redding's "Respect," Rosie's voice came out loud and clear, with a completely different sound. Lorraine started yelling, "Sing it Rosie, yeah, sing it girl."

1990 Later that night, when they had left, Jimmy asked me, "Precious, what did you think of Rosie's singing?" I replied, Rosie is your singer. She needs some practicing, and she tends to go flat, her breathing is off, but she was nervous and has not sung much." He replied, "My God, we're starting to think alike, perhaps you should be the band leader."

1990 Months later, with Jimmy practicing with Rosie, he began to feel like what Clarence Williams must have felt like when he went down south to get Bessie Smith-"The Empress of The Blues." He taught and coached Rosie, and now when she started singing the blues, you knew she meant it, she was loving the blues.

1990 One evening when Jimmy was playing his clarinet and Rosie was singing, I thought I was listening to Jimmie Noone Sr. playing with Bessie Smith. I immediately noticed the difference in her delivery, her voice was now harsh yet soft, low but not too low, and her blues were like none I had heard before.

1990 Rosie was a married woman, with five children. She was extremely attractive, her skin had no blemishes, she had black hair fixed in corn rows. She was of medium built, about 5'5', and her children names were: Alisa, Tanya, Tamara, Marquies, and Aisha. I wondered how she managed raising kids, as she was employed by a hospital to guard prisoners, who were awaiting trials, but need treatments. Rosie had now become an accomplished singer under Jimmy's assistance, in a noticeably fleeting period of time.

1990 About the second week in September, I flew to San Francisco, to visit my brother David and his wife Cynthia. My oldest son Andre (nickname-Andy) was thirty and was about to be married to a beautiful girl by the name of Sheila Carmella Andrews. Jimmy had airplane tickets to meet me, while I had tickets to go three days early to help my sister-in-law prepare a formal dinner, for the wedding party. It also allowed me time to meet Sheila's parents, and to spend some time with my son before his wedding.

1990 Jimmy was set to arrive September 15th early Friday evening, he did not arrive on his scheduled flight. When I called the house, the recorder was on, so I knew he had left. I never heard from Jimmy until Saturday morning, the day of the wedding.

1990 Jimmy told us he had missed his flight, and ended up coming in late that Friday night, so he stayed at a motel, rather than wake us up. Jimmy was scheduled to play several solos for my son's wedding with his clarinet. Finally, everything was going pretty smooth, until after the wedding, when the family portrait pictures were being taken. Jimmy watched me as I talked to my ex-husband, and I could see jealously boiling within him.

1990 Jimmy looked like a boiling tea kettle, which was whistling because the water was finally getting hot. He never thought that me and my ex-husband had not seen or talked to each other in at least twelve or fifteen years. He also looked jealous for the young man that was my escort in the wedding, who held my arm walking down the aisle, who was my son's best friends. I had no idea that Jimmy so jealous and possessive, over what was nothing.

1990 After the wedding Jimmy and my brother David, left the reception, and never returned. Me and my sister-in-law, and the rest of the women with us, had to beg for a ride from Oakland back to San Francisco.

1990 The men returned back to San Francisco drunk. They said that they had been at a bar. The women were mad because we were left stranded, and the whole episode turned into a big argument. Me and Jimmy had a big fight over the entire day.

1990 It was almost the end of the year and me and Jimmy had taken time off from writing and composing. We really enjoyed buying a Christmas tree, selecting presents, and Jimmy felt so proud that he had purchased a gift for his daughter. He told me, "Lorraine and I never reached the closeness that we could have had, but I love my daughter so much. And I am so proud of her."

1990 We had invited Lorraine over for Christmas dinner, along with some friends and my relatives, but she never came over the house or called. After waiting for her to come over and get her gifts for several weeks, Jimmy took them to her job. This was the first time that I had seen Jimmy really in a sentimental way over a holiday, and it surprised me.

1990 Jimmy was now probably about thirty or more pounds overweight, but he carried it good for his short height and body built. He was not looking fat, rather stocky. He was really drinking up the beer, and he did not care what type. He liked draft, ale's, light/low calorie, Budweiser and Coor's banquet lager, and Coor's light lager beer. As far as cigarettes go, Jimmy could smoke almost any brand, he usually liked Carlton, Marlboro, and Kent's. But he would always forget that he had laid a cigarette down and then would smoke another one.

On the furniture that we had, he was so careless with burning cigarettes, that finally I purchased a few smoke detectors, just to ease my mind somewhat.

1991 In January, Jimmy's waist when I first started dating him was twenty-nine inches, and now he had reached a waist of thirty-six inches.

1991 It became success for Jimmy, because now he had his New Orleans band, and Rosie was his singer. Jimmy was now bragging about his band and how good they were starting to sound, and his singer Rosie, he knew that she could sing.

1991 Right about this time is when he met Robert Reynolds and Catherine Luminais promotors of a business called Crescent City Promotions. Robert and Catherine were boyfriend and girlfriend and in business together as promoters, and when I first met them, I was impressed. They were honest, sharp, and ambitious and I realized that they could manage Jimmy's promotions. They knew that Jimmy was introducing latest music, and they had accepted the challenge to further his career.'

1991 January, this is when Jimmy's personality and musical capabilities changed and made him into a different person. Jimmy in all reality, was not living his normal life, he had become his father, and his father's son. He had begun living up to the public's expectations of being the son of a famous musician.

1991 Jimmy had named his band "The New Orleans Good Times Society and Marching Band, and they had even practiced doing what is called, 'Second Line'. The Second Line is an old New Orleans tradition that Jimmy seen as a child, and whom bands such as the Eureka Bras Band participated in and became part of New Orleans cultural heritage.#11

1991 Jimmy had become very hard-nosed with Rosie his singer, with her he wanted perfection and he was pushing her to exceed to a higher level of singing. And quickly she reached that level. She exceeded the level he was looking for. He also attacked the band members in about the same way, he knew that he only had a few weeks, before the band would play their first performance.

1991 Everything that people had expected him to become, from his heritage, had made its appearance. Questions that people often asked were: Did he play like his father, Did they both look alike? How influenced was he from his father's recordings? And now in the year 1991, he was finally able to answer a "Yes," to all the questions asked.

1991 When I said that "Jimmy became his father, and his father's son," I meant that he had become and stayed throughout this last cycle of his life, almost non-human. Jimmy became almost supernatural or spiritual. By that I mean, his reasons for a life of existence were different from that of all other human beings.

1991 For example, he really did not care about anything but music. Music was everything in his life. His total ambition in his life was to re-create his father's music—to re-produce the Apex Band. How he now felt about his life was this saying he had, "I celebrate life every day, as if it was my last." He also used to say, "Love me when I am here, not after I've left."

1991 I knew that Jimmy was living for only one thing, and that he was about to reach the height of his popularity, and his death could be like that of his father—he would die just when becoming successful. We had talked about it so much, that it scared me. I had reached a point where I was afraid for him, because—let us face it—me and Jimmy knew what the future was to bring. And I knew that there was nothing that I could do about it.

1991 Jimmy called me from a phone booth in downtown San Diego, to tell me that he had news for me, and he was on his way home, with a bottle of champagne. When he arrived, he told me about the contract he had just signed with the manager of a hotel and with his promoters, Catherine, and Rob.

1991 His promoters had landed him a series of possibly five weekend engagements at the U.S. Grant Hotel, which is located at 326 Broadway. The best accurate description of this luxury collection hotel is that it is a plush five-star hotel, elegantly decorated, and known for its excellent service, located at 326 Broadway. It is located in the Gaslamp quarters, which is San Diego's most vibrant district. I did not even ask Jimmy how much his pay he would receive as a band leader, because it was so irrelevant. All we both cared about was that this was his first opportunity to show his musical abilities, at one of the finest hotels in our city.

1991 He then played a recorded cassette tape of his new band, that David Crowne had recorded for him to listen to. It also included Rosie singing with the band, and she sounded superb. They had advance to a New Orleans Creole Band, and we both felt great over the accomplishment. While we drank champagne and listened, he started picking out the good qualities of the band versus the bad, and what really needed improvements.

1991 After playing that tape for hours, Jimmy asked me, "What is your opinion of this tape?" I told him the truth, as I knew he relied on my opinion. "I believe that the band needs at least four more rehearsals, before you can hit the stage. Also, I noticed three errors that you made on the clarinet, when playing APEX BLUES and YOU RASCAL YOU. Plus, the drummer tried to rush the beat on APEX BLUES, and when Rosie sings, the band need to play a little softer."

1991 It was almost time for the band to make their first playing date, and Jimmy had listened to me, and the band was performing exactly as he preferred. Jimmy had named the band, "The New Orleans Good Time Society and Marching Band." I told him the name was too long, but he disagreed completely, so the name remained.

1991 At the beautiful U.S. Grant Hotel, Jimmy's band made their first appearance, and the room was filled to capacity, with many people standing. An example of the songs played that night were as follow: IT'S TIGHT LIKE THAT, LET'S SOW A WILD OAT, FOUR OR FIVE TIMES, RHYTHM MAN, SLEEPY TIME DOWN SOUTH, YOU RASCAL YOU, APEX BLUES, and SWEET LORRAINNE.

1991 During the performance the band did several songs, which included second lining. Second Lining is a sort of a foot parade led by a brass band, with a type of strutting or swaggering dance step. It has become a New Orleans tradition at parades. And Jimmy's band pulled it off exactly as he watched it while living in New Orleans as a youngster.#11

1991The similarity between Jimmie Noone Sr. and Jimmy Noone Jr's clarinet playing is indeed close. The resemblance can be compared on the song Sweet Lorraine. Jimmy Jr. learned the trill quite well at six years old from his father, and it still burst through out this song.

1991 I can remember when Jimmy was a teenager and played the tune Sweet Lorraine—then he played it from knowing the notes and from rehearsals over the years. Now—decades later, he played with the New Orleans Style, as if it were embedded within him.

1991 Jimmy's band performed at the U.S. Grant Hotel, Jimmy proved to me and the audience that night, that he was a master clarinet player. He captured the attention of the audience with his New Orleans style playing of the high register, and then being able to sweep into the low register, and play back and forth in both registers, precisely like his father did on every song.

Index for Chronological Dates
for Jimmy Noone, Jr.

#1 Rita Noone Floyd passed away. Rita worked at the May Company Store in Mission Valley, as a salesperson. She was employed in 1960. Jimmy said, "No one at the May Company store she worked at knew that she was Black, she was not trying to pass as white, everyone just assumed that she was white. She attended Saint Rita's church, in Southeast San Diego, and she was a devote Catholic, and attended mass every Sunday." Her burial was at Greenwood Cemetery, where she was laid to rest next to her deceased husband, Troy Floyd.

#1A November 1983 Jimmy recorded live a local jam session in San Diego that featured the Cottonmouth D'Arey's. It consisted of five songs: Blues My Naughty Sweetie Gives To Me and Perdido Street Blues, featurning Stan Kling.
On tuba, and Jimmy on clarinet. The third song: Tight Like That, featured Jimmy singing vocals and playing Clarinet. Song four featured Jimmy on tenor sax, entitled: Blue And Sentimental, and the fifth song was: *Oh Daddy*, Featuring Chris Norris, vocals, and Jimmy on Alto Sax.

#2. Jimmy Noone recorded Hal Smith's Creole Sunshine Orchestra. Songs recorded were: Creole Song, Blues.
For Jimmie Noone, Mahogany Hall Stomp, Do What Ory Say, Savoy Blues, All the Girls Go Crazy, All the Jazz Band Ball, Dippermouth Blues, Bucket's got a Hole In It, High Society, Blues My Sweetie Naughty Sweetie Gives to Me, Balling The Jack, Get Out of Here. On Stomp Off Records #SOS 1078. The musicians: Bob Jackson (tr, voc,) Dick Shooshan (p), Hal Smith (dr), Jimmy Noone Jr. (cl, voc,) Michael Fay (b), Mike Duffy(b,voc), and Roger Jamieson (tb).

#3.The Cheatham band released a new album titled, "Homeward Bound," in December 1987 for Concord Jazz, Songs written by Jeannie and Jimmy Cheatham, with guest Eddie "Cleanhead Vinson," and Jimmy Noone doubling on clarinet. The songs: Permanent Solution, Goin' Down Slow, Daddy-O, Trouble In Mind, Homeward Bound, You don't Have To Go, Hello, Little Boy, Detour Ahead, Sometimes It Be That Way. The musicians: Soloists, Jimmy Noone Jr., and Dinky Morris, altoist, Curtis Peagler, trumpet Snooky Young, brass trombonist, Jimmy Cheatham, bassist, Red Callender, and drummer John "Ironman" Harris.

#4.Summer 1988Jimmy was in his recording studio and created a song called, "Cecile," that was written for Me, and it had a sort of medium bossa nova beat combined with a New Orleans style phrasing, while the Clarinet played an arpeggiated embellished counter lines with Jimmy's vocalizing inflection. The words for Cecile is as follows:

Cecile You're a walk in the warm summer sun
Cecile, you're the cool of night, when day is done
Not all the stars in the skies match
The loveness in your eyes
Cecile you're the one I adore
2nd verse
Cecile you are the music that lives
In my soul
Cecile you're the song that will
Never grow old
You came into my life from yesterday,
Child of November won't you stay?
Cecile you're the one I adore.

I was flabbergasted that he would compose a song about me. He told me "I want this song to become my Theme song when I form my new band, your song will be what "Sweet Lorraine," was to my father. Soon you Will be my wife and we'll live happy forever."

#5 Jimmy records a demo tape in his recording room a self-contained orchestra. This is his list of songs:

Tatum, and Linnette Hunting
Sister—Jimmy Noone, Vocals, and clarinet
San Francisco—Jimmy Noone, clarinet, and alto sax
Confessing my Love—Jimmy Noone, vocals, alto sax, and organ
Somewhere—Jimmy Noone, vocals, flute, alto and soprano sax
Cecile—Jimmy Noone, vocals, flute, alto and soprano sax
Recorded in San Diego, this tape went out to various recording labels, but it was never sold.

#6 Dr. Oliver Luck was the author of a paperback book called, "Music Is Math," It was published by his own Publishing company, called Owl Publishing. It detail's the method for reading and counting. He taught music in public schools including general music, band orchestra, chorus, marching band, and jazz. He had played with Duke Ellington, Louis Bellson, Cab Calloway, and Jimmy Noone. Jim Merod is a recorded legendary for jazz and blues. He has recorded with Herbie Hancock, Ella Fitzgerald, Sarah Vaughn. He played a very important role for Jimmy, as a jazz critic who recognized Jimmy's capabilities.

#7 As a jazz musician. Jim Merod was able to capture the essence of July 12, 1988, in his published article entitled:
Mike Wofford's Solar Wind, printed in the Jazz Link, Volume 1 issue 3, listed is some of his quotes. "The latest informal version of Mike Wofford jam session genius hit the Bella Via as the proud foreguts of a Building hurricane. From the opening churn of Blues In The Closet through the sassy run of three tightly stitched Sets, the five musicians assembled a conversation. The musicians were: Mike Wofford (piano), Oliver Luck (trombone) Jimmy Noone Jr. (alto, soprano sax), Chuck McPherson (drums) and Chris Conner (bass.). The first of many individual highlights showed up in Jimmy Noone's gorgeous reading of the Ellington/webster Standard, "I got It Bad" which was a set piece for the incomparable Johnny Hodges so much as it recreates the Creamy satin texture of hodges' intonation…a timbre considerably at odds with the sharp, somewhat grainy rough-Ness of Noone's soprano. Noone doesn't occupy the

bandstand; he invades it. A one-man cheering section, commenting on fellow soloists. In the midst, his running dialogue with tradition and with immediate events masters an invisible honey sunshine. That lures musical conversations into motion. And such motion this group gathers is like a rolling carnival.

#8 August 1988, Jimmy had been called upon at the request of FRO Brigham (he was one of San Diego's finest Musician,) to assist in a salute to jazzman Leon Petties. Leon Belonged to an old San Diego family, whose kids went.
To school with me and Jimmy. Leon had started as a musician with Fro way back in 1947 (along with Harold Land (saxophonist,) before he joined the ranks of Nat King Cole, as his drummer. On September 4, 1988, hundreds of People crowded into the OASIS CLUB on 3184 Market Street. Remembering a few musicians that attended and gave an outstanding performance were: Mike Wofford, Don Glaser (piano). Marshall Hawkins (bass) Peggy Claire and Lila Brown (vocals,) Gary Le Febvre and Jimmy Noone (sax).
And Cottonmouth D'Arcy's Jazz Vipers. (these musicians also performed at my brother's Teddy's memorial Concert.)

#9 The members of the Sweet Baby Blues Band were: Curtis Pegler, (saxophonists), Cora Bryant (trumpet), Ricky Woodward (clarinet), Jimmie Cheatham (trombone, and arranger), Jeannie Cheatham (piano and vocalists), Red Callender (brass), John "Ironman" Harris (drums), Dinky Morris (bar, sax), Nolan "Cat Daddy" Smith (trumpet) and Jimmy Noone Jr. (sax, clarinet).

#10 Red Callender, for over fifty years has either performed or recorded with an endless list of jazz artists. To Name a few: Louis Armstrong, Lester Young, Duke Ellington, Lena Horne, Erroll Garner, Art Tatum, Billie Holiday, Charlie Mingus, and Charlie Parker. Red is also known as starting a new revived interest in the tuba, although the bass is his instrument. He Has also composed and arranged for numerous bands. There are two songs that George (Red) Callender and His wife Mary Lou Callender composed together: See You Later, So Long, and Merry Go Round.

#11 Second Lining is associated with marching bands when they became popular with New Orleans Jazz music and is now considered a tradition. Alphonse Picou who became famous for his rendition of developing the clarinet.

Part for the song "High Society," played in numerous marching bands including the Excelsior Brass Band and then Freddie Keppard's Olympia Orchestra, which included second lining in the streets of New Orleans.

In 1961 when Alphonse Picou, a French Creole, who played jazz clarinet, passed away, his funeral was considered the largest second lining jazz funeral parade in history. The brass band members met in front of Picou's Food Store. to begin his burial parade. This is why Jimmy Noone included the second lining in his music to continue that old New Orleans jazz tradition.

The first time that I had seen a recording being made was when my brother, Teddy, recorded his album "Experience." But this recording was made with a different type of enthusiasm. I think because the Musicians had just gotten back from New Orleans. This recording is not one to be classified as "neat, cute, or stylish, it is boogie that will wake you up. The Compositions have been conducted and arranged by Jimmy Cheatham, into a "funky Kansas City Blues," sound.

Jeannie Cheatham has a way with a piano, which when combined with her pure unmistakable alto voice, Creates emotion, and excitement. Her execution on all ten songs is energizing. This recording was entitled Luv In The Afternoon, thru the Concord Jazz Label, #CCD-4420. Their guest Performer is CLARENCE "GATEMOUTH" BROWN, on guitar, who appears by courtesy of REAL RECORDS INC.

The performers on this C.D. are all outstanding artist, they are skilled, versed, and adept musician's, who Everyone loves and respect. They are JEANNIE CHEATHAM (PIANO, VOCALS); JIMMY CHEATAM (BRASS TROMBONE): RED CALLENNDER (bass); JOHN "IRONMAN" HARRIS (drums); DINKY MORRIS (tenor and baritone saxophone); JIMMY NOONE (clarinet, soprano, tenor saxophone); CURTIS PEAGLER (alto, tenor, saxophone); NOLAN "CAT DADDY" SMITH (trumpet & flugelhorn)t; SNOOKY YOUNG (trumpet, flugelhorn); CLARENCE, "GATEMOUTH" BROWN (guitar.). The glee club singing on the last tune, RAUNCHY RITA, is many voices, including myself (I now have Recorded music), that was directed by SNOOKY YOUNG. Everyone in the studio was singing at the End of the session, and it was a lot of fun.

On this album is the following tunes: MESSIN' ROND WITH THE BOOGIE;

LUV IN THE AFTERNOON, MAMA'S BLUES, COMIN' BACK TO SOUTH CHICAGO, TRAV'KLIN' LIGHT, DON'T YOU FEEL MY LEG: YOU WON'T LET ME GO; WEE BABY BLUES; BABY PLEASE DON'T GO; RAUNCHY RITA.

Endnotes

[1] Shapiro, N. and Hentoff, N., *Hear Me Talkin' To Ya*, pg 106.

[2] Barker, D. and Buerkle, J. V., *Bourbon Street Black*, Oxford University Press, pg 17.

[3] Shapiro, N. and Hentoff, N., *The Story of Jazz, Hear Me Talkin' to Ya*, New York: Dover Publications, Pg 23.

[4] Brooks, T., *America's Black Musical Heritage*, Englewood Cliffs, New Jersey: Prentice-Hall, Inc., pg 66.

[5] Copland, A., *What to Listen For In Music, A Mentor Book,* McGraw-Hill Co. Inc., pg 63.

[6] Lyons, L. and Perlo, D., *Jazz Portraits, The Lives and Music of The Jazz Masters*, New York: Quill, William Morrow, pg 394.

[7] Chilton, J., *Sidney Bechet, The Wizard of Jazz*, New York: Oxford University Press, pg 16.

[8] Barker, D. and Buerkle, J. V., *Bourbon Street Black*, Oxford University Press, pg 17.

[9] Shapiro, N. and Hentoff, N., *"Hear Me Talkin' To Ya,"* by Nat Shapiro and Nat Hentoff, New York: Dover Publications, Inc., pg 22.

[10] Schuller, G*., Early Jazz, Its Roots and Musicial Development*, New York: Oxford University Press, pg 57.

[11] Clayton, P. and Gammond, P., *The Guinness Jazz Companion*, Guinness Publishing, pg 32.

[12] Clayton, P. and Gammond, P., *The Guinness Jazz Companion*, Guinness Publishing, pg 227.

[13] Clayton, P. and Gammond, P., *The Guinness Jazz Companion*, Guinness Publishing, pg 174.

[14] Chilton, J., *Sidney Bechet, The Wizard of Jazz*, New York: Oxford University Press, pg 29.

[15] Chilton, J. and Bechet, S., *The Wizard of Jazz*, New York: Oxford University, pg 28.

[16] Chilton, J. and Bechet, S., *The Wizard of Jazz*, New York: Oxford University, pg 28.

[17] Williams, M., *Jazz Masters of New Orleans*, New York: MacMillan Co., pg 91.

[18] Shapiro, N. and Hentoff, N., *Hear Me Talkin' To Ya*, New York: Dover Publications, Inc., pg 87.

[19] Shaw, A., *The Jazz Age, Popular Music in the 1920s*, New York: Oxford University Press, pg 18.

[20] Collier, J. L., *The Making Of Jazz*, Boston: Houghton Mifflin Co., pg 128.

[21] Shapiro, N. and Hentoff, N., *Hear Me Talkin' To Ya*, New York: Dover Publications, Inc., pg 116.

[22] Shaw, A., *The Jazz Age*, New York: Oxford University Press, pg 287.

[23] Shaw, A., *The Jazz Age*, New York: Oxford University Press, pg 287.

[24] Schuller, G., *Early Jazz, Its Roots and Musical Development*, New York: Oxford University Press, pg 204.

[25] Shapiro, N. and Hentoff, N., *Hear Me Talkin' To Ya*, New York: Dover Publications, Inc., pg 88.

[26] Lyons, L. and Perlo, D., *The Lives And Music Of The Jazz Masters*, New York: Quill, William Morrow, pg 168, 394.

[27] Shaw, A., *The Jazz Age, Popular Music in the 1920s*, New York: Oxford University Press, pg 287.

[28] Lyons, L. and Perlo, D., *Jazz Portraits, The Lives And Music of The Jazz Masters*, pg 394.

[29] Shapiro, N. and Hentoff, N., *Hear Me Talkin' To Ya*, New York: Dover Publications, Inc., pg 88.

[30] Collier, J. L., *The Making Of Jazz*, Boston: Houghton Mifflin Co., pg 128.

[31] Shapiro, N. and Hentoff, N., *Hear Me Talkin' To Ya*, New York: Dover Publications, Inc., pg 98.

[32] Clayton, P. and Gammond, P., *The Guinness Jazz Companion*, Great Britain: Guinness Publishing Ltd., pg 207.

[33] Shapiro, N. and Hentoff, N., *Hear Me Talkin' To Ya*, New York: Dover Publications, Inc., pg 173.

[34] Stroff, S. M., *Discovering Great Jazz*, New York: New Market Press, pg 14.

[35] Stroff, S. M., *Discovering Great Jazz*, New York: New Market Press, pg 27.

[36] Shapiro, N. and Hentoff, N., *Hear Me Talkin' To Ya*, New York: Dover Publications, Inc., pg 96.

[37] Shapiro, N. and Hentoff, N., *Hear Me Talkin' To Ya*, New York: Dover Publications, Inc., pg 104, 105.

[38] Schuller, G., *Early Jazz, Its Roots and Musical Development*, New York: Oxford University Press.

[39] Schuller, G., *Early Jazz, Its Roots and Musical Development*, New York: Oxford University Press, pg 205.

[40] Stroff, S. M., *Discovering Great Jazz*, New York: New Market Press, pg 27, 28.

[41] Collier, J. L., *The Making Of Jazz*, Boston: Houghton Mifflin Co., pg?

[42] Schuller, G., *Early Jazz, Its Roots and Musical Development*, New York: Oxford University Press, pg 204, 205.

[43] Stroff, S. M., *Discovering Great Jazz*, New York: New Market Press, pg 18.

[44] Sagawe, H., *Jimrnie Noone Bio-Discography*, New Orleans, LA: Tulane University Library, pg 2.

[45] Collier, J. L., *The Making Of Jazz*, Boston: Houghton Mifflin Co., pg 92.

[46] Simmen, J., 'Storyville 41', New Orleans, LA: Tulane University Achives, pg 177.

[47] Shapiro, N. and Hentoff, N., *Hear Me Talkin' To Ya*, New York: Dover Publications, Inc., pg 130.

[48] Shapiro, N. and Hentoff, N., *Hear Me Talkin' To Ya*, New York: Dover Publications, Inc., pg 130.

[49] Collier, J. L., *The Making Of Jazz*, Boston: Houghton Mifflin Company, pg 126.

[50] Collier, J. L., *The Making Of Jazz*, Boston: Houghton Mifflin Company, pg 126.

[51] Collier, J. L., *The Making Of Jazz*, Boston: Houghton Mifflin Company, pg 92.

[52] Shapiro, N. and Hentoff, N., *Hear Me Talkin' To Ya*, Dover Publications, Inc., pg 27.

[53] Williams, M., *Jazz Masters of New Orleans*, New York: The Mac Millan Co., pg 188.

[54] Arnaud, G. and Chesnel, J., *Masters Of Jazz*, New York: Chambers Encyclopedic Guides, pg 72.

[55] Stroff, S. M., *Discovering Great Jazz*, New York: New Market Press, pg 27.

[56] Schuller, G., *Early Jazz, Its Roots and Musical Development*, New York: Oxford University Press, pg 206.

[57] Schuller, G., *Early Jazz, Its Roots and Musical Development*, New York: Oxford University Press, pg 206.

[58] Collier, J. L., *The Making Of Jazz*, Boston: Houghton Mifflin Company, pg 93.

[59] Collier, J. L., *The Making Of Jazz*, Boston: Houghton Mifflin Company, pg 93.

[60] Collier, J. L., *The Making Of Jazz*, Boston: Houghton Mifflin Company, pg 93.

[61] Panassie, H., *Jazz Information Magaine*, New Orleans, LA: Tulane University.

[62] Lyons, L. and Perlo, D., *Jazz Portraits*, New York: William Morrow, pg 394.

[63] Lyons, L. and Perlo, D., *Jazz Portraits*, New York: William Morrow, pg 395.

[64] Lyons, L. and Perlo, D., *Jazz Portraits*, New York: Quill, pg 37.

[65] Clayton, P. and Gammond, P., *The Guinness Jazz Companion*, Guinness Books, pg 191.

[66] Hentoff, N. and Mc Carthy, A., *Jazz, A New Perspective of The History of Jazz*, New York: Da Capo Press, pg 145.

[67] Article written by Hugues Panassie, possibly around the 1940s, from the archives files of Tulane University, New Orleans.

[68] Article written by Hugues Panassie, possibly around the 1940s, from the archives files of Tulane University, New Orleans.

[69] Shaw, A., *The Jazz Age*, New York: Oxford University Press, pg 81.

[70] Shaw, A., *The Jazz Age*, New York: Oxford University Press, pg 81.

[71] Shaw, A., *The Jazz Age*, New York: Oxford University Press, pg 81.

[72] Shaw, A., *The Jazz Age*, New York: Oxford University Press, pg 103.

[73] Shaw, A., *The Jazz Age*, New York: Oxford University Press, pg 223.

[74] "The Jazz Information," by Hugues Panassie, Article reprinted dated 21/3/41.

[75] "Clarinet Kings," by William Schaefer, The Mississippi Rag Newspaper, donated by Tulane University, Howard-Tilton Memorial Library, New Orleans, article dtd 9/83.

[76] Collier, J. L., *The Making Of Jazz*, Boston: Houghton Mifflin Company, pg 91.

[77] Travis, D. J., *An Autobiography of Black Jazz*, Urban Research Institute.

[78] Shapiro, N. and Hentoff, N., *Hear Me Talkin' To Ya*, New York: Dover Publications, Inc., pg 114.

[79] (79)Article written by Hugues Panassie, possibly around the 1940s, from the archives files of Tulane University, New Orleans.

[80] Schuller, G., *Early Jazz*, New York: Oxford University Press, pg 206.

[81] Shapiro, N. and Hentoff, N., *Hear Me Talkin' To Ya*, New York: Dover Publications, Inc., pg 190.

[82] Hentoff, N. and Mc Carthy, A., *Jazz, A New Perspective*, New York: Da Capo Press, pg 183.

[83] Travis, D., *An Autobiography of Black Jazz*, Urban Research Institute, pg 391.

[84] Ostransky, L. R., *Jazz City, The Impact Of Our Cities On The Development Of Jazz*, New Jersey: Prentice Hall, Inc., pg 157.

[85] "Storyville," by Johnny Simmen, Article from Tulane University Archives, pg 177.

[86] Travis, D., *An Autobiography of Black Jazz*, Urban Research Institute, pg 393.

[87] Travis, D., *An Autobiography of Black Jazz*, Urban Research Institute, pg 393.

[88] Ostransky, L. R., *Jazz City,* New Jersey: Prentice Hall, Inc., pg 222.

[89] Collier, J. L., *The Making Of Jazz*, Boston: Houghton Mifflin Company, pg 92.

[90] Collier, J. L., *The Making Of Jazz*, Boston: Houghton Mifflin Company, pg 294.

[91] Travis, D., *An Autobiography of Black Jazz*, Chicago: Urban Research Institute, Inc., pg 36.

[92] Travis, D., *An Autobiography of Black Jazz*, Chicago: Urban Research Institute, Inc., pg 391.

[93] Shapiro, N. and Hentoff, N., *Hear Me Talkin' To Ya*, New York: Dover Publications, Inc., pg 214.

[94] Travis, D. J., *An Autobiography Of Black Jazz*, Chicago: Urban Research Institute, Inc., pg 113.

[95] Travis, D. J., *An Autobiography Of Black Jazz*, Chicago: Urban Research Institute, Inc., pg 114.

[96] Thomas and Aylesworth, V., *The Glamour Years (1919–1941),* New York: W.H. Smith Publishers, Inc., pg 85–87.

[97] Schuller, G., *Early Jazz, Its Roots and Musical Development*, New York: Oxford University Press, pg 6–7.

[98] Simon, G. T., *The Big Bands*, New York: MacMillan Publishing Co. Inc., pg 85.

[99] Lyons, L. and Perlo, D., *Jazz Portraits*, New York: Quill, pg 585.

[100] Chilton, J., *Sidney Bechet, The Wizard Of Jazz*, New York: Oxford University Press, pg 125.

[101] Hentoff, N. and McCarthy, A. J., *Jazz, New Perspectives*, New York: Da Capo Press, pg 354.

[102] Lyons, L. and Perlo, D., *Jazz Portraits*, New York: Quill, pg 52.

[103] Gitler, I., *Jazz Masters of the Forties*, New York: MacMillan Company, pg 12.

[104] Travis, D. J., *An Autobiography Of Black Jazz*, Chicago: Urban Research Inst. Inc., pg 470.

[105] Travis, D. J., *An Autobiography Of Black Jazz*, Chicago: Urban Research Inst. Inc., pg 394.

[106] Fox, T., Rinehart, H. and Winston, *Showtime, At The Apollo*, New York, pg 133.

[107] Williams, M., *Jazz Masters of New Orleans*, pg 212.

[108] Hentoff, N. and McCarthy, A. J., *Jazz, New Perspectives*, New York: Da Capo Press, pg 317.